McGRAW-HILL'S ASVAB BASIC TRAINING FOR THE AFQT

Second Edition

Dr. Janet E. Wall

Former Manager, ASVAB Career Exploration Program

Department of Defense

New York   Chicago   San Francisco   Lisbon   London   Madrid   Mexico City
Milan   New Delhi   San Juan   Seoul   Singapore   Sydney   Toronto

ISBN 978-0-07-163282-9
MHID 0-07-163282-4

McGraw-Hill books are available at special quantity discounts to use as premiums and sales promotions, or for use in corporate training programs. To contact a representative please e-mail us at bulksales@mcgraw-hill.com.

The views expressed in this book are those of the author and do not reflect the official position of the Department of Defense or any other agency of the U.S. Government.

ASVAB is a registered trademark of the United States Department of Defense, which was not involved in the production of, and does not endorse, this product.

CONTENTS

Introduction

If you want to do well on the Armed Forces Qualifying Test (AFQT), this book is for you. The AFQT is the primary score that determines whether or not you can get into the military. The higher you score on the AFQT, the more kinds of military training and jobs you have as options. The higher your AFQT score, the more likely it is that you will have your pick of jobs that are of interest to you. This book is designed to maximize your AFQT so that you have more control over your life in the military.

The AFQT is made up of four of the eight tests found on the Armed Services Vocational Aptitude Test Battery (ASVAB). If you want to know about the whole ASVAB, get the book *McGraw-Hill's ASVAB*. That book will help you understand the other, non-AFQT tests.

This book, *McGraw-Hill's ASVAB Basic Training for the AFQT*, is jam-packed with information and advice to help you do your best on the test. If you pay close attention to the advice you'll find here, you can get a much better AFQT score. You can maximize your job options with a high score.

The contents of this book are based on the very latest reports and documents provided and sponsored by the U.S. Department of Defense (DoD) available as of this writing. On occasion, DoD may make some small changes that are not reflected here. You should know, however, that some of the testing advice that DoD provides to ASVAB test takers does not give an accurate description of the actual tests. This book is far more accurate in that regard. It should help you understand what to expect and help you score better on the AFQT.

Part 1 of this book describes the ASVAB, the AFQT, and what it takes to qualify for military service. It focuses on the AFQT and how it is calculated and used. Other requirements for military entrance are also listed.

This section of the book also describes the paper-and-pencil version of the ASVAB and the computerized version. The differences between the two are listed. Special strategies for taking each version are outlined for you.

This section of the book ends with information about the question types in each of the four tests that make up the AFQT so that you know what to expect on the test.

Part 2 of this book will give you the most comprehensive review of the AFQT test topics that you are likely to encounter. No other book currently on the market and no existing Web site will provide you with as complete a content review as this book does. These topic reviews are key to the AFQT and, if you do the work, can definitely help you get a higher score on the AFQT. The reviews can also help you score high on other tests, such as the SAT and ACT, and on school exit exams and other mandated tests.

This section gives you review and advice on topics related to the Word Knowledge, Paragraph Comprehension, Mathematics Knowledge, and Arithmetic Reasoning tests that make up the AFQT. Relevant sections start with a quiz. After scoring your quiz, a chart is provided that will show you if your knowledge is good enough or if you will need to work harder to improve your skills.

To help you improve your scores, a complete and comprehensive review of the subject area is provided to get you ready for what you might find on the test. Examples of the types of skills that could be tested, along with example items and explanations of how the answers were determined, are given. Hundreds of practice items and their answers are included so that you can be sure that your skills are the best they can be. Practicing these items until they are second nature to you is the key to your success on the AFQT. Being comfortable with the content will help you answer the questions accurately in the short period of time given to you. The more questions you answer correctly, the higher you will score.

Part 3 contains two full-length, simulated AFQT forms—two tests each of Arithmetic Reasoning, Word Knowledge, Paragraph Comprehension, and Mathematics Knowledge—that are as close as possible to the real thing. This section will also provide you with the exact directions that you will hear from your test administrator and see in your test booklet. No other test preparation book has this information. You'll also find an exact replica of the actual answer sheet you will use with the paper-and-pencil version. At the end of the tests, you will be able to see the answers to the items and explanations that will help you understand why the correct answer is correct and why the other answers are wrong. The information in these explanations can help you even more to prepare for the real AFQT tests.

If you want to get a high AFQT score, you need to feel comfortable with what you will be facing on the day you take the test. This section will help you understand exactly what the real test is like. By knowing what to expect, you will feel more comfortable and less stressed, allowing you to perform better on the test. Once you sharpen your skills, the rest should be easy.

Part 4 provides information on occupations in the military and civilian worlds of work, so that you can see how the verbal and math AFQT test results matter to these careers. Even if you decide not to join the military or after you make the transition out, this information will be helpful for you in deciding what occupations seem right for you, based on your skills and abilities. This edition of Basic Training includes information on how the ASVAB Science and Technology Scores relate to military and Civilian Occupations. Although the tests that make up Science and Technology are not part of the AFQT, they are part of the full ASVAB battery.

A really helpful aspect of this section is showing how your personal interests relate to military and civilian careers. If you want, you can take a quick interest inventory that can give you an idea of your strongest interest areas. You can use your interest areas to look at both civilian and military occupations to determine which ones may be right for you! No other preparation book has this information.

HOW TO USE THIS BOOK

If you don't know much about the ASVAB and AFQT and how they relate to the military

- Read Chapter 1: Introducing the ASVAB.
- Read Chapter 2: The ASVAB, AFQT, and Military Entrance.
- Read Chapter 3: ASVAB Score Reports.
- Read Chapter 4: Taking the CAT-ASVAB.

If you want to know about the computerized ASVAB/AFQT

- Read Chapter 4: Taking the CAT-ASVAB.

If you want to know about the ASVAB and why it is important to the military

- Read Chapter 2: The ASVAB, AFQT, and Military Entrance.
- Read Chapter 3: ASVAB Score Reports.
- Read Chapter 4: Taking the CAT-ASVAB.

If you want to learn about the various AFQT question types and requirements

- Read Chapter 5: AFQT Question Types.

If you want to determine your vocabulary skills and improve your vocabulary

- Review Chapter 6: Sharpen Your Word Knowledge Skills.

If you want to determine your reading skills and improve your reading capabilities

- Review Chapter 7: Sharpen your Paragraph Comprehension Skills.

If you want to determine your math skills and improve those skills

- Review Chapter 8: Sharpen Your Math Skills.

If you want to determine your arithmetic reasoning skills and improve them

- Review Chapter 9: Sharpen Your Word Problem Skills.

If you want to diagnose your strengths and weaknesses in the verbal and math areas

- Take and score the quizzes in Chapters 6, 7, 8, and 9.

If you want to practice your verbal and math skills in order to perform well on the AFQT

- Complete the practice items in Chapter 6.
- Complete the practice items in Chapter 7.
- Complete the practice items in Chapter 8.
- Complete the practice items in Chapter 9.

If you want to refresh your knowledge of the AFQT test areas

- Go to Part 2 of this book, which provides a complete review of every topic tested.

If you want to practice taking the AFQT test

- Go to Part 3 of this book and take AFQT Practice Test Forms 1 and 2 under actual test conditions.

If you want to know about how well you have to score for specific jobs and training programs in the military

- Go to Part 4 of this book.

If you want to see how your interests and skills relate to civilian and military occupations

- Go to Part 4 of this book.

This book does not guarantee that it contains the actual ASVAB test questions. There are several forms of the paper-and-pencil version of the ASVAB and AFQT and many hundreds of items on the computerized version of the test. However, if you use this book as we recommend, it will certainly give you a major advantage in scoring high on the ASVAB. This will give you increased job and training opportunities that will help you in your military career and later in civilian jobs.

Good luck in your efforts! I hope you are inspired by the following quotes.

Learning is not attained by chance, it must be sought for with ardor and attended to with diligence.

—Abigail Adams

Desire is the key to motivation, but it's the determination and commitment to an unrelenting pursuit of your goal, a commitment to excellence, that will enable you to attain the success you seek.

—Mario Andretti

The quality of a person's life is in direct proportion to their commitment to excellence, regardless of their chosen field of endeavor.

—Vince Lombardi

If you work hard, if you're well-prepared, if you learn from your failures, and if you always do the very best you can, then your chances of success are increased a hundred times.

—Colin Powell

ALL ABOUT THE ASVAB AND THE AFQT

Introducing the ASVAB

WHAT IS THE ASVAB?

Everyone who wishes to join any branch of the U.S. Armed Forces must take the Armed Services Vocational Aptitude Battery (ASVAB). The education level of military personnel is a major concern, and the military does not take just anyone who wants to enlist. The ASVAB is one tool that the military uses to measure the abilities of potential recruits. The ASVAB is also given to civilian high school students to help them explore their aptitudes for different careers. Results from the high school assessment can be used for military entrance.

The ASVAB is actually a group of individual aptitude tests. The tests are listed in the charts that follow. Each test measures something important for either military entrance or acceptance into training programs for certain military jobs. Your scores on certain tests determine whether you are eligible for enlistment. Once you are accepted into the military, your ASVAB scores are used to qualify you for various military occupations. The higher your scores, the more choices you will have for training in different occupations.

Different Versions of the ASVAB

The ASVAB comes in two formats. Persons who take the ASVAB in schools and at certain other locations in the country are given a paper-and-pencil test battery. This version of the test has 200 items

and takes a little over two hours to complete. The test taker reads the questions in a test booklet and answers them by filling in bubbles on a machine-readable answer sheet. The sheets are taken to a scoring location, and the results are returned to the school and to recruiters. There are four separate forms of the paper-and-pencil version of the test. The following chart shows the subtests that make up the paper-and-pencil ASVAB.

In recent years, the Department of Defense has implemented a computer version of the test. Individuals who take this form of the ASVAB sit in a room with computers and answer the questions using the keyboard. One of the special characteristics of the computer version is that the test is adapted to the ability level of each individual. This feature is called computer adaptive testing (CAT), so this version of the ASVAB is called CAT-ASVAB.

The CAT-ASVAB has fewer items than the paper-and-pencil version and takes less time. Because the items are tailored to your ability level, you will not receive many easy items or many items that are far too difficult for you. Items are selected based on whether or not you get the previous answer correct. The items that are given to you are drawn from a very large pool of items, and no two people get exactly the same test. The chart on p. 5 shows the subtests that make up the CAT-ASVAB.

It doesn't matter which version of the ASVAB you take because you will end up with the same military enlistment score.

The Paper-and-Pencil ASVAB

Subtest	Minutes	Questions	Description
General Science	11	25	Measures knowledge of physical, earth and space, and biological sciences
Arithmetic Reasoning	36	30	Measures ability to solve basic arithmetic word problems
Word Knowledge	11	35	Measures ability to select the correct meaning of words presented through synonyms
Paragraph Comprehension	13	15	Measures ability to obtain information from written material
Mathematics Knowledge	24	25	Measures knowledge of high school mathematics concepts and applications
Electronics Information	9	20	Tests knowledge of electrical current, circuits, devices, and electronic systems
Auto and Shop Information	11	25	Measures knowledge of automotive maintenance and repair, and wood and metal shop practices
Mechanical Comprehension	19	25	Measures knowledge of the principles of mechanical devices, structural support, and properties of materials.

WHO TAKES THE ASVAB?

About 1.3 million people take the ASVAB each year, making it the most popular aptitude test in the country. The ASVAB can be taken by students in grades 10, 11, and 12 and by those in postsecondary schools. It is used in about 14,000 schools across the country. Many students take the ASVAB in order to help them identify their strengths and weaknesses and to help them seek out and explore careers and jobs.

Scores of students in grades 11 and above are acceptable for use in the military enlistment process if the scores are no more than two years old. If you took the ASVAB more than two years ago, you must take the test again if you are interested in enlisting in the military. If you have never taken the ASVAB in school, you can contact a recruiter or visit a local recruiting station to request the test.

Hundreds of thousands of people take the ASVAB at government locations for the purpose of enlisting in the military. If you take the ASVAB at a government location, you must be 17 years of age or older for your scores to count for enlistment purposes.

WHERE CAN YOU TAKE THE ASVAB?

There are several places where you can take the ASVAB: at your school, at a Military Entrance Processing Station (MEPS), or at a Mobile Examining Team site (METS).

Your School

About 800,000 students take the ASVAB at their school every year. If you are a student at a high

THE CAT-ASVAB

Subtest	Minutes	Questions	Description
General Science	11	25	Measures knowledge of physical, earth and space, and biological sciences
Arithmetic Reasoning	36	30	Measures ability to solve basic arithmetic word problems
Word Knowledge	11	35	Measures ability to select the correct meaning of words presented through synonyms
Paragraph Comprehension	13	15	Measures ability to obtain information from written material
Mathematics Knowledge	24	25	Measures knowledge of high school mathematics concepts and applications
Electronics Information	9	20	Tests knowledge of electrical current, circuits, devices, and electronic systems
Auto and Shop Information	11	25	Measures knowledge of automotive maintenance and repair, and wood and metal shop practices
Mechanical Comprehension	19	25	Measures knowledge of the principles of mechanical devices, structural support, and properties of materials
Assembling Objects	16	9	Measures the ability to interpret diagrams showing spatial relationships and how objects are related and connected.

school or postsecondary school, it is very likely that the ASVAB is offered at your school at least once a year. It is offered at more than 14,000 schools across the United States. There is no charge to students for taking the ASVAB.

Watch for school announcements that mention testing dates and times. Keep your eye out for announcements on the bulletin board. Visit your career center and ask about the ASVAB testing dates scheduled for your school. Ask your school counselor when the ASVAB will be offered at your school or a nearby school. Your school counselor will have received information about the ASVAB from a local representative and should be able to tell you where and when it will be offered. If the ASVAB is not offered at your school, your counselor can arrange to include you in a testing session at a nearby school.

Unlike taking the SAT or the ACT, taking the ASVAB at your school does not cost you anything except your time and effort.

The ASVAB test can be taken by students in grades 10 through 12 and also by students at the postsecondary level. Scores at the tenth-grade level cannot be used for military entrance, but taking the test in tenth grade is a good idea because it can give you an idea of how you will do on an ASVAB test that counts for military enlistment. It is good practice for other tests that you will take in your lifetime as well.

Scores from ASVAB tests taken in grades 11 and 12 and at the postsecondary level can be used for military entrance for up to two years. If you took the test in eleventh or twelfth grade, but you think that you could score higher, you may wish to retake the ASVAB at a MEPS to see if you can exceed your high school scores.

If you take the ASVAB at a school, you will probably take it with a group of students. The administration procedures should be professionally delivered by competent government test administrators. This is important because you need to perform your very best on this test and any other tests you may take.

The MEPS

You can take the ASVAB test at a local Military Entrance Processing Station (MEPS). There are 65 MEPS located all across the United States. (See the list of MEPS in this chapter.) At a MEPS, you will take the computer version of the test. This test will seem different from the paper-and-pencil version, as it will have fewer items, but those items will be tailored by the computer to your level of ability. As discussed earlier, this ASVAB test is tailored or adapted to your particular ability level. The directions will be self-explanatory, and you will determine the pace of the test. It is likely that you will finish the CAT-ASVAB in less time than it would take you to finish the paper-and-pencil instrument.

Don't worry about taking the CAT-ASVAB, as you will receive the same scores as you would on the paper-and-pencil version.

Later on in this book you will learn more about how the CAT-ASVAB works and what you should expect.

MET Sites

There are about 500 mobile examining team (MET) sites across the country. They have been set up to qualify military applicants at locations that may be remote or distant from a MEPS. If you live a long way away from the nearest MEPS, you can take the ASVAB at a MET site, That way, you and the recruiter can determine whether you are qualified to enter the military without spending the time and money it would take you to travel to a MEPS.

At a MET site you will receive a paper-and-pencil version of the test, not the CAT-ASVAB. Note, however, that this may change in the future. The test you will take includes Assembling Objects.

WHO ADMINISTERS THE ASVAB?

The answer to this question depends on where you take the test battery. If you take the ASVAB at a school or at a MET site, you will have a trained, civilian test administrator from the Office of Personnel Management. These are individuals who are contracted by the federal government to adhere to the strict timing and directions of ASVAB administration.

If you take the ASVAB at a MEPS, you will have a military administrator who will help you get started on the CAT-ASVAB.

CAN YOU TAKE THE ASVAB MORE THAN ONCE?

If you have taken the ASVAB within the past two years, you can retake the test as long as you follow certain rules.

The rules about retaking the ASVAB are as follows. First, you must take the entire test battery— that is, all eight subtests, not just one. Military applicants who have taken an initial ASVAB (student or enlistment) can retake the test after one calendar month has elapsed. For example, if you first took the test on February 3, the earliest you could retake it would be March 3. If you wished to retake the test a second time, you would have to wait until April 3. After that, you would need to wait at least six months before you could take the test again. In other words, if you first took the test on February 3, took a retest on March 3, and took a second retest on April 3, you would have to wait until October 3 before you could take a third retest.

Retesting with the same version of the ASVAB that was used on any previous test is strictly prohibited for at least six months. If an applicant is retested with the same test version within a six-month period, the retest score will be invalidated and the previous valid test score will stand as the score of record. However, if the condition is the result of a procedural or administrative error by a MEPS or OPM test administrator, the MEPS

Sample Retesting Schedule

3 Feb	3 March	3 April	3 May	3 June	3 July	3 Aug	3 Sept	3 October
Initial test	First retest	Second retest						Third retest

commander may authorize an immediate retest using a different ASVAB version.

Applicants who are dismissed for cheating or disruptive behavior will have their test invalidated and are not authorized to be retested for six months from the date of the invalid test.

If you are taking the ASVAB in order to enlist in the military and your AFQT score on your most recent test is 20 points or higher than your score on an ASVAB you took less than six months previously, you will be required to complete a confirmation test.

Retaking the ASVAB for Enlistment if You Took It in High School

If you took the test in high school, should you take it again if you want to join the military? Remember that you can retake the test every six months and that your highest score will be the one used for military enlistment purposes. That being the case, it is a good idea to take the test again if you think you can get a better score.

Contact Information for the Military Entrance Processing Stations

ALABAMA
Montgomery
Maxwell Air Force Base—Gunter Annex
705 McDonald Street
Building 1512
Montgomery, AL 36114-3110

PHONE: (334) 416-6377, ext. 203
FAX: (334) 416-5034
E-MAIL: mntg-sec@mepcom.army.mil

ALASKA
Anchorage
1717 "C" Street
Anchorage, AK 99501

PHONE: (907) 274-9142
FAX: (907) 274-7268
E-MAIL: anch-sec@mepcom.army.mil

ARIZONA
Phoenix
1 North 1st Street
Suite 613
Phoenix, AZ 85004-2357

PHONE: (602) 258-1703
FAX: (602) 258-8206
E-MAIL: phoe-sec@mepcom.army.mil

ARKANSAS
Little Rock
1520 Riverfront Drive
Little Rock, AR 72202-1724

PHONE: (501) 666-6377
FAX: (501) 663-5863
E-MAIL: nirk-sec@mepcom.army.mil

CALIFORNIA
Los Angeles
5051 Rodeo Road
Los Angeles, CA 90016

PHONE: (323) 292-2202, ext. 221
FAX: (323) 292-0004
E-MAIL: losa-sec@mepcom.army.mil

Sacramento
3870 Rosin Court
Suite 105
Sacramento, CA 95834-1648

PHONE: (916) 564-0253
FAX: (916) 564-0268
E-MAIL: sato-sec@mepcom.army.mil

San Diego
4181 Ruffin Rd
Suite B
San Diego, CA 92123

Phone: (858) 874-2400, ext. 261
Fax: (858) 874-0415
E-mail: sndi-sec@mepcom.army.mil

San Jose
546 Vernon Avenue
Mountain View, CA 94043

Phone: (650) 603-8223
Fax: (650) 603-8225
E-mail: snjo-sec@mepcom.army.mil

COLORADO
Denver
275 New Custom House
19th and Stout Streets
Denver, CO 80202

Phone: (303) 623-1020, ext. 223
Fax: (303) 623-5506
E-mail: denv-sec@mepcom.army.mil

FLORIDA
Jacksonville
4051 Phillips Highway
Jacksonville, FL 32207-7299

Phone: (904) 737-6861
Fax: (904) 448-6794
E-mail: jacv-sec@mepcom.army.mil

Miami
7789 NW 48th Street
Suite 150
Miami, FL 33166

Phone: (305) 463-0891, ext. 248
Fax: (305) 629-8923
E-mail: miam-sec@mepcom.army.mil

Tampa
3520 West Waters Avenue
Tampa, FL 33614-2716

Phone: (813) 932-0079, ext. 1105
Fax: (813) 932-8763
E-mail: tamp-sec@mepcom.army.mil

GEORGIA
Atlanta
1500 Hood Avenue, Building 720
Fort Gillem, GA 30297-5000

Phone: (404) 469-3090
Fax: (404) 469-5367
E-mail: atla-sec@mepcom.army.mil

HAWAII
Honolulu
490 Central Avenue
Pearl Harbor, HI 96860

Phone: (808) 471-8725
Fax: (808) 471-2888
E-mail: hono-sec@mepcom.army.mil

IDAHO
Boise
550 West Fort Street
MSC 044
Boise, ID 83724-0101

Phone: (208) 334-1450, ext. 202
Fax: (208) 334-1580
E-mail: bois-sec@mepcom.army.mil

ILLINOIS
Chicago
1700 South Wolf Road
Des Plaines, IL 60018

Phone: (847) 803-6111
Fax: (847) 803-4626
E-mail: chic-sec@mepcom.army.mil

INDIANA
Indianapolis
5541 Herbert Lord Drive
Indianapolis, IN 46256

Phone: (317) 554-0531, ext. 201
Fax: (317) 554-0541
E-mail: indi-sec@mepcom.army.mil

IOWA
Des Moines
7105 NW 70th Avenue
Building S-71
Johnston, IA 50131

Phone: (515) 224-0125, ext. 312
Fax: (515) 224-4906
E-mail: desm-sec@mepcom.army.mil

KENTUCKY
Louisville
600 Dr. Martin Luther King, Jr., Place
Room 477
Louisville, KY 40202

Phone: (502) 582-5921, ext. 2222
Fax: (502) 582-6566
E-mail: lvil-sec@mepcom.army.mil

LOUISIANA
New Orleans
4400 Dauphine Street
Building 603-1C
New Orleans, LA 70146-5900

PHONE: (504) 943-0470, ext. 225
FAX: (504) 943-5670
E-MAIL: newo-sec@mepcom.army.mil

Shreveport
2715 Alkay Drive
Shreveport, LA 71118-2509

PHONE: (318) 671-6080, ext. 203
FAX: (318) 671-6097
E-MAIL: shrv-sec@mepcom.army.mil

MAINE
Portland
510 Congress Street
3rd Floor
Portland, ME 04101-4103

PHONE: (207) 775-3408
FAX: (207) 775-2947
E-MAIL: porm-sec@mepcom.army.mil

MARYLAND
Baltimore
850 Chisholm Avenue
Fort Meade, MD 20755

PHONE: (301) 677-0422
FAX: (301) 677-0440
E-MAIL: balt-sec@mepcom.army.mil

MASSACHUSETTS
Boston
Barnes Building
495 Summer Street
4th Floor
Boston, MA 02210

PHONE: (617) 753-3100
FAX: (617) 426-7486
E-MAIL: bost-sec@mepcom.army.mil

Springfield
551 Airlift Drive
Westover JARB
Springfield, MA 01022-1519

PHONE: (413) 593-9543, ext. 200
FAX: (413) 593-9485
DSN: 589-111
E-MAIL: spri-sec@mepcom.army.mil

MICHIGAN
Detroit
1172 Kirts Blvd.
Troy, MI 48084-4846

PHONE: (248) 244-8534
FAX: (248) 244-9352
E-MAIL: detr-sec@mepcom.army.mil

Lansing
120 East Jolly Road
Lansing, MI 48910

PHONE: (517) 887-1714
FAX: (517) 877-9160
E-MAIL: lans-sec@mepcom.army.mil

MINNESOTA
Minneapolis
Bishop Henry Whipple Federal Building
1 Federal Drive
Suite 3300
Fort Snelling, MN 55111-4080

PHONE: (612) 725-1772
FAX: (612) 725-1749
E-MAIL: minn-sec@mepcom.army.mil

MISSISSIPPI
Jackson
664 South State Street
Jackson, MS 39201

PHONE: (601) 355-3835, ext. 203
FAX: (601) 352-5708
E-MAIL: json-sec@mepcom.army.mil

MISSOURI
Kansas City
10316 NW Prairie View Road
Kansas City, MO 64153-1350

PHONE: (816) 891-9490
FAX: (816) 891-8258
E-MAIL: kans-sec@mepcom.army.mil

St. Louis
Robert A. Young Federal Building
1222 Spruce Street
St. Louis, MO 63103-2816

PHONE: (314) 331-4040
FAX: (314) 331-5699
E-MAIL: stlu-sec@mepcom.army.mil

MONTANA
Butte
22 West Park Street
Butte, MT 59701
PHONE: (406) 723-8883, ext. 222
FAX: (406) 782-7797
E-MAIL: butt-sec@mepcom.army.mil

NEBRASKA
Omaha
5303 "F" Street
Omaha, NE 68117-2805
PHONE: (402) 733-7474, ext. 4
FAX: (402) 733-7660
E-MAIL: omah-sec@mepcom.army.mil

NEW JERSEY
Fort Dix
Building 5645 Texas Avenue
Fort Dix, NJ 08640
PHONE: (609) 562-6050, ext. 2306
FAX: (609) 562-5207
E-MAIL: dixx-sec@mepcom.army.mil

NEW MEXICO
Albuquerque
505 Central Ave NW
Suite A
Albuquerque, NM 87102-3113
PHONE: (505) 246-8020
FAX: (505) 246-8861
E-MAIL: albq-sec@mepcom.army.mil

NEW YORK
Albany
Leo W. O'Brien Federal Building
North Pearl Street & Clinton Avenue
Albany, NY 12207
PHONE: (518) 320-9860
FAX: (518) 320-9869
E-MAIL: alba-sec@mepcom.army.mil

Buffalo
2024 Ent Avenue
Building 799
Niagara Falls ARS, NY 14304-5000

PHONE: (716) 501-9012
FAX: (716) 501-9027
E-MAIL: buff-sec@mepcom.army.mil

New York
Fort Hamilton Military Community
116 White Avenue
Brooklyn, NY 11252-6700
PHONE: (718) 630-4646
FAX: (718) 833-1037
E-MAIL: newy-sec@mepcom.army.mil

Syracuse
6001 East Malloy Road
Building 710
Syracuse, NY 13211-2100
PHONE: (315) 455-3012
FAX: (315) 455-7807
E-MAIL: syra-sec@mepcom.army.mil

NORTH CAROLINA
Charlotte
6125 Tyvola Centre
Charlotte, NC 28217-6447
PHONE: (704) 665-6620
FAX: (704) 665-6678
E-MAIL: char-sec@mepcom.army.mil

Raleigh
2625 Appliance Court
Raleigh, NC 27604
PHONE: (919) 834-7787
FAX: (919) 755-1303
E-MAIL: rale-sec@mepcom.army.mil

NORTH DAKOTA
Fargo
225 Fourth Avenue North
Fargo, ND 58102
PHONE: (701) 234-0473
FAX: (701) 234-0597
E-MAIL: farg-sec@mepcom.army.mil

OHIO
Cleveland
20637 Emerald Parkway Drive
Cleveland, Ohio 44135-6023
PHONE: (216) 267-1286
FAX: (216) 522-9860
E-MAIL: clev-sec@mepcom.army.mil

Columbus
775 Taylor Road
Gahanna, OH 43230
PHONE: (614) 868-8430, ext. 220
FAX: (614) 856-9065
E-MAIL: cooh-sec@mepcom.army.mil

OKLAHOMA
Oklahoma City
301 Northwest 6th Street
Suite 150
Oklahoma City, OK 73102
PHONE: (405) 609-8700
FAX: (405) 609-8639
E-MAIL: okcy-sec@mepcom.army.mil

OREGON
Portland
7545 NE Ambassador Place
Portland, OR 97220-1367
PHONE: (503) 528-1630
FAX: (503) 528-1640
E-MAIL: poro-sec@mepcom.army.mil

PENNSYLVANIA
Harrisburg
4641 Westport Drive
Mechanicsburg, PA 17055
PHONE: (717) 691-6180
FAX: (717) 691-8039
E-MAIL: hari-sec@mepcom.army.mil

Pittsburgh
William S. Moorehead Federal Building
1000 Liberty Avenue
Suite 1705
Pittsburgh, PA 15222-4101
PHONE: (412) 395-5873
FAX: (412) 281-0859
E-MAIL: pitt-sec@mepcom.army.mil

PUERTO RICO
San Juan
Highway 28
GSA Building 651
Guaynabo, PR 00968
PHONE: (787) 277-7500
FAX: (787) 277-7507
E-MAIL: snju-sec@mepcom.army.mil

SOUTH CAROLINA
Fort Jackson
2435 Marion Avenue
Fort Jackson, SC 29207
PHONE: (803) 751-5141
FAX: (803) 751-5744
E-MAIL: jack-sec@mepcom.army.mil

SOUTH DAKOTA
Sioux Falls
2801 South Kiwanis Avenue
Suite 200
Sioux Falls, SD 57105
PHONE: (605) 334-0280
FAX: (605) 332-8412
E-MAIL: siou-sec@mepcom.army.mil

TENNESSEE
Knoxville
9745 Parkside Drive
Knoxville, TN 37922
PHONE: (865) 531-8221, ext. 221
FAX: (865) 531-8741
E-MAIL: kxvl-sec@mepcom.army.mil

Memphis
480 Beale Street
Memphis, TN, 38103-3232
PHONE: (901) 526-2100
FAX: (901) 527-7832
E-MAIL: memp-sec@mepcom.army.mil

Nashville
4751 Trousdale Drive
Nashville, TN 37211
PHONE: (615) 833-1347, ext. 112
FAX: (615) 833-2570
E-MAIL: nash-sec@mepcom.army.mil

TEXAS
Amarillo
1100 South Fillmore
Suite 100
Amarillo, TX 79101
PHONE: (806) 379-9037
FAX: (806) 374-9332
E-MAIL: amar-sec@mepcom.army.mil

Dallas

Federal Building
207 South Houston Street
Suite 400
Dallas, TX 75202

Pʜᴏɴᴇ: (214) 655-3200
Fᴀx: (214) 655-3213
E-ᴍᴀɪʟ: dall-sec@mepcom.army.mil

El Paso

6380 Morgan Avenue
Building 6380, Suite E
El Paso TX 79906-4610

Pʜᴏɴᴇ: (915) 568-3505
Fᴀx: (915) 568-4477
E-ᴍᴀɪʟ: elpa-sec@mepcom.army.mil

Houston

701 San Jacinto Street
P.O. Box 52309
Houston, TX 77052-2309

Pʜᴏɴᴇ: (713) 718-4220
Fᴀx: (713) 718-4228
E-ᴍᴀɪʟ: hous-sec@mepcom.army.mil

San Antonio

1950 Stanley Road
Suite 103
Fort Sam Houston, TX 78234-5102

Pʜᴏɴᴇ: (210) 295-9031
Fᴀx: (210) 295-9151
DSN: 421-9031
E-ᴍᴀɪʟ: snan-sec@mepcom.army.mil

UTAH

Salt Lake City

2830 South Redwood Road
Salt Lake City, UT 84119-2375

Pʜᴏɴᴇ: (801) 975-3701
Fᴀx: (801) 975-3715
E-ᴍᴀɪʟ: salt-sec@mepcom.army.mil

VIRGINIA

Ft. Lee

2011 Mahone Avenue
Ft. Lee, VA 23801-1707

Pʜᴏɴᴇ: (804) 765-4180
Fᴀx: (804) 765-4190
E-ᴍᴀɪʟ: leee-sec@mepcom.army.mil

WASHINGTON

Seattle

4735 East Marginal Way South
Seattle, WA 98134-2385

Pʜᴏɴᴇ: (206) 766-6400, ext. 7525
Fᴀx: (206) 766-6430
E-ᴍᴀɪʟ: seat-sec@mepcom.army.mil

Spokane

Federal Building
920 West Riverside Avenue
2nd Floor
Spokane, WA 99201

Pʜᴏɴᴇ: (509) 353-3105
Fᴀx: (509) 353-3104
E-ᴍᴀɪʟ: spok-sec@mepcom.army.mil

WEST VIRGINIA

Beckley

409 Wood Mountain Road
Glen Jean, WV 25846

Pʜᴏɴᴇ: (304) 465-0208
Fᴀx: (304) 465-3194
E-ᴍᴀɪʟ: beck-sec@mepcom.army.mil

WISCONSIN

Milwaukee

11050 West Liberty Drive
Milwaukee, WI 53224

Pʜᴏɴᴇ: (414) 359-1315
Fᴀx: (414) 359-1390
E-ᴍᴀɪʟ: milw-sec@mepcom.army.mil

Chapter 2

The ASVAB, the AFQT, and Military Entrance

READ THIS CHAPTER TO LEARN:

- **What parts of the ASVAB make up the AFQT**
- **How AFQT scores are used to determine eligibility for enlistment**
- **What are the other educational requirements for military recruits**
- **What happens during the rest of the military entrance process**

WHAT IS THE AFQT?

The Armed Forces Qualifying Test (AFQT) is a part of the ASVAB. It is made up of the four subtests Word Knowledge, Paragraph Comprehension, Arithmetic Reasoning, and Math Knowledge. When you take the ASVAB, one of the scores you will receive will be your AFQT score (also called the Military Entrance Score). This is the most important score for the purpose of entrance into the military. You will need to achieve a certain AFQT score in order to be eligible for initial enlistment. The purpose of this book is to help you raise your AFQT score.

HOW ARE AFQT SCORES CALCULATED?

The AFQT score is calculated by combining your scores on the Word Knowledge and Paragraph Comprehension tests into a composite called Verbal Ability (VE) and adding to it your scores on Math Knowledge (MK) and Arithmetic Reasoning (AR). In math terms, the formula is $AFQT = 2VE + MK + AR$. That score is then compared to the scores of a nationally representative sample of other test takers aged 18 to 23 to produce a percentile score. The percentile indicates how well you ranked in comparison to these individuals. The higher the AFQT score, the higher the percentile.

HOW ARE AFQT SCORES USED?

Your AFQT percentile score determines where you fit into what are called AFQT categories. The Armed Services use these categories to set recruiting goals. Recruiters prefer to recruit people in the highest categories because they are generally smarter and easier to train in the various occupations needed by the military. It is also more economical for the Department of Defense to recruit smarter individuals because they learn what is needed much more quickly and they perform better on the job.

Persons in Categories I and II are above average in trainability. Category III recruits tend to be average in trainability, and Category IV recruits are below average in trainability. Applicants scoring in Category V are forbidden by law to be accepted into the military. In addition, applicants in Category IV who do not have a high school diploma are generally forbidden to enter the military.

The Armed Services are required to enlist at least 60 percent of recruits from AFQT Categories I through IIIA, and no more than 4 percent of the recruits can come from Category IV. To give you an idea of the percentages of recruits in each AFQT category, look at the following table. You can see that very few recruits come from Category IV and none come from Category V.

Armed Forces Qualification Test (AFQT) Categories and Corresponding Percentile Score Ranges

AFQT Category	Percentile Score Range
I	93–99
II	65–92
IIIA	50–64
IIIB	31–49
IV	10–30
V	1–9

AFQT Scores of Active Component NPS Accessions, by Gender and Service (Percent)

AFQT Category	Army	Navy	Marine Corps	Air Force	DoD	18- to 23-Year-Old Civilians
			Males			
I	7.2	7.1	5.3	8.2	7.0	8.1
II	37.0	38.1	37.3	46.8	39.0	29.0
IIIA	28.8	24.9	27.2	27.8	27.5	15.3
IIIB	26.0	29.9	29.5	16.3	25.8	18.4
IV	0.7	0.0	0.6	0.0	0.4	19.6
V	0.3	0.0	0.1	1.0	0.3	9.6
Total	100.0	100.0	100.0	100.0	100.0	100.0
			Females			
I	4.0	3.9	4.0	3.9	3.9	7.6
II	30.3	33.8	36.9	39.5	34.0	26.4
IIIA	29.7	32.1	31.7	34.1	31.5	15.8
IIIB	34.9	30.1	27.2	21.9	29.9	19.2
IV	0.8	0.0	0.2	0.0	0.4	21.9
V	0.3	0.1	0.0	0.6	0.3	9.2
Total	100.0	100.0	100.0	100.0	100.0	100.0

Columns may not add to total due to rounding.
Source: Defense Manpower Data Center

OTHER EDUCATIONAL REQUIREMENTS

The amount of education you have obtained also affects your eligibility to enter military service. The Department of Defense uses a three-tier classification of education credentials. The three tiers are:

Tier 1. Regular high school graduates, adult diploma holders, and nongraduates with at least 15 hours of college credit.

Tier 2. Alternative credential holders, including those with a General Education Development (GED) certificate of high school equivalency.

Tier 3. Those with no education credential.

The reason for this classification system is that there is a strong relationship between education credentials and successful completion of the first term of military service. That is, if you have a good AFQT and good educational credentials, you are more likely to complete your required service and not drop out partway through (an outcome that would waste the taxpayer dollars spent to train you).

The Armed Services are required to ensure that at least 90 percent of first-time recruits are high school graduates. Individual services often set even higher educational standards, sometimes requiring nearly 100 percent of the recruits in their enlistment pool to be high school graduates. If you don't have a high school diploma, you will need a high AFQT score.

There are different AFQT scoring standards for individuals in each tier. Generally, Tier 3 applicants must have higher AFQT test scores than Tier 2 applicants, who must have higher test scores than applicants in Tier 1. The Air Force and Marine Corps follow these differential standards, requiring different minimum test scores for each tier. The Army and Navy require applicants with alternative credentials (Tier 2) and those with no credentials (Tier 3) to meet the same AFQT standards, which are more stringent than those for high school graduates (Tier 1).

So if you want to enlist in the military, your chances are much better if you have graduated from high school with a traditional diploma and score high on the AFQT.

BEYOND THE ASVAB
Physical Condition and Moral Character Requirements

If you achieve a satisfactory ASVAB score and continue the application process, you will be scheduled for a physical examination and background review at one of the 65 Military Entrance Processing Stations (MEPS). The examination determines your fitness for military service. It includes measurement of blood pressure, pulse, visual acuity, and hearing; blood testing and urinalysis; drug and HIV testing; taking of a medical history; and possibly tests of strength and endurance. If you have a fixable or temporary medical problem, you may be required to get treatment before proceeding. It is possible but very difficult to obtain a waiver of certain disqualifying medical conditions before being allowed to enlist.

To enter one of the services, you must meet rigorous moral character standards. You will be screened by the recruiter and will undergo an interview covering your background. You may undergo a financial credit check; a computerized search for a criminal record may also be conducted. Some types of criminal activity are clearly disqualifying; other cases require a waiver. The service to which you applied will examine your circumstances and make an individual determination of your qualification. Since it has been shown that applicants with existing financial problems generally do not overcome those problems on junior enlisted pay, your credit history may be part of the decision to allow you to enlist or not.

Military Occupational Counseling

If your ASVAB scores, educational credentials, physical fitness, and moral character qualify you for entry and you wish to proceed with the process, you will meet with a service classification counselor at the MEPS to discuss options for enlistment. The counselor has the record of your qualifications and computerized information on available service training and skill openings, schedules, and enlistment incentives.

A recruit can sign up for a specific skill or for a broad occupational area (such as the mechanical or electronics area). In the Army, most recruits (95 percent) enter for specific skill training; the others are placed in a military occupational specialty during basic training. Approximately 70 percent of Air Force recruits enter for a specific skill, while the rest sign up for an occupational area and are classified into a specific skill while in basic training. In the Navy, approximately 79 percent of recruits enlist for a specific skill, while the rest go directly to the fleet in airman, fireman, or seaman programs after basic training. Approximately 86 percent of Marine Corps enlistees enter with a guaranteed occupational area and are assigned a specific skill within that area after recruit training; the rest either enlist with a specific job guarantee or are assigned to a job after recruit training.

Your counselor will discuss your interests with you and will explain what the particular service has to offer. Typically, the counselor will describe a number of different occupations to you. In general, the higher your test scores, the more choices you will have. The counselor may suggest incentives to encourage you to choose hard-to-fill occupational specialties. You are free to accept or reject these offers. Many applicants do not decide immediately, but take the time to discuss their options with their family and friends; others decide not to enlist. The Armed Services do not discriminate based on race, religion, or gender, but females are barred from entering certain combat occupations. In fact, about 22 to 23 percent of the Armed Forces are female.

What Happens Next

When you accept an offer and sign a contract, you will need to choose between two options. One option is to proceed directly to a recruit training center within a month of signing the contract. However, very few people select this option. Most people choose the second option, which is to enter the Delayed Entry Program (DEP). This allows you up to a year before you need to report for duty. During this time, you can continue your education, obtain your high school diploma, take advantage of a supervised exercise program, and, in general, become acclimated to the military. The length of time you are in the DEP depends on the training opportunities for the occupation you have selected.

If you are selected, you will be one of the nearly 400,000 individuals each year who have elected to serve and protect their country by joining the Armed Forces of the United States.

Preparing for a Day at the MEPS

1. Discuss any childhood medical problems with your parents and bring documentation with you.
2. Bring your Social Security card, birth certificate and driver's license.
3. Remove all piercings.
4. Profanity and offensive wording or pictures on clothing are not tolerated.
5. Hats are not permitted inside the MEPS.
6. If you wear either eyeglasses or contacts, bring them along with your prescription and lens case.
7. Bathe or shower the night before your examination.
8. Wear underclothes.
9. Get a good night's sleep before taking the ASVAB.
10. Wear neat, moderate, comfortable clothing.
11. Don't bring stereo headphones, watches, jewelry, excessive cash or any other valuables.
12. Ask your recruiter for a list of recommended personal items to bring to basic training.
13. Processing starts early at the MEPS—you must report on time.

Chapter 3

ASVAB Score Reports

READ THIS CHAPTER TO LEARN:

- **What information will be on your score report**
- **How standard scores differ from percentile scores**
- **What ASVAB score reports look like**

Once you take the ASVAB, the score report you receive will depend on where you took the test. The amount of information you receive will also depend on whether you took the paper-and-pencil version or the computer adaptive version of the ASVAB.

IF YOU TAKE THE ASVAB AT A SCHOOL

If you take the ASVAB at a school, a score report will be sent to your school within 14 days after the test. Your score report will include a number of different scores, as discussed here.

Subtest Scores and AFQT Score

Your score report will include scores for each of the subtests in the test battery. It will also include your Armed Forces Qualifying Test (AFQT) score, the score that determines whether you are eligible for military enlistment. The AFQT score is also called the Military Entrance score.

Career Exploration Scores

Your score report will also show three Career Exploration Scores: Verbal Skills, Math Skills, and Science and Technical Skills. These are composite scores that combine your scores on several ASVAB subtests. The Verbal Skills score includes Word Knowledge and Paragraph Comprehension. The Math Skills score includes Arithmetic Reasoning and Mathematics Knowledge. The Science and Technical

Skills score includes General Science, Electronics Information, and Mechanical Comprehension.

The ASVAB Career Exploration Scores are a good indicator of the kinds of tasks that test takers do well and the kinds of tasks that they may find difficult.

- *Verbal Skills* is a general measure of the vocabulary and reading skills covered in the Word Knowledge and Paragraph Comprehension tests. People with high Verbal Skills scores tend to do well on tasks that require good vocabulary or reading skills, while people with low scores have more difficulty with such tasks.
- *Math Skills* is a general measure of the mathematics skills covered in the Mathematics Knowledge and Arithmetic Reasoning tests. People with high Math Skills scores tend to do well on tasks that require knowledge of mathematics, while people with low scores have more difficulty with these tasks.
- *Science and Technical Skills* is a general measure of the science and technical skills that are covered in the General Science, Electronics Information, and Mechanical Comprehension tests. People with high Science and Technical Skills scores tend to do well on tasks that require scientific thinking or technical skills, while people with low scores have more difficulty with such tasks.

Standard Scores and Percentile Scores

Each of the scores just described is reported in two ways: as a standard score and as a percentile score.

The standard score is calculated by applying statistical methods to the student's raw score. This produces a numerical score with a short range of possible statistical error above and below it. Most students who take the ASVAB achieve standard scores between 30 and 70. This means that a standard score of 50 is an average score and a score of 60 is an above-average score. The score report shows the numerical standard scores and a graph on which the scores appear with bands above and below them indicating the range of possible statistical error. According to the report, if you took the test again, your new score would most likely fall within this range.

The percentile scores on the ASVAB score report indicate how well the student did in relation to others in the same grade. For each test and composite, students receive a same grade/same sex, same grade/opposite sex, and same grade/combined sex percentile score. For example, if you are a female eleventh grader, you will get percentile scores showing how well you did compared to other females in the eleventh grade, males in the eleventh grade, and all eleventh graders. If you scored a same grade/same sex percentile of 72 on Math Skills, that means that you scored as well as or better than 72 out of 100 eleventh-grade females in Math Skills.

Because the experiences of males and females differ, they can score somewhat differently on tests. On the more technically oriented tests, such as Electronics Information, the mean performance of males is higher than that of females. This does not mean that women cannot learn this information or that they should be discouraged from considering occupations in related areas. Typically, this difference occurs because more males than females have had exposure to electronics principles. As a result, it is fairer to report how students do compared to others of their own sex, but also to let them know how they compare to members of the opposite sex on tests that might be important to them. For example, a female student might be interested in a career in mechanics, surveying, or civil engineering. Knowing how she scores relative to both her own sex and the opposite sex is useful information. In the past, these career fields have traditionally been dominated by males. Since she will be competing with males, it is important for her to know how she stands relative to males. The same is true for males interested in occupations that have traditionally been dominated by females.

IF YOU TAKE THE PAPER-AND-PENCIL ASVAB AT A MILITARY FACILITY

If you take the ASVAB at a military facility called a MET site, you will be given a paper-and-pencil version of the test. You won't receive as much information about your results as those who take the ASVAB at a high school or other postsecondary school.

The sample report shown on pages 19–21 shows the only information you will receive: the AFQT percentile.

IF YOU TAKE THE CAT-ASVAB AT A MEPS

The CAT-ASVAB report provides your scores on every subtest of the ASVAB, your AFQT, and your general scores for qualifying for services occupations. (See Part IV for information on how your scores qualify you for various jobs in each of the services.) The score report shown on page 22 is a sample of the CAT-ASVAB score report.

ASVAB SUMMARY RESULTS

Student
12th Gr Female (Form: 23G)
SSN: XXX-XX-9999
Test Date: Jul 11, 2005
Old Dominion Hs
Hometown DC

Print No 0005

ASVAB Results

	Percentile Scores			12th Grade Standard Score Bands	12th Grade Standard Scores
	12th Grade Females	12th Grade Males	12th Grade Students		
Career Exploration Scores					
Verbal Skills	97	95	96		65
Math Skills	22	17	19		42
Science and Technical Skills	81	48	64		53
ASVAB Tests					
General Science	91	81	86		61
Arithmetic Reasoning	43	30	37		47
Word Knowledge	98	95	96		66
Paragraph Comprehension	92	91	91		62
Mathematics Knowledge	14	12	13		37
Electronics Informations	13	10	11		38
Auto and Shop Information	53	21	37		45
Mechanical Comprehension	95	76	85		59

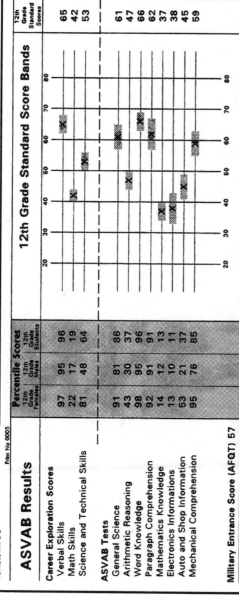

Military Entrance Score (AFQT) 57

EXPLANATION OF YOUR ASVAB PERCENTILE SCORES

Your ASVAB results are reported as percentile scores in the three highlighted columns to the left of the graph. Percentile scores show how you compare to other students - males and females, and for all students - in your grade. For example, a percentile score of 65 for an 11th grade female would mean she scored the same or better than 65 out of every 100 females in the 11th grade.

For purposes of career planning, knowing your relative standing in these comparison groups is important. Being male or female does not limit your career or educational choices. There are noticeable differences in how men and women score in some areas. Viewing your scores in light of your relative standing both for men and women may encourage you to explore areas that you might otherwise overlook.

You can use the Career Exploration Scores to evaluate your knowledge and skills in three general areas (Verbal, Math, and Science and Technical Skills). You can use the ASVAB Test Scores to gather information on specific skill areas. Together, these scores provide a snapshot of your current knowledge and skills. This information will help you develop and review your career goals and plans.

EXPLANATION OF YOUR ASVAB STANDARD SCORES

Your ASVAB results are reported as standard scores in the above graph. Your score on each test is identified by the "X" in the corresponding bar graph. You should view these scores as estimates of your true skill level in that area. If you took the test again, you probably would receive a somewhat different score. Many things, such as how you were feeling during testing, contribute to this difference. This difference is shown with gray score bands in the graph of your results. Your standard scores are based on the ASVAB tests and composites based on your grade level.

The score bands provide a way to identify some of your strengths. Overlapping score bands mean your true skill level is similar in both areas, so the real difference between specific scores might not be meaningful. If the score bands do not overlap, you probably are stronger in the area that has the higher score band.

The ASVAB is an aptitude test. It is neither an absolute measure of your skills and abilities nor a perfect predictor of your success or failure. A high score does not guarantee success, and a low score does not guarantee failure, in a future educational program or occupation. For example, if you have never worked with shop equipment or cars, you may not be familiar with the terms and concepts assessed by the Auto and Shop Information test. Taking a course or obtaining a part-time job in this area would increase your knowledge and improve your score if you were to take it again.

USING ASVAB RESULTS IN CAREER EXPLORATION

Your career and educational plans may change over time as you gain more experience and learn more about your interests. Exploring Careers: The ASVAB Career Exploration Guide can help you learn more about yourself and the world of work, to identify and explore potential goals, and develop an effective strategy to realize your goals. The Guide will help you identify occupations in line with your interests and skills. As you explore potentially satisfying careers, you will develop your career exploration and planning skills.

Meanwhile, your ASVAB results can help you in making well-informed choices about future high school courses.

We encourage you to discuss your ASVAB results with a teacher, counselor, parent, family member or other interested adult. These individuals can help you to view your ASVAB results in light of other important information, such as your interests, school grades, motivation, and personal goals.

DD FORM 1304-5(S)

Sample score report from an ASVAB taken at a school

ASVAB SCORE AND TEST DESCRIPTIONS

Verbal Skills is a general measure of language and reading skills which combines the Word Knowledge and Paragraph Comprehension tests. People with high scores tend to do well in tasks that require good language or reading skills, while people with low scores have more difficulty with such tasks.

Math Skills is a general measure of mathematics skills which combines the Mathematics Knowledge and Arithmetic Reasoning tests. People with high scores tend to do well in tasks that require a knowledge of mathematics, while people with low scores have more difficulty with these kinds of tasks.

Science and Technical Skills is a general measure of science and technical skills which combines the General Science, Electronics Information, and Mechanical Comprehension tests. People with high scores tend to do well in tasks that require scientific thinking or technical skills, while people with low scores have more difficulty with such tasks.

General Science (GS) tests the ability to answer questions on a variety of science topics drawn from courses taught in most high schools. The life science items cover botany, zoology, anatomy and physiology, geology, meteorology, and oceanography. The physical science items are based on astronomy, geology, earth and space science items measure force and motion mechanics, energy, fluids, atomic structure, and chemistry.

Arithmetic Reasoning (AR) tests the ability to solve basic arithmetic problems one encounters in everyday life. One-step and multi-step word problems require addition, subtraction, multiplication, and division, and choosing the correct order of operations when more than one step is necessary. The items include operations with whole numbers, operations with rational numbers, ratio and proportion, interest and percentage, and measurement. Arithmetic reasoning is one factor that helps characterize mathematics comprehension and it also assesses logical thinking.

Word Knowledge (WK) tests the ability to understand the meaning of words through synonyms - words having the same or nearly the same meaning as other words. The test is a measure of one component of reading comprehension since vocabulary is one of many factors that characterize reading comprehension.

Paragraph Comprehension (PC) tests the ability to obtain information from written material. Students read different types of passages of varying lengths and respond to questions based on information presented in each passage. Concepts include identifying stated and reworded facts, determining a sequence of events, drawing conclusions, identifying main ideas, determining the author's purpose and tone, and identifying style and technique.

Mathematics Knowledge (MK) tests the ability to solve problems by applying knowledge of mathematical concepts and applications. The problems focus on concepts and algorithms and involve number theory, numeration, algebraic operations and equations, geometry and measurement, and probability. Mathematics knowledge is one factor that characterizes mathematics comprehension; it also assesses logical thinking.

Electronics Information (EI) tests understanding of electrical current, circuits, devices, and systems. Electronics information topics include electrical circuits, electrical and electronic systems, electrical currents, electrical tools, symbols, devices, and materials.

Auto and Shop Information (AS) tests aptitude for automotive maintenance and repair and wood and metal shop practices. The test covers several areas commonly included in most high school auto and shop courses such as automotive components, automotive systems, automotive tools, troubleshooting and repair, shop tools, building materials, and building and construction procedures.

Mechanical Comprehension (MC) tests comprehension of the principles of mechanical devices and properties of materials. Mechanical comprehension topics include simple machines, compound machines, mechanical motion, fluid dynamics, properties of materials, and structural support.

Military Entrance Score (AFQT) is the score used if an individual decides to enter any of the armed services. See your local recruiter for details.

Sample score report from an ASVAB taken at a school — Continued

UNVERIFIED TEST SCORES (SINGLE APPLICANT)
For use of this form, see USMEPCOM Reg 611-1

FOR OFFICIAL USE ONLY

FOR TA USE ONLY

Name		SSN

Date of Test 5 24 09	Test Version 26a	MET Site 4321

Service	AR	NA	(AF)	MC	CG	Component	(Active)	Reserves	National Guard

Enter the percentile score:

    39

AFQT Percentile

USMEPCOM Form 611-1-2-R-E, NOV 01   Replaces USMEPCOM Form 611-1-2-R-E, 1 MAR 00, which is obsolete.

34813(11-01)

Sample score report from an ASVAB taken at a MET site. This is an unofficial score calculated by the local test administrator.

21

FOR OFFICIAL USE ONLY

UNVERIFIED WINDOWS CAT-ASVAB TEST SCORE REPORT

Testing Site ID: 987654   Service: DNR

Testing Session: Date 2008/09/24   Starting Time: 05:00

Applicant: Name: Jay Jones   SSN: 123-45-6789

Test Form: 04D   Test Type: Initial

	GS	AR	WK	PC	MK	EI	AS	MC	AO	VE
Standard Scores:	56	57	56	35	46	37	37	48	40	50

COMPOSITE SCORE:

Army:	GT	CL	CO	EL	FA	GM	MM	OF	SC	ST
	108	101	092	092	-94	091	085	093	093	097

Air Force:	M	A	G	E
	38	40	59	47

Navy/CG:	GT	EL	BEE	ENG	MEC	**MEC2**	NUC	OPS	HM	ADM
	107	196	205	083	142	145	201	193	152	096

Marine:	MM	GT	EL	CL
	088	104	098	096

AFQT Percentile Score: 49

Sample CAT-ASVAB score report

Chapter 4

Taking the CAT-ASVAB

READ THIS CHAPTER TO LEARN:

- **The pros and cons of taking the CAT-ASVAB**
- **What directions are given for the computer-based test**
- **Strategies that can raise your CAT-ASVAB score**

HOW THE CAT-ASVAB WORKS

The CAT-ASVAB is the computer-based version of the test that is offered to potential recruits at the military facilities called MEPS. If you take this version of the test, you will be seated in front of a computer and monitor in a room with others. The test comes up on the screen. As you answer the test questions, the program records each answer, scores it, and then calculates your ability level. Based on that information, another item is selected. If you got the first answer wrong, the computer will give you an easier item. If you got it correct, the computer will give you a more difficult item. This process continues until you have completed the items provided to you. After you have completed the test, the AFQT and composite scores will be calculated. See Chapter 3 for a sample CAT-ASVAB score report.

Possible Advantages

One advantage of taking the CAT-ASVAB is that it takes less time than the paper-and-pencil version. Also, the test can be scored immediately, and scoring errors are reduced because of the automation. The test can be administered with minimal advance notice, whereas administration of the paper-and-pencil ASVAB needs to be scheduled well in advance.

Unlike scores on the paper-and-pencil ASVAB, the CAT-ASVAB score you get is not based solely on the number of items you answered correctly. Some people have claimed that the CAT-ASVAB is easier and can give you better scores because

you get more "points" for answering more difficult items.

Possible Disadvantages

Unlike the paper-and-pencil ASVAB, the CAT-ASVAB does not give you an opportunity to go back to questions you answered previously to change your answer or think about the question again. You also cannot skip questions and go on to other questions that you might know the answer to. If you get items wrong, the computer will give you easier items, but your score will be lower than if you correctly answered a few difficult items.

CAT-ASVAB Directions

When you arrive to take the CAT-ASVAB, you will be escorted to a waiting room. You will complete various forms, if you haven't done so already. Your social security number will be verified. There you will get a briefing similar to the one that follows.

Briefing

(Your Test Administrator will read aloud to you the following.)

Welcome; I am (Administrator's name), and I will be administering your test today. First of all, has anyone here taken the Armed Services Vocational Aptitude Battery at any time in the past, either in a high school or another testing site, and has not

indicated this on the USMEPCOM Form 680-3AE you provided? It is extremely important to identify this because your test will be checked against a nationwide computer file for Armed Forces applicants. If it is discovered that you previously tested, but did not tell us, the results from today's test may not be valid for enlistment.

(If anyone raises their hand, the administrator will check their USMEPCOM Form 680-3AE to ensure that they have marked the retest box and entered the previous forms.)

It is important that you are physically fit to take this test. Is there anybody here that doesn't feel well enough to take the examination?

[If anyone says he or she doesn't feel well, the Administrator will remove that person from the session group, inform the service (if available), and indicate the reason for removal on USMEPCOM Form 680-3AE.]

The test you are about to take is administered by computer. Instructions for taking the test are on the computer, and the guidelines are very easy to follow. If you need assistance during any part of the test, press the red "HELP" key, raise your hand, and I'll assist you.

No electronic devices are allowed in the testing room. It is best not to take cellphones into the MEPS as the phones will not be secured while you are being tested. In addition, coats, jackets, and bags will be left in the CAT-ASVAB waiting room.

The use of calculators, crib sheets, or other devices designed to assist in testing are not permitted. No

talking is allowed while in the testing room. Use the scratch paper and pencil on the side of your computer for any figuring you need to do while taking the test. If you need more paper or another pencil, press the red "HELP" key and then raise your hand.

Do not touch any other keys except for the letter choices, the red "HELP" key, or the "ENTER" bar.

After completing the examination, give your scratch paper to me and then you are released. If you are staying at the hotel, wait at the front desk for transportation.

Does anyone have any questions?

What Happens Next?

After the briefing by the Test Administrator, you will be brought into the testing room and assigned a seat.

The CAT-ASVAB is designed so that individuals with very little or no computer experience can take the exam. It is recommended that you practice using a computer before you take the CAT-ASVAB. A recruiter may be able to give you some of this practice. The bottom line is to be prepared—well prepared.

The keyboard has been modified to make it easy for you to find the keys. The computer program will give you the directions on how to answer the items. It will also tell you about the time limits and give you the chance to do some practice items to be sure that you know how to navigate the keyboard.

The directions are quite simple. If you need help during the session, you need only to press the HELP key. The administrator will come by to assist you. You should only do this if you are experiencing technical problems with the test, or if you are in need of more scratch paper or another pencil to use for your calculation. When you press the HELP key, the clock on the test will stop. It will restart when you restart the test.

You will answer each item by pressing the key that represents your answer. To register your response, hit the enter key, which is the space bar. The next item will then be presented to you.

Recent Changes

Recently, the Department of Defense began a rollout of a new Windows-based version of the CAT-ASVAB. It has a Windows look and feel, and you can use a mouse instead of the keyboard to record your answers. The modified keyboard described earlier can still be used if that is more comfortable for you.

Changes have been made in the look of the on-screen items, and the graphics have been improved. You can click on buttons for the various answer choices, or you can type the letter of the response.

This new system should be in place before you take the CAT-ASVAB.

SPECIAL STRATEGIES FOR TAKING THE CAT-ASVAB

Except where noted, the strategies for taking the CAT-ASVAB are the same as those for the paper-and-pencil test. Here are some special things to keep in mind.

- To raise your scores, try your very best to answer every item correctly. Take your time, especially with the early items in each test. If you get the early items correct, the computer will give you more difficult questions, and these carry more value. If you get the early items wrong, the computer will give you easier items, and even if you answer these correctly, your score will be lower than if you answered the same number of more difficult items. Unlike on the paper-and-pencil tests, guessing is not necessarily a good strategy.
- Focus hard and give the test your full attention.
- Pay attention to the directions. Directions will not be given to you verbally. They will only be on the computer screen to be read.
- Try hard to finish all the items. For every item you do not finish, there is a penalty.

CAT-ASVAB Myths

Myth	Reality
The CAT-ASVAB is harder than the paper-and-pencil ASVAB.	The CAT-ASVAB may seem harder to many people because the items are selected based on a person's previous answers. For example, a person with high ability will be able to skip over the easier questions which would be found on the paper-and-pencil version of the instrument.
	A lot of research has been done to assure that the score you would get on the paper-and-pencil or computer adaptive versions will be the same.
The paper-and-pencil ASVAB is easier than the CAT-ASVAB.	For persons of lower ability the paper-and-pencil version may seem easier because the questions are generally arranged from easy to hard within each subtest. As a result you will receive many easier items to answer before you are challenged with the more difficult ones.
	On the CAT-ASVAB, once your general ability level is determined, you will be getting more difficult items to answer to see how well you do. The easier items are skipped.

Chapter 5

AFQT Question Types

READ THIS CHAPTER TO LEARN:

- **What is the format of each AFQT subtest**
- **What kinds of questions are on each AFQT subtest**

In earlier chapters in this book, you learned that the AFQT, the portion of the ASVAB that determines your eligibility for military service, consists of four subtests: Arithmetic Reasoning, Mathematics Knowledge, Word Knowledge, and Paragraph Comprehension. This chapter will look more closely at each of these four subtests. You will review how many questions there are in each subtest and how much time you will have to answer them. Then you will learn what topics each subtest covers and see samples of the different question types.

WORD KNOWLEDGE

The ASVAB Word Knowledge test measures your ability to understand the meaning of words through synonyms. *Synonyms* are words that have the same or nearly the same meaning as other words. Your ability to recognize synonyms is an indicator of how well you comprehend what you read. The Word Knowledge test, along with the Paragraph Comprehension test, is part of the verbal ability portion of the AFQT.

Some Word Knowledge questions present a vocabulary word and ask you which of four answer choices the word "most nearly means." Other Word Knowledge questions present a vocabulary word in a sentence. You can use the meaning of the sentence to help you decide which of the four answer choices has the same meaning as the vocabulary word. The tested vocabulary words are not difficult scientific or technical terms. They are words that you are likely to encounter in your ordinary reading or conversation but that may be unfamiliar to you. This chapter will teach you ways to figure out the

meaning of unfamiliar words and improve your score on the Word Knowledge test.

ASVAB Word Knowledge Test

Number of questions:

- Paper-and-pencil ASVAB: 35
- CAT-ASVAB: 16

Time limit:

- Paper-and–pencil ASVAB: 11 minutes
- CAT-ASVAB: 8 minutes

Question types:

- Define a single word
- Define a word in a sentence

If you take the CAT-ASVAB, you will have only about half a minute to answer each Word Knowledge question. If you take the paper-and-pencil ASVAB, you'll have even less time, so you'll have to work fast if you want to get a good score. That's why it pays to spend time studying ways to build your vocabulary and tackling plenty of sample ASVAB Word Knowledge questions.

Here are some sample Word Knowledge questions:

1. The wind is <u>variable</u> today.

    A. mild
    B. steady
    C. shifting
    D. chilling

2. <u>Rudiments</u> most nearly means

    A. politics
    B. minute details
    C. promotion opportunities
    D. basic methods and procedures

ANSWERS

1. **C.** *Variable* means "constantly or regularly changing." *Mild, steady,* and *chilling* do not share the meaning of the word *variable.* Thus choice C, *shifting,* is the best answer.
2. **D.** The *rudiments* of something are its fundamental elements. *Politics, minute details,* and *promotion opportunities* do not share this meaning. The best answer is choice D, *basic methods and procedures.*

Answering ASVAB Word Knowledge Questions

When you take the ASVAB Word Knowledge test, follow these steps to improve your score:

1. *Look for context clues.* If the word appears in a sentence, there may be clues in the context—that is, in the surrounding words.
2. *Mentally guess at the meaning of the word.* Try to think of another word that has the same meaning.
3. *Scan the answer choices.* Is the word you thought of among them? Pick the word that is the closest match—the *best* answer. Mark it and go on.
4. If the word you thought of is not among the choices, *try picking the word apart.* Look for prefixes, roots, and suffixes.
5. *Guess if you must.* If you cannot decide which answer choice is correct, *try to eliminate choices that are clearly wrong.* Then guess, even if you cannot eliminate more than one or two choices. The more choices you are able to eliminate, the better your chances of guessing correctly. There is no penalty for wrong answers on the paper and pencil version, so be sure to mark an answer for every question, even if you have to guess.

Chapter 6 of this book provides review and practice for Word Knowledge questions. You'll learn about context clues, prefixes, suffixes, and word roots. You'll also have the opportunity to practice with questions just like those on the real test.

PARAGRAPH COMPREHENSION

The ASVAB subtest called Paragraph Comprehension is designed to find out how well you obtain information from written material. Basically, it measures your reading comprehension skills. Paragraph Comprehension is especially important because it is part of the AFQT, the primary score for entering the military. To get in and get good job and training opportunities, you need to score well on this test. Just think about it. During your basic and specialized training, you will need to understand written material provided to you by your instructors. You will need to read and understand manuals that relate to your job. The military, regardless of branch, needs you to have a good understanding of everything you read.

ASVAB Paragraph Comprehension Test

Number of questions:
- Paper-and-pencil ASVAB: 15
- CAT-ASVAB: 11

Time limit:
- Paper-and-pencil ASVAB: 13 minutes
- CAT-ASVAB: 22 minutes

Topics covered: history, health, science, social studies, sports, current events, culture

Question types:
- Recognizing the main idea
- Finding specific information
- Interpreting what you read
- Determining the meaning of words in context

Each item on the Paragraph Comprehension test consists of a paragraph or paragraphs followed by multiple-choice questions. You will need to read the paragraphs in order to answer the questions. The paragraphs will cover a wide variety of topics. Note, however, that you won't need to know anything more about any topic than what is in the paragraph. The paragraph will contain everything you need to know to answer the question.

If you do the math, you will see that on the paper-and-pencil ASVAB, you have only 52 seconds to answer each item, including reading the passage. That means that you will need a test-taking strategy that allows you to approach the test both quickly and accurately. This chapter gives you some practical advice on how to approach the test, what kinds of questions to expect, and how to prepare yourself to get your best score on the ASVAB Paragraph Comprehension test.

Here is a sample Paragraph Comprehension question.

From a building designer's standpoint, three things that make a home livable are the client, the building site, and the amount of money the client has to spend.

According to this statement, to make a home livable,

A. the prospective piece of land makes little difference.
B. it can be built on any piece of land.
C. the design must fit the owner's income and site.
D. the design must fit the designer's income.

ANSWER: C

Answering ASVAB Paragraph Comprehension Questions

When you take the ASVAB Paragraph Comprehension test, follow these steps to improve your score:

1. *Read the questions before you read the paragraph.* This is an absolute must—no exceptions. You need to do this so that you can focus on the pertinent parts of the paragraph and ignore the remainder. Remember that you have a very limited amount of time and you need to get to the right answer as quickly as possible.
2. *Read the paragraph next.* When you read the paragraph, focus on the answers to the questions and ignore all the extraneous information that might be in the paragraph. There will be a lot of fluff in the passage that has nothing to do with the questions you are being asked. Don't try to fully understand all the information that is given. Your job is to answer the question, not to become an expert in the subject at hand.
3. In your mind, *try to answer the question* as you read each paragraph. Try to guess the answers in you own mind. Your answer will probably be similar to one of the answer choices.

4. *Now look at the answer choices again* to see which one matches the answer you reached in your mind. If one of the choices matches your answer or is close, mark it and go on.
5. If you cannot decide which answer choice is correct, *try to eliminate choices that are clearly wrong, then guess,* even if you cannot eliminate more than one or two choices. The more choices you are able to eliminate, the better your chances of guessing correctly. Remember that there is no penalty for a wrong answer on the paper and pencil version.

Chapter 7 of this book provides review and practice for Paragraph Comprehension questions. You'll learn how to highlight important parts of a passage, how to identify the main idea, how to write notes to yourself about a passage, and how to search a passage for important details. You'll also have the opportunity to practice with questions just like those on the real test.

ARITHMETIC REASONING

The ASVAB Arithmetic Reasoning test measures your ability to solve the kinds of arithmetic problems that you encounter every day at home or on the job. All of the questions on the test are word problems. That is, each one presents a real-life situation with a problem that must be solved using an arithmetic operation such as addition, subtraction, multiplication, or division. Arithmetic Reasoning problems also involve other arithmetic concepts, such as fractions, decimals, percents, exponents, and square roots.

ASVAB Arithmetic Reasoning Test

Number of questions:

- Paper-and-pencil ASVAB: 30
- CAT-ASVAB: 16

Time limit:

- Paper-and–pencil ASVAB: 36 minutes
- CAT-ASVAB: 39 minutes

Topics covered:

- Operations with whole numbers
- Operations with rational numbers
- Ratio and proportion
- Interest and percentage
- Measurement

Here are some sample Arithmetic Reasoning questions:

1. Dave is on a kayaking trip. On the first day he travels 15 miles. On the second day he travels 35 miles, and on the third day he rests. On the fourth day he travels 57 miles, and on the fifth day he travels 43 miles. What is the average number of miles that he travels per day?

    A. 25
    B. 27
    C. 30
    D. 32

2. Blythe sees a computer that she wants to buy. It costs $1,600. The store manager says that next week the computer will be on sale for $350 less. What percent will Blythe save if she waits a week before purchasing the computer?

    A. 12.8%
    B. 15.3%
    C. 21.9%
    D. 31.3%

ANSWERS

1. **C.** To calculate the average, add the number of miles Dave travels each day, then divide by the number of days.

    $15 + 35 + 0 + 57 + 43 = 150$
    150 (total miles) $\div$ 5 (number of days) $= 30$ (average number of miles per day)
    Don't forget to divide by 5, even though Dave traveled 0 miles on one of the five days.

2. **C.** To calculate the percent one number is of another, divide the first number by the second:

    $350 = x\%$ of 1,600
    $350 \div 1,600$ Divide.
    $= 0.21875$
    $\approx 21.9\%$

Answering ASVAB Arithmetic Reasoning Questions

When you take the ASVAB Arithmetic Reasoning test, follow these steps to improve your score:

1. *Read the problem all the way through.* Don't start making any calculations until you know exactly what you are supposed to find out.
2. *Be sure you understand what the problem is asking.* Are you supposed to find how far someone will travel? How fast something is moving? How much something costs?
3. *Decide what you need to do to find the answer.* Do you need to add? Subtract? Multiply? Divide?
4. *Test your answer.* Be sure that the number you found answers the question that was asked.
5. *Look at the answer choices.* Is one of them the answer you calculated? Remember that on a multiple-choice test like this one, one of the answer choices has to be correct. If your answer is one of the choices, mark it and move on.
6. *Guess if you have to,* as there is no penalty for a wrong answer on the paper and pencil version.

Chapters 8 and 9 of this book provide review and practice for Arithmetic Reasoning questions. In Chapter 8, you'll review basic topics in arithmetic, algebra, and geometry. You'll study sample problems with solutions, and you'll have the opportunity to solve practice problems on your own. In Chapter 9, you'll learn effective procedures for solving the kinds of arithmetic and geometry word problems that appear on the Arithmetic Reasoning test. You'll also measure your test readiness by taking a word problems quiz.

MATHEMATICS KNOWLEDGE

The ASVAB Mathematics Knowledge test measures your ability to solve problems using concepts taught in high school math courses. These concepts include various topics in algebra and probability. You'll need to know about solving equations, setting up ratios and proportions, graphing on a coordinate plane, and determining the probability of a given event.

Along with problems in algebra and probability, the ASVAB Mathematics Knowledge test also includes problems in geometry. To do well on this portion of the test, you'll need to know the basic geometry concepts taught in high school math courses. Topics tested include classifying angles; identifying different kinds of triangles and parallelograms; calculating perimeter, area, and volume; finding the circumference and area of circles; and identifying different kinds of solid figures.

ASVAB Mathematics Knowledge Test

Number of questions:

- Paper-and-pencil ASVAB: 25
- CAT-ASVAB: 16

Time limit:

- Paper-and–pencil ASVAB: 24 minutes
- CAT-ASVAB: 18 minutes

Topics covered:

- Number theory
- Numeration
- Algebraic operations and equations
- Geometry and measurement
- Probability

Here are some sample Mathematics Knowledge questions:

1. If $x + 6 = 7$, then x is equal to

   A. –1
   B. 0
   C. 1
   D. 7/6

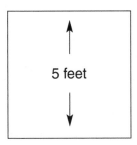

5 feet

2. What is the area of this square?

   A. 1 square foot
   B. 5 square feet
   C. 10 square feet
   D. 25 square feet

ANSWERS:

1. **C**

   $x + 6 = 7$ Subtract 6 from both sides of the equation.
   $\quad -6 \; -6$
   $\qquad x = 1$

2. **D** The formula for finding the area of a square is $A = s \times s$ or $A = s^2$.

   If the figure is a square, then the dimension shown will be the same as the length of each side.

   $A = s^2$
   $\quad = 5^2$ Substitute numbers into the formula
   $\quad = 25$ square feet

Answering ASVAB Mathematics Knowledge Questions

When you take the ASVAB Mathematics Knowledge test, follow these steps to improve your score:

1. *Be sure you understand what the problem is asking.* Are you supposed to find out the measure of a certain angle? The factors of a certain expression? The square root of a certain number?
2. *Decide what you need to do to find the answer.* Do you need to multiply? Divide? Arrange numbers in order? Substitute numbers for unknowns in an expression?
3. *Test your answer.* Be sure that the number you found answers the question that was asked.
4. *Look at the answer choices.* Is one of them the answer that you calculated? If your answer is one of the choices, mark it and move on.
5. *If your answer is not one of the choices, test each answer choice by substituting it into the problem.* Remember that on a multiple-choice test like this one, one of the answer choices has to be correct.
6. *Guess if you have to,* as there is no penalty for a wrong answer on the paper and pencil version.

The review of arithmetic, algebra, and geometry in Chapter 8 of this book will help you with the ASVAB Mathematics Knowledge test as well as with the Arithmetic Reasoning test. The sample questions with solutions are just like the ones on the Mathematics Knowledge test. By carefully studying the chapter and solving the practice items, you can raise your Mathematics Knowledge score.

Part 2

SHARPEN YOUR SKILLS

Chapter 6

Sharpen Your Word Knowledge Skills

READ THIS CHAPTER TO LEARN:

- **What you can do to build a better vocabulary**
- **How you can use word parts to figure out meanings**
- **What context clues are and how they can help you**

You have learned that ASVAB Word Knowledge questions measure your ability to understand the meaning of words through synonyms. *Synonyms* are words that mean the same thing, or almost the same thing, as a given word. This chapter will help you learn ways to identify synonyms. You'll explore techniques for building your vocabulary, and you'll find out ways to use word parts and context clues (hints in the surrounding sentence) to decode word meanings. You'll also find drills that you can use to improve and sharpen your word knowledge skills. If you work through the exercises in this chapter carefully, you can get a higher ASVAB Word Knowledge score!

START BUILDING A BETTER VOCABULARY

There are several ways to build your vocabulary, and this workbook contains a number of exercises that will help you do this. In general, the following pages have some good advice and excellent practice exercises that will help you build your ASVAB vocabulary.

Memorize

It may help you to memorize some common prefixes, suffixes, and word roots. However, memorizing lists of words will not be particularly helpful,

especially if your study time is limited. You need to use study methods that are far more useful than memorizing words and their definitions.

Read, Read, Read, and Read Some More

Read everything you can get your hands on, including schoolbooks, newspapers, magazines, and fiction and nonfiction books. The more you read, the more new words you'll come across that you can add to your vocabulary.

Develop a Word List

As you read and find words you don't know, start developing a word list. Use the Word List Chart provided at the end of this section. Write down each word you don't know. Take a guess at the meaning, and write down your guess. Then go to a dictionary, your thesaurus, or your word processing program to find synonyms (words that mean the same thing). Write the synonyms in the last column of the chart. You don't need to write down the formal dictionary definition because the synonyms are what the ASVAB asks for. When you hear people say words that you do not know, add them to the Word List Chart as well.

Often just writing down a word and some synonyms will help you retain the meaning. You may also want to use the Word List Chart to create flash

35

cards that you can take with you anywhere to study when you have some free time. Using something like 3" × 5" cards, write the word on one side and some synonyms on the other. Later in this section, you will find a set of words that you can use for these flash cards or whatever other study system you decide to use.

Use a New Word in Your Conversations Each Day

Every time you hear a new word, either on the television or radio, when you hear a person talking on the phone, or when you hear people talk to each other, write down that word, pronounce it to yourself, pronounce it out loud, and use it in a sentence when you talk with someone that day. Do this each day. Saying the word out loud and using it in a sentence will help you retain its meaning.

Review, Review, Review

Once you have developed your word list, listed synonyms, and worked through the sample tests, you still need to keep reviewing. Review on the bus to work or school. Review during TV commercials. Review during your spare time. Review during study sessions. Review before you go to sleep at night. Review with your parents. Review with your friends. Review with a study group. Review in whatever way is most convenient and efficient for you. Be realistic. If reviewing with your friends ends up as a chat session or party, then that's not helping you reach your goal of scoring high on the ASVAB. Stay disciplined. Stay focused. Stay on track.

Decode the Meaning of a Word

Persons who are developing a better vocabulary use a variety of strategies to help them decode unfamiliar words. They apply knowledge of sound and letter patterns and of the structure of words, including compounds, root words, grammatical endings, prefixes, suffixes, and syllable divisions, to help them decode words. They understand that effective readers draw on several sources of knowledge to help them make sense of unfamiliar words besides looking at the individual words themselves: clues from context, experience, text, and sentence structure. This workbook will give you some good strategies

and opportunities to practice these strategies to make your vocabulary larger and more powerful.

USE WORD PARTS TO FIGURE OUT MEANING

Many words are made up of several parts: a *root* (the basic idea) and a *prefix* and/or a *suffix* (short letter combinations that change the meaning in some way). A prefix is attached to the root at the beginning of the word. A suffix is attached to the root at the end of the word. Not all words have prefixes and suffixes, but many do. On the ASVAB test, you will find many words that have roots with prefixes and/or suffixes. If you learn the most common word roots, prefixes, and suffixes, you can use what you know to pick apart unfamiliar words and figure out what they mean.

Below you will find tables of **Common Prefixes**, **Common Word Roots**, and **Common Suffixes.** Study these tables carefully. The more you know about these word parts, the better able you will be to figure out the meaning of unfamiliar words.

Study Some Examples

Now that you have studied these common word parts, you can start using what you know to figure out the meaning of unfamiliar words. Here are a few examples of picking words apart to find their meaning.

- *disagree*: *dis-* is a prefix that means "not do" or "do the opposite." To *disagree* means not to agree.
- *illegal*: *il-* is a prefix that means "not" or "not to." Illegal, then, means not or not to be legal.
- *endless*: *-less* is a suffix that means "without," so this word means without end.
- *perishable*: *-able* is a suffix that means "capable" or "possible." *Perishable* therefore means able to perish.
- *faster*: *-er* is a suffix that suggests a comparison. So, *faster* means that something is more fast than something else.
- *derail*: *de-* is a prefix that means "to undo." To *derail* means to undo from the rail or the track something has been on.
- *childish*: -ish is a suffix that means "to be like." The word *childish* means to be or act like a child.
- *inaudible*: *in-* is a prefix that means "not," *aud* has something to do with sound, and the suffix -ible means "capable of," so the word means something like "not capable of being heard."

Common Prefixes

Prefix	Meaning	Examples
a-, an-	without	amoral, anaerobic
ante-	before	antedate, antechamber
anti-	against, opposing	antipollution, antipathy
auto-	self	autobiography, autopilot
bene-	good or well	beneficial, benediction
bi-	two	bicycle, bipolar
cen-	hundred	century, centennial
circum-	around	circumnavigate, circumvent
co-, com-, con-	together, with	coauthor, complete, congregate
contra-, counter-	against, opposite	contradict, counterclockwise
de-	away from, down, undoing	descend, deactivate
dis-	not do, do the opposite of	disagree, disarm
ex-	out of, away from	exhale, expropriate
extra-	beyond, outside of	extraordinary, extraterrestrial, extramural
hetero-	different	heterogeneous, heterodox
homo-	same	homogenized, homonym
hyper-	above, excessive	hyperbaric, hyperactive, hypertension
il-, in-, ir-	not	illegible, inaudible, irregular
inter-	between	intercontinental, interject
intra-	within	intramural, intranet
mal-	bad or ill	maladjusted, malevolent
micro-	small	microbiology, microscope
milli-	thousandth	millisecond, millimeter
mis-	badly, wrongly	misbehave, misunderstand
mono-	one	monosyllable, monorail
neo-	new	neoclassical, neophyte
non-	not	nonessential, nonconformist
paleo-	old, ancient	paleontology, paleobiology
pan-	all, all over	pandemic, panorama
poly-	many	polygon, polynomial
post-	after, behind	postpone, postnasal
pre-	before	preview, premeditate
pro-	forward, in favor of	promote, pro-labor
re-	again, backward	rewrite, retract
retro-	backward	retrofit, retroactive
semi-	half	semiannual, semifinal
sub-	under, below	submarine, subcabinet
super-	above, over	supersede, supervise
sym-, syn-	together with, at the same time	sympathetic, synchronize
tele-	from a distance	telecommute, telemetry
trans-	across	transcontinental, transatlantic
un-	not	unannounced, unnoticed
uni-	one	unicycle, unify

Common Word Roots

Root	Meaning	Examples
act	do	transact, activate
aero	air	aerobics, aerospace
ambu	walk	ambulatory, perambulate
ann, enn	year	annual, perennial
anthrop	human	anthropology, philanthropy
aster, astro	star	asterisk, astrology
audi	hear	audible, auditorium
bibli	book	bibliography, bibliophile
bio	life	biosphere, biography
brev	short	brevity, abbreviate
capit	head	decapitate, capital
card, cord, cour	heart	cardiology, discord, courage
carn	flesh	carnivorous, carnage
cede	go	recede, precede
cent	hundred, hundredth	centipede, centimeter
chron	time	chronology, synchronize
cide	killing	suicide, homicide
cis	cut	precise, scissors
claim, clam	shout, cry out	exclaim, clamorous
cogn	know	cognition, recognize
cracy, crat	rule	autocratic, democracy
culp	blame	culpable, exculpate
dem	people	democracy, demographics
dic, dict	speak	dictation, predict
dorm	sleep	dormant, dormitory
fer	carry	transfer, refer
fuge	flee	refuge, centrifugal
geo	earth	geography, geologic
gram	something written or recorded	telegram, cardiogram
graph	to write	graphic, calligraphy
jac, ject	throw	ejaculate, trajectory
jur	law	jury, jurisprudence
labor	work	laboratory, collaborate
loc	place	location, collocation
log	discourse, speech	dialogue, travelogue
logy	expression, science	dermatology, phraseology
luc	light	lucid, translucent
manu	hand	manuscript, manufacture
mill	thousand	millennium, millenarian
meter	measure	barometer, metric
morph	form	morphology, amorphous
mort	die	mortuary, mortal

Root	Meaning	Examples
omni	all	omnipresent, omnipotent
oper	work	opera, operate
path	feeling, suffering	empathy, pathetic
ped, pod	foot	pedal, podiatry
phil	love	bibliophile, philanthropy
phob	fear	claustrophobic, hydrophobia
phon	sound	phonograph, stereophonic
photo	light	photographic, photokinesis
phys	of nature	physical, physician
scrib	write	scribble, transcribe
stro, stru	build	destroy, construction
terr	earth, land	extraterrestrial, territory
therm	heat	hypothermal, thermometer
tor	twist	torsion, contort
vac	empty	evacuate, vacuous
verb	word	proverb, verbose
vert, vers	change	conversion, revert
vid, vis	see	video, television
vol, volv	turn, roll	evolution, revolve

Common Suffixes

Suffix	Meaning	Examples
-able, -ible	capable or worthy of	likable, possible
-ful	full of	healthful, joyful
-fy	to make or cause	purify, glorify
-ish	like	impish, devilish
-ism	act of, state of	capitalism, socialism
-ist	one who does	conformist, cyclist
-ize	make into	formalize, legalize
-ment	state of being	entertainment, amazement
-oid	like or resembling	humanoid, trapezoid
-ty	state of being	purity, acidity

- *audiovisual*: *audio-* is a prefix that has something to do with hearing, and *visual* relates to seeing, so *audiovisual* involves both hearing and seeing.
- *antibiotic*: *anti-* is a prefix that means "against," and *bio* is a root that means "life," so the word has something to do with "against life." An *antibiotic* is a substance that attempts to kill germs
- *precede*: *pre-* is a prefix that means "before," and *cede* is a root that means "to go," so the word means something like "going before."

- *captain*: *capit* is a root that means "head," so the word relates to the head of something (in this case, a ship's crew)
- *capital*: *capit* is a root that means "head," so the word has something to do with the head of something (in this case, the symbolic "head" of a country, the location of the government).
- *chronometer*: *chron-* is a prefix that has to do with time, and *meter* relates to measuring, so the word has to do with measuring time
- *pedicure*: *pedi-* is a prefix that has to do with "foot," so this word has to do with something related to feet
- *visage*: *vis* has something to do with seeing or looking, so the meaning of this word is "how a person looks."
- *transform*: *trans-* is a prefix that means "go across," so this word means "going across" or "changing form."
- *microbiology*: *micro-* is a prefix that means "small," *bio* is a root that has to do with life, and *-ology* means "the study of," so the word has to do with studying small living things
- *multitalented*: *multi-* is a prefix that means "many," so this word has to do with many talents
- *thermometer*: *therm-* has to do with heat, and *meter* means "measuring," so this word has to do with measuring heat.
- *geology*: *geo* is a root that means "earth," and *-ology* means "the study of," so this word has to do with studying the earth.

- *revolve*: *re-* is a prefix that means "again," and *"volve* means "to turn," so this word has something to do with turning again or turning repeatedly.
- *mispronounce*: *mis-* is a prefix that means "wrong" or "to do wrongly," so this word has to do with pronouncing something in a wrong way.
- *vacate*: *vac* means "empty," so this word has to do with making something empty or leaving an empty space.
- *aerate*: *aero* is a root that has to do with air, so this word has to do with putting or placing air in a particular place.
- *lyricist*: *-ist* is a suffix that means "one who does." A *lyricist* is some one who creates lyrics to a song.
- *biology*: *-ology* means "the study of," and *bio* is a root word that means life. *Biology* therefore means the study of life or living things.
- *misrepresent*: *mis-* is a prefix that means "wrong" or "to do wrongly," so this word has to do with presenting something in a wrong way or incorrectly.
- *extraordinary*: *extra-* is a prefix that means "outside of" or "beyond." *Extraordinary* means beyond the ordinary.
- *deconstruct*: *de-* is a prefix that means "move away from." *Deconstruct* means to move away from or make something different from the original or to break it apart or into pieces.
- *disrespect*: *dis-* is a prefix that means "do the opposite of." *Disrespect* means not to respect.

Start Using What You Know

Use the following activity to further expand and strengthen your vocabulary.

Activity 1: Use Prefixes, Roots, and Suffixes to Figure Out Meaning

The following words contain common prefixes, roots, and suffixes. Read each word and try to guess its meaning. Write your guess. Then look up the dictionary meaning and write it in the space provided. From the dictionary or a thesaurus, list at least one synonym.

Word: *achromatic*

My Guess Machine	Synonym: achromous, colorless, diatomic, neutral
Dictionary Meaning a. free from color b. able to emit, transmit, or receive light without separating it into colors.	

Word: *ambidextrous*

My Guess Powerful	Synonym: skillfull
Dictionary Meaning able to use both hands equally well • an ambidextrous baseball player.	

Word: *amoral*

My Guess Guard, defense	Synonym: abandoned, corrupt, depraved, uncontrollable, unmoral, unruly
Dictionary Meaning having or showing no concern about whether behavior is morally right or wrong.	

Word: *antipathy*

My Guess against some happy feeling	Synonym: aversion, dislike, antagonism, hostility, disgust, hatred
Dictionary Meaning a strong feeling of dislike	

anti-prefix against opposing
path-root feeling, suffering

Word: *antiseptic*

My Guess shot to prevent sickness	Synonym: aseptic, disinfectant, germicidal sterile, sanitary
Dictionary Meaning a substance that prevents infection in a wound by killing bacteria. anti - prefix against opposing	

Word: *antisocial*

My Guess don't interact or be social with others	Synonym: 1. disruptive, rebellious, interactable 2. unsociable, estranged, solitary
Dictionary Meaning 1. violent or harmful to people, 2 not friendly to other people. anti - prefix against opposing	

Word: *apathetic*

My Guess Something not crazy	Synonym: indifferent, unfeeling, unresponsive emotionless, uncaring, impassive.
Dictionary Meaning Not having or showing much emotion or interest a - prefix - without path - root - feeling, suffering	

Word: *atypical*

My Guess Not typical, not ordinary.	Synonym: unusual, abnormal
Dictionary Meaning Not typical: not usual or normal a - prefix - without	

Word: *benefit*

My Guess Something that you will have or need that is good.	Synonym: profit, advantage, boon, blessing, help, good, assist
Dictionary Meaning a good or helpful result or effect bene - prefix - good or well	

Word: *biography*

My Guess	study of the world	Synonym:	life, lifestory, lifehistory
Dictionary Meaning	the story of a real person's life written by someone other than that person.		

bio -root -life
graph - root -to write

Word: *biosphere*

My Guess	atmosphere life ___	Synonym:	environment, habitat
Dictionary Meaning	the part of the earth in which life can exist		

bio -root -life

Word: *cacophony*

My Guess	a growing cacoon	Synonym:	discord, harshness, noise,
Dictionary Meaning	unpleasant loud sounds		

phon -root- sound

Word: *chronic*

My Guess	Something sharp	Synonym:	long-lasting, continuing, prolonged lingering, persistent
Dictionary Meaning	1. medical: continuing or occuring again and again for a long time		

Chron- root- time

Word: *chronicle*

My Guess	Temporary, limited	Synonym:	history, archives, record, journals, calendar.
Dictionary Meaning	A description of events in the order that they happened.		

Chron- root- time

Word: *chronological*

My Guess evidence	Synonym: sequential, in sequence, in order, dated, ordered, successive
Dictionary Meaning arranged in the order that things happened or came to be	

chron - root - time

Word: *cognizant*

My Guess intelligent	Synonym: aware, informed, knowing, understanding, recognizing
Dictionary Meaning aware of something	

cogn - root - know

Word: *contiguous*

My Guess addictive	Synonym: touching, next, adjoining, proximate, close, nearby
Dictionary Meaning used to describe things that touch each other or are immediately next to each other.	

con - prefix - together with

Word: *contradict*

My Guess solving ahead	Synonym: deny, disagree, gainsay, refute, dispute, contravene
Dictionary Meaning to say the opposite of (something that someone else has said); to deny the truth of (something)	

con - prefix - together, with
dict - root - speak

Word: *contrarian*

My Guess fixing a problem	Synonym: adverse, anti, contradictory, opposed
Dictionary Meaning a person who takes an opposite or different position or attitude from other people.	

con - prefix - together, with
an - prefix - without

Word: *decompress*

My Guess de-attach, remove, seperate	Synonym: relax, loosen up, depressurized uncompress
Dictionary Meaning to release or reduce the physical pressure on something.	

de - prefix - away from

Word: *defile*

My Guess	not file, no filing	Synonym:	corrupt, befool, besmirch, dirty, pollute, smear, sully
Dictionary Meaning	to make something dirty.		

de - prefix - away from

Word: *democracy*

My Guess	People power	Synonym:	commonwealth, equalitarianism emancipation, equality, justice
Dictionary Meaning	A form of government in wich people choose leaders by voting.		

demo - root - people
cracy - root - rule

Word: *demography*   study of human population

My Guess	Population graph	Synonym:	anthropology, population. analysis, population density
Dictionary Meaning	the study of changes (such as the # of births, death, marriages and illness.) that occur over a period of time in human population.		

demo - root people
graph - root to write

Word: *deregulate*

My Guess	release control	Synonym:	
Dictionary Meaning	to give up control of (something such as industry) by removing laws.		

de - prefix - away from
reg root - rule

Word: *destruction*

My Guess		Synonym:	
Dictionary Meaning			

Word: *devalue*

My Guess		Synonym:	
Dictionary Meaning			

Word: *fratricide*

My Guess	Synonym:
Dictionary Meaning	

Word: *geography*

My Guess	Synonym:
Dictionary Meaning	

Word: *genocide*

My Guess	Synonym:
Dictionary Meaning	

Word: *geopolitical*

My Guess	Synonym:
Dictionary Meaning	

Word: *hemisphere*

My Guess	Synonym:
Dictionary Meaning	

Word: *interact*

My Guess	Synonym:
Dictionary Meaning	

Word: *interject*

My Guess	Synonym:
Dictionary Meaning	

Word: *interrupt*

My Guess	Synonym:
Dictionary Meaning	

Word: *metrics*

My Guess	Synonym:
Dictionary Meaning	

Word: *microclimate*

My Guess	Synonym:
Dictionary Meaning	

Word: *micrometer*

My Guess	Synonym:
Dictionary Meaning	

Word: *microwave*

My Guess	Synonym:
Dictionary Meaning	

Word: *patricide*

My Guess	Synonym:
Dictionary Meaning	

Word: *polychromatic*

My Guess	Synonym:
Dictionary Meaning	

Word: *prologue*

My Guess	Synonym:
Dictionary Meaning	

Word: *retrograde*

My Guess	Synonym:
Dictionary Meaning	

Word: *retrorocket*

My Guess	Synonym:
Dictionary Meaning	

Word: *semiretired*

My Guess	Synonym:
Dictionary Meaning	

Word: *substandard*

My Guess	Synonym:
Dictionary Meaning	

Word: *subterranean*

My Guess	Synonym:
Dictionary Meaning	

Word: *subversive*

My Guess	Synonym:
Dictionary Meaning	

Word: *terrestrial*

My Guess	Synonym:
Dictionary Meaning	

Word: *transact*

My Guess	Synonym:
Dictionary Meaning	

Word: *transform*

My Guess	Synonym:
Dictionary Meaning	

Word: *translate*

My Guess	Synonym:
Dictionary Meaning	

Word: *unable*

My Guess	Synonym:
Dictionary Meaning	

Word: *unappreciative*

My Guess	Synonym:
Dictionary Meaning	

Word: *underachieve*

My Guess	Synonym:
Dictionary Meaning	

USE CONTEXT CLUES TO FIGURE OUT MEANING

One good way to figure out the meaning of an unfamiliar word is to use what are called *context clues*. The *context* of a word is the phrases and sentence or sentences that surround it. Often, even if you have never heard a word before, you can guess its meaning by looking at the context in which it appears. The context may give you clues to help you figure out the meaning.

Study Some Examples

Here are some examples of how to use context clues to figure out the meaning of an unfamiliar word.

- The argument was so logical and comprehensive that any additional information was *nonessential*. (*Nonessential* must mean "not important" or "not needed.")
- Despite his love for her, his actions toward her were *undemonstrative*. (*Undemonstrative* must mean "not shown.")
- George's *stamina* in the boxing ring allowed him to finish the fight and defeat the champion. (*Stamina* must have something to do with strength and endurance.)

- The *spectators* watched carefully as the matador put the bull through its paces in the coliseum. (*Spectators* must mean "people who watch.")
- The room was so *spacious* that it felt larger than a football field. (*Spacious* must mean "open" or "roomy.")
- She *rummaged* through her bulging purse trying to find the theater tickets she thought she placed there. (*Rummage* must mean "to search or look through.")
- The judge *reversed* the jury's decision because the penalty was far too harsh for the crime. (*Reverse* must mean "to change.")
- The *recumbent* bicycle was much more comfortable for her to ride because she did not have to lean forward. (*Recumbent* must mean "to lie back.")
- She was so angry at being stood up that he needed to *placate* her with a promise of dinner and dancing next weekend. (*Placate* must mean "to pacify or appease.")
- He seemed to have this *innate* ability to know exactly what to say no matter the circumstances. (*Innate* must mean "inner.")

Start Using What You Know

Use the activities that follow to further expand and strengthen your vocabulary.

Activity 2: Guess the Meaning of Words in Context

In this activity, a sentence is given and a word is boldfaced. By reading the sentence, guess the meaning of the word. Write your guess. Then look up the dictionary meaning and write it in the space provided. List at least one synonym.

Sentence: The electronic game was so **ingenious** that the children were entertained for hours upon end.	
My Guess:	**Synonym:**
Dictionary Meaning:	

Sentence: After 20 years of teaching high school social studies, Mr. Jones decided to treat himself to a **furlough** by going back to school and studying a new subject.	
My Guess:	**Synonym:**
Dictionary Meaning:	

Sentence: You could hear the **furor** across America when they heard that the accused person was found not guilty.	
My Guess:	**Synonym:**
Dictionary Meaning:	

Sentence: So many people showed up at the same time at the "by invitation only" theater production that trying to check invitations was a **fiasco**.	
My Guess:	**Synonym:**
Dictionary Meaning:	

Sentence: The shopping mall was in **deplorable** condition after so many years of neglect by its owners.	
My Guess:	**Synonym:**
Dictionary Meaning:	

Sentence: Only **credentialed** journalists were allowed to attend the president's news conference.

My Guess:	Synonym:

Dictionary Meaning:

Sentence: He was so relieved after passing his final exams that he celebrated with his friends by **carousing** at a local diner.

My Guess:	Synonym:

Dictionary Meaning:

Sentence: His appetite for sports was so **voracious** that he subscribed to four different magazines on the subject.

My Guess:	Synonym:

Dictionary Meaning:

Sentence: The waves hitting the beach were so violent that you could feel the **tremor** on the ground.

My Guess:	Synonym:

Dictionary Meaning:

Sentence: Dane's friends tried to convince him to go to graduate school, but his lack of funds made his decision to get a job **immutable**.

My Guess:	Synonym:

Dictionary Meaning:

Sentence: Chad stubbornly believed that he was right on this issue, so he was **impervious** to any new information.

My Guess:	Synonym:

Dictionary Meaning:

Activity 3: Fill In the Blank

The list that follows has 10 words. Write the proper word from the list in the blank in each sentence. Each word is used only once.

miscellaneous	remarkable
implicit	preemptive
artifact	magnanimous
irrational	nominate
unconventional	premiere

1. The conclusion was _____ in the clues given by the author.

2. The _____ of the film was shown at the Regal Theater in New York City.

3. If we couldn't categorize the objects into the groups of red or green, we put them in a category called _____.

4. The improvement in Salvador's grades in the last six months was truly _____.

5. Before his parents could discover the trouble he was in, Lance took a(n) _____ approach by confiding in them immediately.

6. Kevin brought back a(n) _____ from the art show that represented the Aztec culture.

7. The high school class worked hard to raise money for the orphans; their generosity was truly _____.

8. Immediately after the accident, the victim was _____ when questioned by the police.

9. The group wanted to _____ Cassidy for homecoming queen.

10. Rhonda's skill with poetry was _____ when compared to traditional poets.

Activity 4: Fill In the Blank

The list that follows has 10 words. Write the proper word from the list in the blank in each sentence. Each word is used only once.

predisposed	unwieldy
predetermined	oration
incessant	indisputable
tumultuous	ingredient
perseverance	indulge

1. Stephanie was _____ to view other people as friends.

2. After the final exams, the students felt they could _____ themselves in some extensive time off.

3. Their relationship was friendly and committed, but on occasion their disagreements would cause _____ arguments.

4. At school the number of homework assignments was often considered so _____ that students would protest at the difficulty.

5. That Chad would go to medical school was almost _____ by the history of his family.

6. The _____ was not only pertinent, but well delivered by the speaker.

7. Her persistence was the major _____ in her successful career.

8. Bernadine's _____ chatter drove her classmates to distraction.

9. With all the evidence that was presented, the conclusion was _____.

10. David would not give up because he believed that _____ was the key to success.

Activity 5: Fill In the Blank

The list that follows has 10 words. Write the proper word from the list in the blank in each sentence. Each word is used only once.

magnanimous	reticent
acrimonious	unilateral
acquiesced	galvanized
erratic	pending
fervor	modification

1. After holding firm on her position, Edie finally _____ to her opponent on the issue of homeland security.

2. Even though Bill did not believe he was at fault, he made the _____ gesture of apologizing.

3. Alfred was mildly enthusiastic about football and baseball, but he cheered the hockey team with great _____.

4. Steve wanted to make a decision about his summer vacation, but he put off the decision _____ the information on his job promotion.

5. During the storm, it was difficult to hold the umbrella because the wind was so _____.

6. Peggy Jean always voted the party line, but this year she was _____ because she did not like the candidate.

7. Valerie and Samuel generally had discussions that were friendly and polite, but on the subject of local politics their discussions were _____.

8. Betsy and Josh both agreed with the specifics of the remodeling of the kitchen, but at the last minute they made a(n) _____ to the plan.

9. Mrs. Smith generally considered the input of others before making a decision, but on the issue of personnel promotions, she made a(n) _____ decision.

10. The terrorist attack on our country _____ the citizens to pull together and rebuild.

Activity 6: Fill In the Blank

The list that follows has 10 words. Write the proper word from the list in the blank in each sentence. Each word is used only once.

absconded	didactic
antagonist	docile
complacent	dormant
consensus	exorbitant
defensive	fidelity

1. Some germs lie _____ for years until the right conditions trigger them to grow and multiply.

2. Sandy's approach to teaching tended to be _____, not encouraging many questions or discussions from the students.

3. It seemed that whatever group George was in, he was considered a(n) _____ because he always had a different point of view.

4. Jane was considered an exemplary employee by the members of her work group because she was _____.

5. Although the views of the group members were so different, Tom tried to bring the group to some level of _____.

6. Octavia felt that the increase in tuition was so _____ that she filed a complaint with the school administration.

7. Conner always thought he was right, so when his statement about the effects of global warming was challenged by his sister, he became _____.

8. Renee had been treasurer of the organization for many years, so when it was determined that she had _____ with the members' dues, everyone was shocked.

9. Mark's _____ to his wife and family was considered one of his most endearing traits.

10. William tended to enjoy a physically active life by jogging and playing tennis, but today, with the weather cold and rainy, he was _____ about sitting by the fireplace with a good book.

Activity 7: Fill In the Blank

The list that follows has 10 words. Write the proper word from the list in the blank in each sentence. Each word is used only once.

pandemic	amicable
explicit	precocious
premonition	nonessential
loquacious	vicarious
commemorated	convened

1. During the snowstorm, the government sent home all _____ personnel.

2. When giving a person driving directions, you must be very _____ or else the person may make a wrong turn.

3. Even though the family members disagreed about the vacation destinations, their conversation was _____.

4. The chairperson _____ a panel of experts to discuss global warming.

5. They _____ the end of the war by holding a big parade.

6. Even though there was no sign of a problem, Cynthia had a(n) _____ that something would go wrong.

7. Gene was only in fourth grade, but he was _____ in his school subjects because he studied with his older brothers.

8. Scientists are worried that this new disease, which spreads rapidly and for which there is no vaccine, may cause a(n) _____.

9. Though most people in the audience were calm and quiet, little Sally was bubbly and _____.

10. Brian took _____ pleasure in Joan's debut on stage, even though he was not able to attend the performance.

USE IT OR LOSE IT

Many experts say that the best way to learn a new word is to use the word in your speech and writing. When you learn a new word, use it in different sentences. Say the word out loud. Do this several times. If you don't use it, you are likely to forget it. Make up new sentences using the word. Find ways to use the word in your daily life. The following activities will help you practice these skills.

Activity 8: Use New Words in a Sentence

In this activity, you are given several words. If you don't know the meaning of a word, look it up in the dictionary and write the definition. Then create a sentence using the word.

Word	Dictionary Definition	My Sentence
accumulation		
acuity		
adapt		
attentive		
attire		
automation		
avowed		
brevity		

Word	Dictionary Definition	My Sentence
buoy		
calamitous		
component		
cursory		
cyclical		
dampen		
defile		
digress		
evade		
excessive		
fabricate		
futile		

Word	Dictionary Definition	My Sentence
garner		
hotbed		
insert		
jaunt		
jovial		
livid		
lodge		
lustrous		
luxurious		
magnitude		
mundane		
nebulous		

Word	Dictionary Definition	My Sentence
nurture		
overbearing		
pensive		
peripheral		
radiant		
receptive		
solitary		
solvent		
spawn		
thwart		
undermine		
wary		

Activity 9: Find Synonyms

For each word, list at least one synonym. A *synonym* is a word that has the same or nearly the same meaning. Use a dictionary or thesaurus if necessary.

Word	Synonyms
abate	
abhor	
acquit	
cajole	
disdain	
erroneous	
façade	
feasible	
ghastly	
haughty	
incognito	
incriminate	
legitimate	
leverage	
liaison	
meander	
opulent	
purge	
rebuke	
rescind	
sanction	
simulate	

Word	Synonyms
stooped	
tangible	
truncate	
ultimate	
undermine	
vacillate	
vie	
viscous	

Activity 10: Match Words to Definitions

Match the words on the left with the definitions on the right by placing the letter of the definition in the column to the left of each word.

	Word	Definition
	abnormal	A. an affiliation between families, states, parties, or individuals
	abyss	B. capable of catching fire easily and of burning quickly
	alliance	C. a momentous tragic event or situation
	capsize	D. not achieving or producing success
	cartography	E. a discussion expressing opposing views
	catastrophe	F. unusual, not typical, or deviating from the average
	colleague	G. to lose spirit or morale
	comprise	H. an associate in a profession
	controversy	I. the science or art of making maps
	dishearten	J. a bottomless pit
	emphasize	K. to become overturned
	fruitless	L. to cause something unpleasant
	hostile	M. openly opposed or resistant to
	flammable	N. to be made up of
	inflict	O. to stress a point or situation

Activity 11: Match Words to Definitions

Match the words on the left with the definitions on the right by placing the letter of the definition in the column to the left of each word.

	initiate	A. to be conventional or traditional
	malignant	B. to be bright, shining, or glowing
	mortify	C. dull or expressionless or heavy
	orthodox	D. relating to the country or areas outside the city
	procure	E. showing dislike or hesitation
	radiant	F. to move at a fast pace; scamper
	rejuvenate	G. seeming to be real, but not
	reluctant	H. strong, solid, firmly constructed
	rural	I. to subject to embarrassment
	substantial	J. full of energy, expression, or animation
	scurry	K. to obtain possession of something
	sodden	L. to start or facilitate the start of something
	spirited	M. to shrink back involuntarily, as from pain
	virtual	N. to bring back to an original or new state
	wince	O. evil or hurtful in effect

Activity 12: Match Words to Definitions

Match the words on the left with the definitions on the right by placing the letter of the definition in the column to the left of each word.

	aghast	A. to rule, control, or overwhelm
	anecdote	B. capable of making a mistake
	congested	C. to plead, beg, or ask urgently
	consolidate	D. useful or practical
	counterfeit	E. a short description of an interesting or humorous event
	docile	F. running away or intending flight; difficult to grasp or retain
	dominate	G. concentrated in a small or narrow space; clogged
	eloquent	H. to unite or make into a whole
	emit	I. dirty
	entreat	J. reacting with disbelief or horror
	fallible	K. an imitation of something else with intent to fool or trick
	fickle	L. forceful and fluent in speaking or writing
	fugitive	M. to throw or give off
	functional	N. erratic or changing
	grimy	O. easily led

Activity 13: Match Words to Definitions

Match the words on the left with the definitions on the right by placing the letter of the definition in the column to the left of each word.

	incident	A. possibility of becoming real
	inflict	B. standing out or easily noticeable
	iota	C. unusual or different
	maul	D. an occurrence or happening
	mythical	E. unsure about something
	potential	F. to cause something unpleasant
	prominent	G. to make something move faster
	quaint	H. to handle roughly, beat, or bruise
	reluctant	I. to dilute or moderate
	tactful	J. the farthest; last in a series; the best of its kind
	temper	K. not named or identified; done by an unknown person
	ultimate	L. having good relations with others by knowing what to say and how to say something without offending
	uncertain	M. fictitious or imaginary
	accelerate	N. feeling or showing hesitation
	anonymous	O. a tiny amount

Activity 14: Match Words to Synonyms

Match the words on the left with the synonyms on the right by placing the letter of the definition in the column to the left of each word.

	abridge	A. famous
	affable	B. disagreeable
	annihilate	C. upset
	impartial	D. cordial
	lethal	E. force
	compel	F. counterbalance
	legendary	G. sound
	coherent	H. prosper
	flourish	I. destroy
	compensate	J. deadly
	disrupt	K. condense
	theme	L. fair
	obnoxious	M. pious
	sleek	N. composition
	devout	O. glossy

Activity 15: Match Words to Synonyms

Match the words on the left with the synonyms on the right by placing the letter of the definition in the column to the left of each word.

	logical	A. picture
	tangible	B. empty
	rejuvenate	C. negligible
	image	D. rational
	reluctant	E. sufficient
	utilitarian	F. touchable
	foreshadow	G. isolate
	marginal	H. suggest
	void	I. practical
	attribute	J. refurbish
	adequate	K. hesitant
	hospitable	L. judge
	insulate	M. gratify
	arbitrate	N. sociable
	indulge	O. quality

Activity 16: Match Words to Synonyms

Match the words on the left with the synonyms on the right by placing the letter of the definition in the column to the left of each word.

	affable	A. clever
	amiss	B. force
	assert	C. faulty
	brawl	D. sociable
	buoyant	E. hate
	canny	F. first
	compel	G. blunder
	deduce	H. eradicate
	detest	I. glaring
	domestic	J. squabble
	extinguish	K. declare
	flagrant	L. vivid
	flounder	M. infer
	foremost	N. expansive
	graphic	O. related to the home

Activity 17: Match Words to Synonyms

Match the words on the left with the synonyms on the right by placing the letter of the definition in the column to the left of each word.

	gruesome	A. famous
	momentum	B. lying
	notable	C. surmise
	nurture	D. previous
	paradox	E. fury
	perjury	F. consistent
	presume	G. barrage
	prior	H. balance
	proficient	I. impetus
	salvo	J. cultivate
	symmetry	K. watchful
	vigilant	L. contradiction
	wrath	M. clown
	buffoon	N. horrible
	coherent	O. skilled

Activity 18: Match Words to Antonyms

Match the words on the left with the antonyms on the right by placing the letter of the word that means the opposite in the column to the left of each word.

	acclaim	A. static
	acrid	B. build
	bewilder	C. denounce
	dupe	D. simple
	decrease	E foolish
	erode	F. clarify
	dynamic	G. enlighten
	eject	H. perfection
	formidable	I. delicious
	goad	J. obedient
	flaw	K. veteran
	insubordinate	L. start
	fledgling	M. calm
	culminate	N. accept
	prudent	O. increase

Activity 19: Match Words to Antonyms

Match the words on the left with the antonyms on the right by placing the letter of the word that means the opposite in the column to the left of each word.

	animated	A. opaque
	poised	B. copy
	desolate	C. impossible
	irate	D. insecure
	recede	E. hostile
	random	F. cheerful
	functional	G. inert
	lustrous	H. flexible
	transparent	I. calm
	harmonious	J. occasional
	original	K. advance
	plausible	L. impractical
	dogmatic	M. dynamic
	chronic	N. systematic
	static	O. dull

Activity 20: Use Vocabulary Words in a Sentence

For each of the following words, write a brief definition of the word, list at least one synonym and one antonym, and use the word in a sentence. If you cannot think of a one-word antonym, use a short phrase.

Word: insinuate

Synonym:	Antonym:
Definition:	
Word in a sentence:	

Word: indispensable

Synonym:	Antonym:
Definition:	
Word in a sentence:	

Word: vengeance

Synonym:	Antonym:
Definition:	
Word in a sentence:	

Word: melancholy

Synonym:	Antonym:
Definition:	
Word in a sentence:	

Word: despondent

Synonym:	Antonym:
Definition:	
Word in a sentence:	

Word: antagonize

Synonym:	Antonym:
Definition:	
Word in a sentence:	

Word: lethargic

Synonym:	Antonym:
Definition:	
Word in a sentence:	

Word: stalemate

Synonym:	Antonym:
Definition:	
Word in a sentence:	

Word: beneficiary

Synonym:	Antonym:
Definition:	
Word in a sentence:	

Word: innumerable

Synonym:	Antonym:
Definition:	
Word in a sentence:	

Word: seclusion

Synonym:	Antonym:
Definition:	
Word in a sentence:	

Word: vindictive

Synonym:	Antonym:
Definition:	
Word in a sentence:	

Word: momentary

Synonym:	Antonym:
Definition:	
Word in a sentence:	

Word: lavish

Synonym:	Antonym:
Definition:	
Word in a sentence:	

Word: timidity

Synonym:	Antonym:
Definition:	
Word in a sentence:	

Word: fluctuate

Synonym:	Antonym:
Definition:	
Word in a sentence:	

Word: subside

Synonym:	Antonym:
Definition:	
Word in a sentence:	

Word: sustain

Synonym:	Antonym:
Definition:	
Word in a sentence:	

Word: simultaneous

Synonym:	Antonym:
Definition:	
Word in a sentence:	

Word: dismantle

Synonym:	Antonym:
Definition:	
Word in a sentence:	

Word: nomadic

Synonym:	Antonym:
Definition:	
Word in a sentence:	

Word: grueling

Synonym:	Antonym:
Definition:	
Word in a sentence:	

Word: facilitate

Synonym:	Antonym:
Definition:	
Word in a sentence:	

Word: forage

Synonym:	Antonym:
Definition:	
Word in a sentence:	

Word: grievous

Synonym:	Antonym:
Definition:	
Word in a sentence:	

Word: magnitude

Synonym:	Antonym:
Definition:	
Word in a sentence:	

Word: mediate

Synonym:	Antonym:
Definition:	
Word in a sentence:	

Word: cynical

Synonym:	Antonym:
Definition:	
Word in a sentence:	

Word: harmonious

Synonym:	Antonym:
Definition:	
Word in a sentence:	

Word: sagacious

Synonym:	Antonym:
Definition:	
Word in a sentence:	

Word: pretentious

Synonym:	Antonym:
Definition:	
Word in a sentence:	

Word: vanquish

Synonym:	Antonym:
Definition:	
Word in a sentence:	

Word: admonish

Synonym:	Antonym:
Definition:	
Word in a sentence:	

Word: reputable

Synonym:	Antonym:
Definition:	
Word in a sentence:	

Word: allege

Synonym:	Antonym:
Definition:	
Word in a sentence:	

Word: officiate

Synonym:	Antonym:
Definition:	
Word in a sentence:	

Word: patronize

Synonym:	Antonym:
Definition:	
Word in a sentence:	

Word: oppress

Synonym:	Antonym:
Definition:	
Word in a sentence:	

Word: grovel

Synonym:	Antonym:
Definition:	
Word in a sentence:	

Word: legitimate

Synonym:	Antonym:
Definition:	
Word in a sentence:	

Word: legacy

Synonym:	Antonym:
Definition:	
Word in a sentence:	

Word: indelible

Synonym:	Antonym:
Definition:	
Word in a sentence:	

Word: illustrious

Synonym:	Antonym:
Definition:	
Word in a sentence:	

Activity 21: Form Compound Words

A *compound word* is a word that is made by joining together two other words. In the blank space in each of the items that follows, write a word that can be joined with either given word to make a compound word. Here is an example:

     break   fast, neck

1. _____ stand, paper
2. _____ pack, ache
3. _____ tail, pen
4. _____ ache, strong
5. _____ paper, box
6. _____ foot, back
7. _____ sick, shore
8. _____ bug, finger
9. _____ print, nail
10. _____ bag, shake
11. _____ rock, time
12. _____ brow, lid
13. _____ house, leg
14. _____ fall, beat
15. _____ out, let
16. _____ sighted, away
17. _____ stone, storm
18. _____ maiden, writing

WORD LIST CHART

Use the following chart to record unfamiliar words that you read or hear. Write down your guess at the meaning of the word. Then look up the word in a dictionary or thesaurus to identify synonyms. Experts say that if you use this word in everyday conversation, you are more likely to remember its meaning in the future.

Word	My Guess	Synonyms

Word	My Guess	Synonyms

Word	My Guess	Synonyms

ANSWERS

Activity 3: implicit, premiere, miscellaneous, remarkable, preemptive, artifact, magnanimous, irrational, nominate, unconventional

Activity 4: predisposed, indulge, tumultuous, unwieldy, predetermined, oration, ingredient, incessant, indisputable, perseverance

Activity 5: acquiesced, magnanimous, fervor, pending, erratic, reticent, acrimonious, modification, unilateral, galvanized

Activity 6: dormant, didactic, antagonist, docile, consensus, exorbitant, defensive, absconded, fidelity, complacent

Activity 7: nonessential, explicit, amicable, convened, commemorated, premonition, precocious, pandemic, loquacious, vicarious

Activity 10: F, J, A, K, I, C, H, N, E, G, O, D, M, B, L

Activity 11: L, O, I, A, K, B, N, E, D, H, F, C, J, G, M

Activity 12: J, E, G, H, K, O, A, L, M, C, B, N, F, D, I

Activity 13: D, F, O, H, M, A, B, C, N, L, I, J, E, G, K

Activity 14: K, D, I, L, J, E, A, G, H, F, C, N, B, O, M

Activity 15: D, F, J, A, K, I, H, C, B, O, E, N, G, L, M

Activity 16: D, C, K, J, N, A, B, M, E, O, H, I, G, F, L

Activity 17: N, I, A, J, L, B, C, D, O, G, H, K, E, M, F

Activity 18: C, I, F, G, O, B, A, N, D, M, H, J, K, L, E

Activity 19: G, D, F, I, K, N, L, O, A, E, B, C, H, J, M

Activity 21: news, back, pig, head, sand, bare, sea, lady, finger or thumb, hand, bed, eye, dog, down, drop, far, hail, hand,

Chapter 7

Sharpen Your Paragraph Comprehension Skills

READ THIS CHAPTER TO LEARN:

• **What you can do to read more carefully**

• **How to focus on important information in a passage**

• **Tips for answering each type of ASVAB paragraph comprehension question**

You have learned that ASVAB Paragraph Comprehension questions are designed to find out how well you obtain information from written material. Basically, they measure your reading comprehension skills. In this chapter, you'll explore some ways to improve your reading comprehension. You'll also learn the six types of ASVAB Paragraph Comprehension questions, and you'll get practical advice about how to approach each type. In addition, you'll find exercises that you can use to improve and sharpen your reading comprehension skills. If you work through this chapter carefully, you can get a higher ASVAB Paragraph Comprehension score!

START IMPROVING YOUR READING COMPREHENSION

Start your preparation for the ASVAB Paragraph Comprehension test by following these general guidelines.

Read

The best way to improve your reading comprehension skills is to *read, read, read*. The more you read and practice your reading comprehension skills, the better off you will be on the test. The following list suggests a variety of materials that you should be reading.

WHAT TO READ

• *Books on subjects that you like.* Whatever the topic that interests you, there are books about it—and reading those books will help you. If you are a sports fan, read books about great teams and famous games. If you love science fiction, read this year's most popular science fiction stories. If you are a history buff, read about the famous people and events of the past that made our world what it is today. Read autobiographies, books on politics, health books, science books, books on bicycling, nutrition, ice skating, organizing your life, and more. The list is endless. You don't need to buy these books; use your local library. The library is also a great place to read because it is quiet and you won't get distracted.

• *School books.* If you are in school, devour those textbooks. Focus on paragraph headings, see how the information is organized, and highlight critical statements and facts. Reading the textbook not only will expand your knowledge base for the other ASVAB tests, but also will improve your vocabulary and your ability to understand what you are reading.

• *Newspapers.* Daily newspapers, especially those from a large town or city, offer plenty of reading opportunity on a variety of subjects.

• *The Internet.* Be selective about what you read on the Internet. Look for more lengthy passages, such as articles from a newspaper or extracts from a book. Avoid Internet sites where information is short, choppy, and abbreviated. That kind of reading will probably not help your reading comprehension skills. However, reading Internet material can be helpful if you select the right stuff.

Learn New Words

The better your vocabulary, the easier it will be for you to understand what you are reading. The previous chapter of this book explained how to improve your vocabulary for the ASVAB Word Knowledge test. Following those suggestions will help you on the Paragraph Comprehension test as well. (You may wish to go back to the earlier chapter and review it.)

How to Learn Words

- *Develop a word list.* As you are reading, identify words that you don't know or don't know very well. Based on the sentence or paragraph that contains each word, try to guess that word's meaning. Look up the meaning in a dictionary to be sure that you are correct. The previous chapter of this book gave you a Word List Chart for recording these words and their definitions. Use it to help your vocabulary grow.
- *Use context clues.* The *context* of a word is the other words and sentences that surround that word. Often you can determine the meaning of a word from its context. One way to determine the meaning is to see how the word is used in the sentence.
- *Use prefixes, suffixes, and roots.* These word parts can help you decode a word's meaning. The Word Knowledge chapter gives you a whole laundry list of common prefixes, suffixes, and roots.

RECOGNIZE THE SIX TYPES OF PARAGRAPH COMPREHENSION QUESTIONS

There are six different types of ASVAB Paragraph Comprehension questions. Each type asks you something different about the paragraph you read. The following is a list of the question types, along with examples of each type. It is a good idea to learn about these question types so that you know what to expect on the test.

1. Words in Context Questions

Some Paragraph Comprehension questions will ask you to determine the meaning of an unfamiliar word in the paragraph by looking at the context in which that word appears. Recall that the *context* of a word consists of the words and phrases in the surrounding sentences.

Example

Space flight is a somewhat common experience these days. Nowadays the International Space Station generally is the home of several astronauts from the United States and Russia. Astronauts generally spend several months in a weightless condition. They sleep, eat, and work without the effects of gravity. One of the effects of lengthy space travel is the atrophy of major muscle groups and the stress of travel on the heart and lungs. When these space travelers return to Earth, it takes several days for them to adjust back to gravity and to walk normally.

In this instance, the word <u>atrophy</u> means

A. strengthening
B. defining
C. weakening
D. breaking

If the correct meaning was "strengthening" (choice A), then it probably wouldn't take several days for the space travelers to adjust back to gravity. If choice D, "breaking," was the correct answer, then the space travelers would probably not adjust at all, as their muscles would be in very poor shape. "Defining" muscles (choice B) would result from exercise performed against gravity, not exercise in a weightless environment. Choice C, "weakening," is the correct answer because when muscles do not have a chance to work out, they get weaker.

2. Main Idea Questions

Another kind of Paragraph Comprehension question asks about the main idea of the paragraph. In this kind of question, you may be asked to identify the main idea, to choose the best title for the paragraph, or to identify the primary theme of the paragraph.

Example

These days the dancing we see on MTV is usually hip-hop, soul, and funk. You may think that those cool moves are brand new, but can you believe that some of them have been around since the late 1800s? A lot of dancing borrows many moves from gymnastics. Long ago, Arabs performing gymnastic routines used a series of one-armed cartwheels. Have you ever seen someone on the street performing for money? Maybe doing a little song-and-dance routine? Street dancing has been around for years, using moves like standing on one's head and twisting around like a top. It looks pretty similar to the head spin move that is so popular in break dancing today.

Of the following, which statement best represents the main idea of this passage?

A. The Arabs were the original creators of what we now know as break dancing.
B. Break dancing has been around since the 1800s.
C. The break dancing of today has a history of moves going back more than 200 years.
D. Gymnasts' training routines were really break dance routines.

The major idea of this passage is that some of the moves of what we know today as break dancing are rooted in athletic events of the past. Choice C is the correct answer.

Often there will be one sentence in a paragraph that sums up the main idea of the paragraph as a whole. The question may ask you to choose which sentence that is. A sentence that sums up the main idea of a paragraph is called the *topic sentence*. In the following example, the sentences are numbered. As you read, try to pick out the topic sentence.

Example

(1) It was 6 p.m. on a cloudy, frigid day in the forest. (2) It had been sleeting the entire afternoon. (3) Simone was worried because her son hadn't returned home, as he usually did by this time. (4) Todd was always punctual, but tonight was different. (5) Todd had a basketball game after school, and a friend was supposed to drive him home. (6) Simone waited by the window in hopes of seeing Todd's smiling face as he came up the stairs.

Which of the following sentences best reflects the main idea of the paragraph?

A. 1
B. 3
C. 4
D. 5

The best and correct answer is choice B. In most paragraphs, the topic sentence tends to be the first sentence. But in this one, as you might have noticed, it is not. Of the five sentences, sentence 3 best conveys the meaning of the entire paragraph. It tells you that for some reason Todd was supposed to be home and wasn't, and that Simone was worried. Sentence 3 is the topic sentence. Sentences 1 and 2 just give an indication of the setting. Sentences 4 and 5 tell us that Todd was usually on time and that on this day, he had a basketball game. These sentences don't reflect the basic idea of the paragraph: that Simone was worried and why she was worried. Sentence 5 conveys no sense that there was any kind of problem or reason for worry, only that Simone was looking out the window hoping to see Todd.

"Best Title" Questions   Another kind of main idea question will ask you to choose the best title for the paragraph. The best title is the one that best expresses the main idea of the paragraph as a whole. Here is an example.

Example

Katherine Graham started her married life as a devoted but insecure housewife. Her husband was a handsome, brilliant, and engaging newspaperman, editor of the *Washington Post,* and a confidant to powerful people, including U.S. presidents and industrial giants. As time went on, her husband developed a mental illness that would tragically end his life. Rather than let her deep insecurities and personal tragedy rule her actions, she hesitantly took on the responsibility of becoming editor of the powerful newspaper. During her tenure as editor and owner, she exhibited extraordinary courage by battling powerful unions, navigating the crises of the Pentagon Papers and Watergate, lifting the paper from potential bankruptcy to profitability, and building one of the most respected newspapers in the entire world.

Based on this passage, which of the following would be the best title for this passage?

A. A Talented Housewife
B. Housewife or Swan
C. Battling the Unions
D. From Tragedy to Triumph

The main idea in this passage has two parts. The first part is that Katherine Graham was dealt a blow when her husband developed a mental illness and died. The second part is that although she was not anxious to do so, she replaced him as editor of the *Washington Post* and brought the paper from a troubled existence to among the most respected newspapers in the world. The best title for this idea would be choice D.

Example

The white shark is the world's largest predatory fish. White sharks are migratory animals and, as a result, are found in oceans around the world. For short periods of time, they can swim at speeds up to 25 miles per hour, and they have been seen leaping out of the water to chase after their food. They are known as vicious killers, but their reputation is undeserved.

White sharks are the most misunderstood animals in the ocean. The myths about them may have contributed to their global decline They have no natural predators other than humans. They are threatened by human activities such as overfishing and habitat destruction. Conservation programs have been put into place to attempt to stop the decline of the white shark population.

Of the following, which is the best title for this passage?

A. Sharks—Very Big Fish
B. Save the White Shark
C. Sharks, Sharks Everywhere
D. Sharks—Vicious Killers

The passage suggests that the shark's reputation as a vicious killer is undeserved, so choice D cannot be correct. It is true that sharks are very big fish (choice A) and that they are found in many oceans (choice C), but the major thrust of the passage suggests that they are currently threatened by human activity and that their population is declining. This means that the best title is choice B, which expresses the idea that the white shark needs saving.

3. Author's Purpose Questions

Another kind of question will ask you to identify the author's purpose in writing the paragraph. Authors write for a variety of purposes: to describe, to raise issues or concerns, to move readers to action, to persuade readers to think in a particular way, to frighten, to give directions, to describe steps

or procedures, to compare and contrast, and to entertain. Here is an example of this kind of question.

Example

Global warming is an increasingly serious environmental problem. It is caused by "greenhouse gases," which are created by things we do to the environment every day. But there are many little things that people can do to reduce greenhouse gas emissions. You can do your part by carpooling to save gasoline. Four people can ride to school or work in a car pool instead of each person taking a car and driving alone. Save electricity by turning off the lights, the television, and the computer when you are through with them. Save energy by taking the bus or riding your bicycle to school or to run errands. Walk to where you want to go. Recycle your cans, bottles, plastic bags, and newspapers. If you care about the future of this planet, help protect the environment! Get with the program!

In the paragraph above, what is the author's purpose?

A. To entertain readers
B. To describe global warming
C. To offer directions
D. To move readers to action

The best answer is choice D. The purpose of the paragraph is to move you to act to protect the environment. The paragraph makes no attempt to entertain readers (choice A), nor does it really describe what global warming is (choice B). It does give suggestions for fixing global warming, but these are not really directions, so choice C is also incorrect.

4. Author's Attitude or Tone Questions

Another kind of question will ask you to identify the author's attitude or tone. In other words, you will need to determine how the author feels toward the subject of the paragraph. Is the author angry? Discouraged? Excited? Happy? For clues to how the author feels, look at the words he or she has chosen to use. Here is an example.

Example

Shooting a cat with a BB gun or anything else is cruelty to animals and is illegal. The recent incident in our neighborhood should be reported to the Society for the Prevention of Cruelty to Animals, the local humane society, or the police. We must as a community band together to find the perpetrators, prosecute them, and get them into some serious counseling program. It's important for all of us to be watchful and to speak up about this horrific behavior. These incidents *must* be stopped before these individuals cause even more serious harm.

In the above paragraph, which of the following best describes the author's tone?

A. Happy about the situation
B. Biased in favor of cats
C. Angry about the situation
D. Depressed about the situation

The correct answer is choice C, "angry about the situation." The author's anger is apparent in words and phrases like "horrific," "we must as a community band together," "prosecute them," and "these incidents *must* be stopped." There is nothing in the paragraph to support any of the other choices.

5. Specific Details Questions

The fifth kind of ASVAB Paragraph Comprehension question will ask you to pick out specific details in the paragraph that you have read. Often these paragraphs provide a lot of information. You have to find the specific item or detail that the question asks about. For this kind of question, it is very helpful to read the question before you read the paragraph. Here is an example.

Example

Dental assistants perform a variety of patient care, office, and laboratory duties. They work chairside as dentists examine and treat patients. They make patients as comfortable as possible in the dental chair, prepare them for treatment, and obtain their dental records. Assistants hand instruments and materials to dentists and keep patients' mouths dry and clear by using suction or other devices. Assistants also sterilize and disinfect instruments and equipment, prepare trays of instruments for dental procedures, and instruct patients on postoperative and general oral health care.

In the above paragraph, where is the dental assistant when the doctor is examining the patient?

A. Right next to the dentist and the patient
B. In the laboratory
C. Finding dental records
D. Sterilizing instruments

The correct answer is choice A. The detail you are looking for is found in the sentence "They work chairside as dentists examine and treat patients." So the correct answer is "right next to the dentist and the patient." At other times, a dental assistant may be in the laboratory (choice B), finding dental records (choice C), or sterilizing instruments (choice D), but when the dentist is working with the patient, the assistant is right by the dentist's side.

Sequence of Steps Questions One type of specific detail question will ask you about the sequence (order) of steps in a process. The process may be something in nature, or it may be preparing a food item, operating a machine, making a repair, or something similar. To answer this kind of question correctly, you need to pay close attention to the order in which things happen or in which things are done. Reading the question before reading the passage is a very good strategy with this type of item. Here is an example.

Example

Making a Brownie

Preheat the oven to 350° and lightly spray the pan with cooking oil. In a saucepan, combine the butter and chopped chocolate. Set this over a low heat until melted. Stir the mixture and set aside to cool. In a mixing bowl, mix together the flour, cocoa, baking powder, salt, and cinnamon. Measure the sugar into a large bowl and mix in the cooled butter-chocolate mixture. Add the eggs, vanilla, and water. Mix very well. Add the dry ingredients and mix until blended. Spoon the batter into the pan and bake for 23 to 25 minutes. Cool in the pan and cut into squares.

When should you add the eggs, vanilla, and water?

A. After melting the chocolate
B. Before cooling the melted butter and chocolate
C. After spooning the batter into the pan
D. Before adding the dry ingredients

The correct answer is choice D. There is a lot of detail in this paragraph, but the time for adding the eggs, vanilla, and water is after combining the melted butter and chocolate with the sugar and before adding the dry ingredients.

6. Interpretation Questions

The sixth type of ASVAB Paragraph Comprehension question will ask you to interpret something that you read. Often an author will suggest or hint at a certain idea but will not state it directly. It is up to you to figure out the author's meaning by "reading between the lines" and drawing your own conclusion. When you do this, you analyze the author's words, you think about what they mean, and you put your ideas together to create something new and original. This process is called *making an inference.* Here is an example of a question that asks you to make an inference.

Example

The dinosaurs went extinct at the end of the Cretaceous period. The reasons for this event are still undetermined. Some scientists attribute it to a cataclysmic occurrence, such as a meteor that struck the Earth, kicking up vast quantities of dust. Another possibility is the great increase in volcanic activity that is known to have taken place at the end of the Cretaceous period. Either cause could have filled the atmosphere with enough dust and soot to block out the sunlight, thus producing a dramatic climate change. Recent discoveries indicate that in many places on several continents, there is a layer of iridium in geologic strata associated with the Cretaceous period. Iridium is an element associated with lava flows.

An inference test item might look like this:

According to this passage, the dinosaurs went extinct because of which of the following conditions?

A. Disappearance of vegetation
B. Radiation from the sun
C. Climate changes
D. Volcanic activity

The best answer is choice C, "climate changes." The paragraph does not come to a conclusion about which of the two events caused the extinction of the dinosaurs, but with both events, it seems that climate changes were the eventual cause of their disappearance. This conclusion is not stated in the passage. You needed to infer this from reading the passage.

SHARPEN YOUR READING SKILLS TO RAISE YOUR SCORE

In the following pages, you will study reading skills that can help you answer ASVAB Paragraph Comprehension questions. You'll also get opportunities to practice each skill on sample questions just like the ones on the real test. Working carefully through the activities that follow can help you raise your ASVAB score.

Highlight the Pertinent Parts of the Passage

As you read a passage in a book or magazine, or scan a reading passage on a test, it is a good idea to highlight pertinent or important parts of the passage. These pertinent parts are the sections that are most likely to generate test questions. Some tests like the ASVAB don't allow you mark up or to write in the test booklet, but you can mentally highlight the important parts of the passage. Here are some practice activities for you.

Activity 1: Highlight Pertinent Parts of a Passage

The following is a passage that could be found on tests such as the ASVAB. As you read the passage, use a highlighting pen to highlight points that are especially important or pertinent. These points are likely to be the basis for the test questions. Check the next page for suggested answers and the reasons that certain sections were highlighted.

A tsunami (pronounced soo-nahm-ee) is a series of huge waves that form after an undersea disturbance, such as an earthquake or volcano eruption. (The term *tsunami* comes from the Japanese word for "harbor wave.") The waves travel in all directions from the area of the disturbance, much like the ripples that are formed when you throw a rock into a pond. The waves may travel in the open sea at speeds up to 450 miles per hour. As they enter shallow waters along the coast, they grow to a great height and smash into the shore. They can be as high as 100 feet. They can cause a lot of destruction on the shore. They are sometimes mistakenly called "tidal waves," but tsunami have nothing to do with the tides.

Hawaii is the state that is at greatest risk for a tsunami. It is struck by about one a year, with a damaging tsunami happening about every seven years. Alaska is also at high risk. California, Oregon, and Washington experience a damaging tsunami about every 18 years.

In 1946, a tsunami with waves of 20 to 32 feet crashed into Hilo, Hawaii, flooding the downtown area. In 1964, an Alaskan earthquake generated a tsunami with waves between 10 and 20 feet high along parts of the California, Oregon, and Washington coasts.

The Tsunami Warning Centers in Honolulu, Hawaii, and Palmer, Alaska, monitor disturbances that might trigger tsunami. When a tsunami is recorded, the centers track it and issue a warning when needed.

Activity 1: Suggested Answers

A tsunami❶ (pronounced soo-nahm-ee) is a series of huge waves❷ that form after an undersea disturbance, such as an earthquake or volcano❷ eruption. (The term *tsunami* comes from the Japanese word for "harbor wave.") The waves travel in all directions from the area of the disturbance, much like the ripples that are formed when you throw a rock into a pond. The waves may travel in the open sea at speeds up to 450 miles per hour.❸ As they enter shallow waters along the coast, they grow to a great height and smash into the shore. They can be as high as 100 feet.❸ They can cause a lot of destruction on the shore. They are sometimes mistakenly called "tidal waves,"❹ but tsunami have nothing to do with the tides.

Hawaii is the state that is at greatest risk for a tsunami. It is struck by about one a year,❺ with a damaging tsunami happening about every seven years. Alaska❺ is also at high risk. California, Oregon, and Washington❺ experience a damaging tsunami about every 18 years.

In 1946, a tsunami with waves of 20 to 32 feet crashed into Hilo, Hawaii, flooding the downtown area. In 1964, an Alaskan earthquake generated a tsunami with waves between 10 and 20 feet high along parts of the California, Oregon, and Washington coasts.

The Tsunami Warning Centers in Honolulu, Hawaii, and Palmer, Alaska, monitor disturbances❻ that might trigger a tsunami. When a tsunami is recorded, the centers track it and issue a warning when needed.

❶ Subject of the passage
❷ Definition and cause
❸ Speed and height details
❹ What tsunamis are not
❺ States involved in danger and details on the degree of danger
❻ Detail on detection

Activity 2: Highlight Pertinent Parts of a Passage

The following is a passage that could be found on tests such as the ASVAB. As you read the passage, use a highlighting pen to highlight points that are especially important or pertinent. These points are likely to be the basis for the test questions. Check the next page for suggested answers and the reasons that certain sections were highlighted.

It may seem hard to believe that people can actually change the Earth's climate. But scientists think that the things people do that send greenhouse gases into the air are making our planet warmer.

Once, all climate changes occurred naturally. However, during the Industrial Revolution, we began altering our climate and environment through agricultural and industrial practices. The Industrial Revolution was a time when people began using machines to make life easier. It started more than 200 years ago, and it changed the way humans live. Before the Industrial Revolution, human activity released very few gases into the atmosphere, but now, through population growth, fossil fuel burning, and deforestation, we are affecting the mixture of gases in the atmosphere.

Since the Industrial Revolution, the need for energy to run machines has steadily increased. Some energy, like the energy you need to do your homework, comes from the food you eat. But other energy, like the energy that makes cars run and much of the energy used to light and heat our homes, comes from fuels like coal and oil—fossil fuels. Burning these fuels releases greenhouse gases.

You send greenhouse gases into the air whenever you watch TV, use the air conditioner, turn on a light, use a hair dryer, ride in a car, play a video game, listen to a stereo, wash or dry clothes, use a dishwasher, or microwave a meal. To perform many of these functions, you need to use electricity. Electricity comes from power plants. Most power plants burn coal and oil to make electricity. Burning coal and oil produces greenhouse gases.

The trash that you send to landfills produces a greenhouse gas called methane. Methane is also produced by the animals people raise for dairy and meat products and by mining operations that take coal out of the ground. Whenever you drive or ride in a car, you are adding greenhouse gases to the atmosphere. And when factories make the things that you buy and use every day, they too are sending greenhouse gases into the air.

Activity 2: Suggested Answers

It may seem hard to believe that people can actually change the Earth's climate. But scientists think that the things people do that send greenhouse gases into the air are making our planet warmer.❶

Once, all climate changes occurred naturally. However, during the Industrial Revolution, we began altering our climate and environment through agricultural and industrial practices.❷ The Industrial Revolution was a time when people began using machines to make life easier.❸ It started more than 200 years ago,❸ and it changed the way humans live. Before the Industrial Revolution, human activity released very few gases into the atmosphere, but now, through population growth, fossil fuel burning, and deforestation,❹ we are affecting the mixture of gases in the atmosphere.

Since the Industrial Revolution, the need for energy to run machines has steadily increased. Some energy, like the energy you need to do your homework, comes from the food you eat. But other energy, like the energy that makes cars run and much of the energy used to light and heat our homes, comes from fuels like coal and oil—fossil fuels. Burning these fuels releases greenhouse gases.❹

You send greenhouse gases into the air whenever you watch TV, use the air conditioner, turn on a light, use a hair dryer, ride in a car, play a video game, listen to a stereo, wash or dry clothes, use a dishwasher, or microwave a meal. To perform many of these functions, you need to use electricity. Electricity comes from power plants. Most power plants burn coal and oil to make electricity. Burning coal and oil produces greenhouse gases.❹

The trash that you send to landfills produces a greenhouse gas called methane. Methane is also produced by the animals people raise for dairy and meat products and by the mining operations that take coal out of the ground. Whenever you drive or ride in a car, you are adding greenhouse gases to the atmosphere. And when factories make the things that you buy and use every day, they too are sending greenhouse gases into the air.❹

❶ Major idea or main theme of the passage
❷ When the problem first began
❸ Important detail
❹ Causes of greenhouse gases

Learn to Identify the Main Idea

In all your reading, you need to decide what is the main idea or general theme of the passage. This skill is important not just for scoring well on the ASVAB, but also for your everyday and school reading.

Here are some activities in identifying the main idea.

Activity 3: Identify the Main Idea

Read the entire passage. Then go back to the passage and highlight the sentences or phrases that represent the basic or main idea. Write a sentence that summarizes the main idea in the passage. Compare your answers with the ones presented on the next page.

Quilting is the process of taking two pieces of fabric; putting a layer of wool, cotton, or stuffing in between; and stitching them together. People all over the world, from China to Africa to Europe, have been quilting clothing and blankets for centuries.

In America, quilts have been keeping people warm for generations. Patchwork quilting—taking scraps of cloth arranged in geometric designs and then quilting them to make a bed cover—became very popular in the nineteenth century. The stitching or quilting not only keeps the layers together, but also adds a decorative element. Quilting is still very popular in America today.

Making a quilt often means more than just making a really warm blanket; sometimes it's like putting together a scrapbook of memories. In the past, quilts were often sewn from scraps of fabric left over from making the family clothes or from old clothes that couldn't be worn any longer. One piece might be some extra fabric not used for a sister's new Sunday dress, and another part of a father's worn-out favorite work shirt.

Quilts can also tell stories. In the old days, friends and family members would come together for a "quilting bee." At a quilting bee, quilters, usually women, gathered around the quilting frame and exchanged stories while sewing the layers together. Have you heard the saying, "Many hands make light work"? Working together, the women finished the quilt more quickly than if one person had done all the stitching herself. Swapping stories helped pass the time and made the "bee" like a party. Today, quilting remains a fun thing to do with friends.

Quilts are often created to remember people or events. One famous quilt is the AIDS Memorial Quilt, the largest quilt ever made. In 1987, a small group of people decided to make a quilt to remember their friends and loved ones who had died of AIDS. Each square represents one person. Eleven years later, more than 41,000 panels had been made. The AIDS quilt is so large that it can no longer be shown together in one piece, so parts of the quilt are displayed in schools, libraries, and public places around the world.

Summary Sentence: _Quilts has been around for centuries. They can be described a story or use them as memories._

Activity 3: Suggested Answers

Quilting is the process of taking two pieces of fabric; putting a layer of wool, cotton, or stuffing in between; and stitching them together. People all over the world, from China to Africa to Europe, have been quilting clothing and blankets for centuries.

In America, quilts have been keeping people warm for generations. Patchwork quilting—taking scraps of cloth arranged in geometric designs and then quilting them to make a bed cover—became very popular in the nineteenth century. The stitching or quilting not only keeps the layers together, but also adds a decorative element. Quilting is still very popular in America today.

Making a quilt often means more than just making a really warm blanket; sometimes it's like putting together a scrapbook of memories. In the past, quilts were often sewn from scraps of fabric left over from making the family clothes or from old clothes that couldn't be worn any longer. One piece might be some extra fabric not used for a sister's new Sunday dress, and another part of a father's worn-out favorite work shirt.

Quilts can also tell stories. In the old days, friends and family members would come together for a "quilting bee." At a quilting bee, quilters, usually women, gathered around the quilting frame and exchanged stories while sewing the layers together. Have you heard the saying, "Many hands make light work"? Working together, the women finished the quilt more quickly than if one person had done all the stitching herself. Swapping stories helped pass the time and made the "bee" like a party. Today, quilting remains a fun thing to do with friends.

Quilts are often created to remember people or events. One famous quilt is the AIDS Memorial Quilt, the largest quilt ever made. In 1987, a small group of people decided to make a quilt to remember their friends and loved ones who had died of AIDS. Each square represents one person. Eleven years later, more than 41,000 panels had been made. The AIDS quilt is so large that it can no longer be shown together in one piece, so parts of the quilt are displayed in schools, libraries, and public places around the world.

Summary Sentence: *Quilting is a sewing technique practiced in many countries that sometimes is used to preserve memories, tell stories, or highlight a special event or situation.*

Activity 4: Identify the Main Idea

Read the entire passage. Then go back to the passage and highlight the sentences or phrases that represent the basic or main idea in each paragraph. Write a sentence that summarizes the main idea in the passage. Compare your answers with the ones presented on the next page.

You may have heard people talking or seen news reports about West Nile, a virus that is spread by the bite of an infected mosquito. In areas where the West Nile virus has been found, very few mosquitoes have it. It's true that the virus can cause an infection in the brain, but the chances that you will get very sick from any one mosquito bite are re-e-e-ally low. But you still want to protect yourself and pitch in to help cut down on the number of mosquitoes.

Just remember, when you go outside, apply some mosquito repellent to your skin. Repellents that contain DEET are the most effective, but make sure that you rub them on according to the directions. A good rule of thumb from the experts is that kids should use mosquito repellents with less than 10 percent DEET. Get your parents to help you put it on your face so that you don't get it in your mouth or eyes. And wash your hands after you apply it.

Wear light-colored clothing so that you can spot mosquitoes that might land on you, and wear long-sleeved shirts and pants to hide your skin from those pesky pests. Top it off with a hat. You can even spray your clothes with a mosquito repellent to keep them away. Ask your parents to help you spray all those hard-to-reach spots.

While some mosquitoes lay their eggs in ponds and swamps, other mosquitoes like to leave their eggs in standing water, like water left in buckets and wading pools. Think about it . . . the fewer places there are where mosquitoes can lay their eggs, the fewer mosquitoes there will be! Help cut down the number of mosquitoes by checking around your home, yard, deck, or neighborhood for standing water. Empty flowerpot saucers and turn over buckets. If you have a birdbath, clean it at least once a week.

Many types of mosquitoes are "night flyers," so you may be more likely to get bitten around sundown . . . or around sunup, if you're an early riser! So that you don't get bitten at these times, either head indoors around sundown or be extra sure to cover up and use repellent.

Summary Sentence: _There was some news where mosquitoes carry a virus and it is deadly to human but the chances are very low. You can still protect yourself with a spray and wear long sleeve and pants to keep away from mosquito bites._

Activity 4: Suggested Answers

You may have heard people talking or seen news reports about West Nile, a virus that is spread by the bite of an infected mosquito. In areas where the West Nile virus has been found, very few mosquitoes have it. It's true that the virus can cause an infection in the brain, but the chances that you will get very sick from any one mosquito bite are re-e-e-ally low. But you still want to protect yourself and pitch in to help cut down on the number of mosquitoes.

Just remember, when you go outside, apply some mosquito repellent to your skin. Repellents that contain DEET are the most effective, but make sure that you rub them on according to the directions. A good rule of thumb from the experts is that kids should use mosquito repellents with less than 10 percent DEET. Get your parents to help you put it on your face so that you don't get it in your mouth or eyes. And wash your hands after you apply it.

Wear light-colored clothing so that you can spot mosquitoes that might land on you, and wear long-sleeved shirts and pants to hide your skin from those pesky pests. Top it off with a hat. You can even spray your clothes with a mosquito repellent to keep them away. Ask your parents to help you spray all those hard-to-reach spots.

While some mosquitoes lay their eggs in ponds and swamps, other mosquitoes like to leave their eggs in standing water, like water left in buckets and wading pools. Think about it . . . the fewer places there are where mosquitoes can lay their eggs, the fewer mosquitoes there will be! Help cut down the number of mosquitoes by checking around your home, yard, deck, or neighborhood for standing water. Empty flowerpot saucers and turn over buckets. If you have a birdbath, clean it at least once a week.

Many types of mosquitoes are "night flyers," so you may be more likely to get bitten around sundown . . . or around sunup, if you're an early riser! So that you don't get bitten at these times, either head indoors around sundown or be extra sure to cover up and use repellent.

Summary Sentence: *Mosquito bites can cause illness, but there are ways in which you can protect yourself, such as using DEET, eliminating areas where mosquitoes can breed, covering up, and staying indoors at sunrise and sunset.*

Activity 5: Identify the Main Idea

Read the passages and answer the main idea questions.

Passage 1

Bologna, Italy, is a city with 26 miles of covered walkways dating from the 1200s. The atmosphere of this beautiful city envelops you like a warm hug. In the center piazza of the city are two leaning towers, the most notable landmarks. Around the corner is the famous Roxy coffee bar, a hangout for many of the young university students who are studying medicine and political science. The nearby open marketplace bustles with color and excitement. Listening closely, you can hear many languages spoken by the tourists who visit each year.

Which of the following best states the main idea of this passage?

A. Bologna is an old city.
B. University students love Bologna.
C. Bologna is an interesting place to visit.
D. Bologna has two leaning towers.

Passage 2

The evidence is growing and is more convincing than ever! People of all ages who are generally inactive can improve their health by becoming active at a moderate intensity on a regular basis. Regular physical activity substantially reduces the risk of dying of coronary heart disease, the nation's leading cause of death, and decreases the risk for stroke, colon cancer, diabetes, and high blood pressure. It also helps to control weight; contributes to healthy bones, muscles, and joints; and reduces falls among older adults. Surprisingly, physical activity need not be strenuous to be beneficial; people of all ages benefit from participating in regular, moderate-intensity physical activity, such as 30 minutes of brisk walking five or more times a week.

Which of the following best represents the main idea of this passage?

A. Even a moderate amount of exercise has health benefits.
B. People who do not exercise need to be convinced to do so.
C. Exercise cures heart disease and decreases the likelihood of stroke.
D. Strenuous exercise is better than moderate exercise.

Activity 5: Answers

Passage 1

Clearly, choice C is the best and therefore the correct answer. The main idea is that Bologna is an interesting and vibrant city that attracts visitors from many places. The other answers may be true, but they do not sum up the gist of the entire passage.

Passage 2

There is nothing in the passage indicating that people need to be convinced to exercise, so choice B is not a correct option. The same can be said for strenuous versus moderate exercise (choice D), as there are no comparisons made about that in the passage. It is true that exercise is good for reducing the risk of heart disease and stroke, but the passage does not indicate that exercise cures anything (choice C). The main thrust of the passage is that moderate exercise has many positive benefits. Choice A is the correct answer.

Activity 6: Identify the Main Idea

Read the passages and answer the main idea questions.

Passage 1

Almost 800 million people on our planet are not able to eat sufficient food to meet minimal energy and health needs. Around 200 million kids younger than five years old have malnutrition, and about 13 million of those die every year from diseases such as measles, malaria, and pneumonia—diseases that can be prevented. Malnutrition stunts human growth and potential. Adults may be unable to work and earn a living. Children may be too weak to go to school and learn properly. Society bears the burden of higher health care costs and loss of economic productivity. The areas of the world that are most prone to these conditions are Asia and the Pacific, which account for about two-thirds of the undernourished.

Which of the following statements best reflects the main idea of this passage?

A. Malnutrition is a serious problem for millions of people in this world.
B. Children with malnutrition cannot attend school.
C. Health care costs are skyrocketing in many developing countries.
D. Children are more affected by malnutrition than are adults.

Passage 2

Wilma Rudolph was born with the odds stacked against her. She was born prematurely into a large family at a time when African American babies were denied access to the best doctors and hospitals. As a child, she was sick with a long list of diseases, including pneumonia and scarlet fever, which left her left leg partially deformed. Despite all of these obstacles, Wilma Rudolph, with the help of her family, grew up to achieve a list of accomplishments longer than the list of her childhood ailments. For example, she became the first American woman to win three gold medals in one Olympics, winning the 100- and 200-meter races and the 4x100-meter relay. She was so fast, people used to say that if you blinked, you would miss her.

Which of the following is the best description of the main idea of this passage?

A. Wilma Rudolph was a fast and talented runner.
B. Wilma Rudolph had a supportive family.
C. Wilma Rudolph was very sick and diseased for a large part of her life.
D. Wilma Rudolph surmounted her difficulties to become a star athlete.

Activity 6: Answers

Passage 1

The passage does not state that children are more affected by malnutrition than adults (choice D), nor does it say that health care costs are skyrocketing in developing countries (choice C). The passage does indicate that some children are too weak to attend school, but there is nothing preventing them from doing so, as choice B suggests. The main idea of the passage is that malnutrition is a serious problem for millions of people. Thus, choice A is the correct answer.

Passage 2

Although it is true that Wilma was a great runner (choice A), that she had a supportive family (choice B), and that she was ill during her childhood (choice C), those are not the best answers. The best summary of the paragraph is choice D, that she surmounted her difficulties to become a star athlete.

Learn to Choose the Title that Reflects the Main Idea   The best title for a passage is usually one that reflects the main idea. So choosing the best title is really another way of identifying the main idea. The best title will be one that sums up what the passage is about and what the reader should expect in the sentences and paragraphs that follow. Some ASVAB main idea questions ask you to choose the best title for the passage. You can practice that skill by working through the following activities.

Activity 7: Identify the Main Idea

Read the passages and answer the main idea questions by selecting the best title for each passage.

Passage 1

It may be possible in the future to get your vaccinations by eating flowers. There are companies that are experimenting with injecting certain flowering plants with a genetically altered virus. A flower from such a plant, when eaten, would create certain substances that can protect us from diseases such as anthrax, the flu, colds, and the like. Imagine a world with vaccinations from eating flower petals!

Of the following, which might be the best title for this passage?

A. Getting Your Vaccinations
B. No More Flu
C. Flower Power
D. Anticipating the Future

Passage 2

Visiting New York City and taking in a Broadway musical had always been a dream of Kevin's, but he knew that a visit to the big city would be very expensive. He wanted to plan a short vacation to the city over a holiday weekend. Could he visit the city on a limited budget? Searching the Internet, he found opportunities for reduced-price hotels, half-price Broadway play tickets, and a special on train transportation. He was ecstatic as he started to pack his bags.

For the paragraph above, which of the following is the best title?

A. New York—An Expensive City
B. Kevin's Budget
C. Finding Cheap Tickets
D. Kevin Goes to the Big City

Activity 7: Answers

Passage 1

Although the passage does deal with the future (choice D) and with getting vaccinations (choice A), those are not the best answers. The passage does not suggest that we would never get the flu (choice B). Since the passage focuses on how flowers may be used in the future to administer vaccinations, the best title would be choice C, "Flower Power."

Passage 2

Of the options, choice D is the best and therefore the correct answer. You don't know about Kevin's actual budget, so choice B is not correct. You do know that New York City is expensive to visit (choice A), but that is not the major point of the paragraph. Finding cheap tickets (choice C) is part of the process, but it is not by any means the major thrust of the paragraph. Kevin's dream and all its parts is the most important theme of the paragraph.

Note that there are a number of other possible good titles for this paragraph. A few of them would be "Kevin Goes to the Big City," "New York City on a Budget," and "Kevin's Dream Comes True." Each of these titles conveys the main idea of the paragraph and would be a possible correct answer choice.

Annotate the Passage

Another technique that can help you answer ASVAB Paragraph Comprehension questions is to make notes to yourself in the margin as you read. This is called annotating the passage. Here are some ideas for the kinds of notes that will be most useful:

- Circle words that you don't know, look up each word, and write a brief definition of it.
- Indicate words or sentences that are similar to something else you have read.
- Point out inconsistencies.
- Point out important details.
- Relate the passage to any experiences you have had.
- Make connections within the passage.
- Ask questions.
- Interpret a character's actions
- Make comments about the passage or the characters in the passage.
- Link the information to something else or someone else in your life.
- Identify the basic idea of the passage.
- Ask questions that seem to need answering.
- Make inferences or predictions about what would happen next.
- Find relationships between the characters in the passage and people you know.

On the following page you will see an example of an annotated passage.

I think I saw a movie about him — a magician?

Houdini built his career on creating tricks and illusions--freeing himself from chains and making an elephant disappear. He was also interested in exposing fraud and showing how people could be tricked into believing something was real when it wasn't. He was especially critical of the production of "spirit photographs" in which the ghost of a well-known figure appeared to be present with someone. To demonstrate his point, Houdini had himself photographed with the ghost of Abraham Lincoln. Of course, it wasn't really Lincoln-- it was trick photography.

— like David Copperfield does
? When did Houdini live?
being tricked?
spoke out against?
? Why?
Did he then explain how it was done?

Another kind of fraud that Houdini worked to expose was more complicated. At that time, people held séances, which are spiritual meetings when participants communicate with the dead. During these séances, spiritual hands of dead people supposedly would appear and leave fingerprints. This kind of fraud was known as "fingerprinting a spirit." To make this happen, the person committing the fraud would make a mold of a dead person's hand. Then, during a séance with the dead person's relatives, fingerprints from the hand would mysteriously appear. Why do you think it was important to Houdini to expose this kind of behavior?

— like the new TV show "Medium"
How? What kind? Not sure how this was done.
where?

Good question — esp. because Houdini tricked / fooled people

This paragraph answers question

Houdini was very close to his mother and when she died, he was devastated. One reason he wanted to expose this kind of deception was because he wanted to prevent people from taking advantage of grieving relatives. Another reason was because there was big money involved in this kind of deception. In one case, Houdini said that $500,000 "changed hands upon the recognition of the fingerprints of a man who had died two years before."

upset? destroyed?
— shows H. was sympathetic, kind.
— greed!
— What does this quote mean?

Because Houdini challenged these kinds of deceptions and proved that they were unreliable, he suggested that people should not believe everything they see.

So, H. had a sense of "fair play."

can't count on them as real

fraud = deception for personal gain; hurts those who are fooled
magic = deception for entertainment   *??*

Activity 8: Annotate the Passage

Read the following passage. Make notes to yourself about the passage in the margins on the left and right.

Best known as the primary author of the Declaration of Independence, Thomas Jefferson was the third president of the United States. He was a man of many talents—an architect, an inventor, a scientist, and a collector of books and artifacts of American history. He could read more than five languages, and he was the U.S. minister to France for several years.

Almost everyone knows that Thomas Jefferson wrote the Declaration of Independence. The other representatives from the 13 colonies selected Jefferson to write the Declaration because they all agreed that he was the best writer. The words in the document are memorable. "We hold these Truths to be self-evident, that all Men are created equal, that they are endowed by their Creator with certain unalienable Rights, that among these are Life, Liberty and the Pursuit of Happiness"—these words may be the best-known part of the Declaration of Independence.

The declaration explains why the 13 colonies wanted independence from Great Britain. However, the declaration is not the law of the land. The Constitution, which wasn't written until 1787, outlines our form of government and explains what kinds of laws we can make. The declaration is more about the ideals of our country.

Thomas Jefferson contributed greatly to the development of the United States, but his single most important contribution was the Declaration of Independence. His belief that each generation has the chance to remake the country's laws and constitution was truly visionary. Jefferson believed in the blessings of self-government and an ever-changing society in which the people, through their elected representatives, continue to make new laws.

Activity 9: Annotate the Passage

Read the following passage. Make notes to yourself about the passage in the margins on the left and right.

African Americans played baseball throughout the 1800s. By the 1860s, notable black amateur teams, such as the Colored Union Club in Brooklyn, New York, and the Pythian Club in Philadelphia, Pennsylvania, had formed. All-black professional teams began in the 1880s, among them the St. Louis Black Stockings and the Cuban Giants (of New York). Like American society in general, amateur and professional baseball remained largely segregated.

One of the few black players on an integrated professional league team was Moses Fleetwood "Fleet" Walker, a catcher for the minor-league Toledo Blue Stockings. In 1883, the Chicago White Stockings, led by star player Adrian "Cap" Anson, refused to take the field against the Blue Stockings because of Walker's presence. The Blue Stockings manager insisted that the game be played, and Anson relented. When the Blue Stockings joined the American Association in 1884, Walker became the first African American major leaguer. In July of 1887, the International League banned future contracts with black players, although it allowed black players who were already under contract to stay on its teams. These are but two of the events that shaped the unwritten "color line" that segregated professional baseball until the 1940s.

During the 1890s, most professional black players were limited to playing on "colored" teams in exhibition games on the barnstorming circuit. Players on major-league teams also barnstormed in cities and towns after the regular season was over. In some places black teams and white teams played each other, and some blacks played for all-black teams in otherwise all-white leagues. In amateur baseball, some athletes played on integrated teams such as the Navy baseball champions from the USS *Maine*.

Activity 10: Annotate the Passage

Read the following passage. Make notes to yourself about the passage in the margins on the left and right.

Carbon monoxide, or CO, is an odorless, colorless gas that can cause sudden illness and death. Carbon monoxide is found in combustion fumes, such as those produced by cars and trucks, small gasoline engines, stoves, lanterns, burning charcoal and wood, and gas ranges and heating systems. Carbon monoxide from these sources can build up in enclosed or semienclosed spaces. People and animals in these spaces can be poisoned by breathing it.

The most common symptoms of carbon monoxide poisoning are headache, dizziness, weakness, nausea, vomiting, chest pain, and confusion. High levels of carbon monoxide ingestion can cause loss of consciousness and death. Unless it is suspected, carbon monoxide poisoning can be difficult to diagnose because the symptoms mimic those of other illnesses. People who are sleeping or intoxicated can die from carbon monoxide poisoning before ever experiencing symptoms.

Help prevent carbon monoxide poisoning by

- Never using a gas range or oven to heat a home
- Never using a charcoal grill, hibachi, lantern, or portable camping stove inside a home, tent, or camper
- Never running a generator, pressure washer, or any gasoline-powered engine inside a basement, garage, or other enclosed structure, even if the doors or windows are open, unless the equipment is professionally installed and vented
- Never running a motor vehicle, generator, pressure washer, or any gasoline-powered engine outside of an open window or door where exhaust can vent into an enclosed area
- Never leaving the motor running in a vehicle parked in an enclosed or semienclosed space, such as a closed garage.

Think About the Order and Flow of the Passage

Another technique that can help you answer ASVAB Paragraph Comprehension questions is to think about how the passage is organized. Passages are written to tell a story or make a statement in a logical way, with a logical flow. In order to grasp the full meaning, you need to understand the order and see how each paragraph builds upon, relates to, or explains the one before.

The following exercises will help you read carefully and critically to determine the logic and flow of the paragraphs.

Activity 11: Put Paragraphs in Order

Paragraphs A, B, and C are in random order. You need to put them in an order that makes sense and flows correctly. Read the paragraphs, then number them in order from 1 to 3. Write the numbers in the blanks next to the letters.

(A) _____

These days Gwen concentrates on slalom racing. In this kind of racing, paddlers travel down a course that has stretches of whitewater rapids and a series of 25 gates. Each gate consists of two poles that the paddler must go between. During a race, Gwen has to paddle through the gates as quickly as possible. If she misses a gate, or if she touches any of the poles that are used to mark the course, she gets time added to her score. And she has to do all of this on an unpredictable river!

(B) _____

At the age of 12 (and in just her second year of competition), Gwen qualified for the Junior Olympics in the 14 and under class. A race was held with the top kids from all over the country. Gwen says, "It was especially exciting because we didn't race on a real river—instead, we raced on a whitewater ride at a theme park in Charlotte, North Carolina! Just being in the race was like riding on a roller coaster!"

(C) _____

Gwen Greeley first started kayaking at age 10 when her family moved to a house right by the water. Her father wanted to try a sport that the whole family could enjoy, so he bought kayaks and signed them up for classes at their local YMCA. Gwen says, "At first I was scared that the boat might flip over and throw me into the water, but really there wasn't anything scary about it." Gwen and her family started slowly, learning to paddle and control the boat in a swimming pool first before heading outdoors. Their instructor taught them how to get out of the boat safely if it flipped over, and the basics of paddling the boat from place to place. Once Gwen and her family became more experienced on the water, they learned how to right the boat while they were still in it, and how to get back in the boat if it tipped over.

Answers

1 (C)

2 (B)

3 (A)

Activity 12: Put Paragraphs in Order

Paragraphs A, B, C, and D are in random order. You need to put them in an order that makes sense and flows correctly. Read the paragraphs, then number them in order from 1 to 4. Write the numbers in the blanks next to the letters.

(A) _____

You can get flesh-eating disease if a cut gets infected with certain types of germs (bacteria called group A strep), but it's super rare. The best thing to do to protect yourself is to wash your hands after coughing and sneezing, before making food or eating, and after using the bathroom. If you got flesh-eating bacteria and they multiplied like wildfire, they would eat away at you—but that almost never happens. And one thing is for sure: no one has ever gotten flesh-eating disease from *bananas!* The reason is that flesh-eating bacteria can live inside the body, but once they get out—like onto a banana—they usually die right away.

(B) _____

There are some crazy body and mind stories out there. Some of them are true, some are false, and some are still being checked out by disease detectives. Don't let the rumors fool you. Here's the lowdown—spread the word!

(C) _____

You *can* get lots of energy from bananas, and they also have potassium, which keeps your muscles strong. So eat up! Just peel and gobble them, or try a banana berry smoothie.

(D) _____

Can you get flesh-eating disease from bananas? We don't know if you've seen it or not, but there is an e-mail floating around that says that you can get flesh-eating disease (necrotizing fasciitis) from Costa Rican bananas. Well, it's totally wrong.

Answers

2 (D)

4 (C)

1 (B)

3 (A)

Activity 13: Put Paragraphs in Order

Paragraphs A, B, C, and D are in random order. You need to put them in an order that makes sense and flows correctly. Read the paragraphs, then number them in order from 1 to 4. Write the numbers in the blanks next to the letters.

(A) _____

In addition to these locations, many states offer registration opportunities at public libraries, post offices, unemployment offices, and public high schools and universities, and through organizations such as the League of Women Voters.

(B) _____

It is everyone's civic responsibility to vote, but in order to do so, you must be registered. Requirements for registration and registration deadlines vary from state to state and the District of Columbia. North Dakota is the only state that does not require voters to register.

(C) _____

Any citizen of the United States who is over the age of 18 and who meets certain state requirements may vote in federal elections. This has not always been the case. When the United States first won its independence, there were many restrictions on who could vote. In some states, only white male landowners over the age of 21 could vote. Beginning in 1870, however, a series of constitutional amendments (the fifteenth, seventeenth, nineteenth, twenty-third, twenty-fourth, and twenty-sixth) and passage of certain pieces of legislation have extended voting privileges to more and more citizens.

(D) _____

Registration forms may be obtained from the local election officials in your county or from the state's election office. You can also register to vote when applying for services at

- State departments of motor vehicles or drivers' licensing offices
- State offices providing public assistance
- State offices providing state-funded programs for the disabled
- Armed forces recruitment offices

Answers

3 (D)

1 (C)

2 (B)

4 (A)

Activity 14: Put Paragraphs in Order

Paragraphs A, B, C, D, and E are in random order. You need to put them in an order that makes sense and flows correctly. Read the paragraphs, then number them in order from 1 to 5. Write the numbers in the blanks next to the letters.

(A) _____

Today, while the Cold War is over, the Berlin Wall is down, and new maps have been drawn, the CIA's work is far from done. In this new world, the agency reveals much more about its work to keep Americans safe from cybercrime, weapons proliferation, drug trafficking, and terrorists. But what can be revealed can never compete with the thrillers that Hollywood continues to produce to entertain the public and . . . spies like us.

(B) _____

James Bond, Maxwell Smart, and Illya Kuryakin were among the fictional spy characters who captured Americans' imaginations in the 1960s and let them dream of a life filled with intrigue and adventure.

(C) _____

The Shoe Phone and the Pen Communicator were but fantasy precursors to today's wireless communications, and James West's sleeve gun device was a variation on the Office of Strategic Services' glove pistol from World War II, fulfilling the spy world's need for concealment. These are examples of art imitating life. Conversely, located near the cold war exhibit at the CIA is the Spy Fi exhibit, a private collection of real-life spy memorabilia owned by H. Keith Melton. It contains devices used by the fictional spies' real-world counterparts: the U.S. Office of Strategic Services, the USSR's KGB, and East Germany's Stasi.

(D) _____

The Spy Fi Archives is an entertaining look at how Hollywood viewed intelligence work during the Cold War and beyond. When President John F. Kennedy revealed his fondness for Ian Fleming's James Bond novels in the early 1960s, the spy fiction craze began in the United States and internationally. While the CIA's intelligence officers were tight-lipped about their sometimes life-and-death Cold War mission, the movie industry eagerly filled the void with glamour, intrigue, and even humor—with some interesting implications for the real world of intelligence.

(E) _____

Among those caught up in the spy fiction craze was Danny Biederman, a Hollywood screenwriter, author, and consultant specializing in movie and TV spy fiction, who realized at an early age that collecting spy show memorabilia was safer than actually being a spy. The Central Intelligence Agency's Fine Arts Commission hosted the first major exhibition of 400 props, photographs, and works of art from Biederman's private collection of 4,000 items from August 10, 2000, through January 5, 2001. They called it the Spy Fi Archives.

Answers

2 (E)

3 (D)

4 (C)

1 (B)

5 (A)

Search for Details

Another technique that can help you answer ASVAB Paragraph Comprehension questions is knowing how to search the passage for important details. Many test questions will ask you to identify or find details in a written passage. Here is an exercise that will give you some practice in finding details. Check your answers with those given on the next page.

Activity 15: Search for Details

Read the passages and select the best response to each detail question.

Passage 1

Shanghai is the most populous city in China. It was established more than 700 years ago and has become a booming commercial center. Its population grew most rapidly in the years just before the 1950s, but has since reached a level of equilibrium as a result of strict family planning policies and a decentralization program that encouraged the development of satellite towns.

According to the passage, when did Shanghai's population grow most rapidly?

A. 700 years ago
B. Before the city became a commercial center
C. After the decentralization program was started
D. In the years before the 1950s

Passage 2

Court reporters make word-for-word reports of court cases, meetings, speeches, and other events. Court reporters play a critical role in legal proceedings. They are expected to create a complete and accurate legal record. Accuracy is crucial. Legal appeals can depend on the court reporter's transcript. Many court reporters organize official records. They may also search them for specific information. Court reporters provide closed-captioning and translating services for deaf and hard-of-hearing persons. Court reporters must have excellent listening skills. In addition, speed and accuracy are important. Good writing skills are also needed.

According to the passage, which of the following is a court reporter's most important job?

A. Organizing official records
B. Providing translating services
C. Writing clearly and accurately
D. Creating a complete and accurate legal record

Activity 15: Answers

Passage 1

According to the passage, Shanghai's population grew most rapidly in the years just before the 1950s. Choice D is the correct answer.

Passage 2

The passage states that court reporters are expected to create a complete and accurate legal record. Choice D is the correct answer.

Chapter 8

Sharpen Your Math Skills

It is important that you do well on the Mathematics Knowledge test because it is one of the four ASVAB tests that are used to calculate the AFQT—your military entrance score. That's why it pays to spend time reviewing topics in basic arithmetic, algebra, and geometry and tackling plenty of sample questions.

Section 1 of this chapter offers a quick but important overview of the basic arithmetic that you need to know in order to score well on the ASVAB. **Section 2** provides review and practice of basic algebra and probability, while **Section 3** covers

basic geometry concepts. Make sure that you carefully review and test yourself on every topic covered in this chapter. Also make sure that you learn how to use all of the problem-solving methods presented in the examples.

There is much more to basic math than this, but if you master the core information presented here, you will be able to answer ASVAB Mathematics Knowledge questions with relative ease. You will also need these basic skills to correctly answer the Arithmetic Reasoning ASVAB questions covered in the next chapter.

SECTION 1: ARITHMETIC

READ THIS SECTION TO LEARN:

- **What arithmetic topics you need to know for the ASVAB**

- **Techniques for solving every kind of ASVAB arithmetic problem**

- **Tips and strategies to help you raise your ASVAB Arithmetic Reasoning and Mathematics Knowledge scores**

Suggested Review Plan for Arithmetic

- Take the Arithmetic Quiz and score it.
- Mark those problems that you got wrong and those that you were not sure of.
- Study any problems that you answered incorrectly or were hesitant about.
- Reread the corresponding review section.
- Pay special attention to the examples.

- Work until you understand how to solve the example problems given.
- Complete the practice items.
- Work the Arithmetic Quiz again.

Remember that while you probably won't get these exact problems on the ASVAB, knowing how to solve them will help you do your best on the actual test.

ARITHMETIC QUIZ

Circle the letter that represents the correct answer. Check your answers with those on page 144. If any of your answers were wrong, go back and study the relevant section of the math review.

1. Add:

    $336 + 789$

    A. 1,025
    B. 1,110
    C. 1,125
    D. 1,126

2. Subtract:

    3475
    -397

    A. 83
    B. 82
    C. 78
    D. 68

3. Which of the following symbols means "is less than"?

    A. $\approx$
    B. $\neq$
    C. $<$
    D. $\perp$

4. Which of the following means to multiply 3 times 6?

    A. $(3)(6)$
    B. $3 \div 6$
    C. $3/6$
    D. $3 * 6$

5. $3 + 5(6 - 3) =$

    A. 18
    B. 24
    C. 30
    D. 32

6. $4 + (19 - 4^2)^2 =$

    A. -240
    B. 13
    C. 85
    D. 240

7. $2^3 - (2 \times 3) + (-4) =$

    A. -2
    B. 7
    C. 17
    D. 19

8. $3(10 - 6)(3 - 7) =$

    A. -48
    B. -43
    C. 18
    D. 48

9. Round to the nearest thousand:

    $34,578$

    A. 34,000
    B. 34,080
    C. 34,600
    D. 35,000

10. Round to the nearest tenth:

    12.8892

    A. 12.0
    B. 12.890
    C. 12.9
    D. 13.0

11. $4 + (-8) + 2 + (-6) =$

    A. 10
    B. 4
    C. -8
    D. -20

12. Subtract:

    18
    -2

    A. 20
    B. 16
    C. 12
    D. -16

13. Subtract:

— and a neg is positive

$$-15$$
$$--12$$

A. −27
B. −3
C. 3
D. 27

14. (−5)(−3)(−2) =

A. 30
B. 13
C. −10
D. −30

15. (14)(2)(0) =

A. 28
B. 16
C. 0
D. −28

16. Reduce to lowest terms:

$$\frac{18}{36} =$$

A. 1/4
B. $\frac{1}{2}$
C. 2/4
D. 3/6

17. Rename this fraction as a mixed number:

22/7 =

A. 2 4/7
B. 2 6/7
C. 3 1/7
D. 4

18. Rename this mixed number as a fraction:

$$5\frac{3}{4} =$$

A. 4/15
B. 15/4
C. 19/4
D. 23/4

19. Add the following fractions:

$$\frac{1}{2} + \frac{3}{4} + \frac{3}{12} = \quad ?$$

A. 7/24
B. 7/12
C. 1 1/2
D. 1 3/4

20. Subtract the following fractions:

$$\frac{3}{4} - \frac{1}{2} =$$

A. $\frac{1}{4}$
B. 1/2
C. $\frac{4}{4}$
D. 1

21. Subtract the following fractions:

$$3\frac{1}{2}$$
$$-2\frac{7}{8}$$

A. − 1 7/8
B. 5/8
C. 7/8
D. 1 7/8

22. Multiply the following fractions:

$$\frac{3}{8} \times \frac{9}{18} =$$

A. $\frac{27}{144}$
B. 3/16
C. 1/5
D. 78/54

23. Divide the following fractions:

$$\frac{1}{9} \div \frac{2}{3} =$$

A. $\frac{2}{27}$
B. $\frac{1}{6}$
C. $\frac{3}{11}$
D. $\frac{2}{6}$

24. Multiply the following mixed numbers:

$2\frac{3}{4} \times 4\frac{1}{3}$

A. 8 1/3
B. 8 2/3
C. $11\frac{11}{12}$
D. $12\frac{1}{6}$

25. Divide the following mixed numbers:

$3\frac{1}{3} \div 4\frac{2}{9} =$

A. $3\frac{1}{7}$
B. $\frac{45}{57}$
C. $\frac{16}{21}$
D. $\frac{15}{19}$

26. Change the following fraction to a decimal:

$\frac{3}{4} =$

A. 0.34
B. 0.50
C. 0.75
D. 0.80

27. Change the following decimal to a fraction:

0.008 =

A. 8/50
B. 8/100
C. 4/100
D. $\frac{1}{125}$

28. Add the following decimals:

12.51 + 3.4 + 6.628 =

A. 21.52
B. 22.528
C. 22.538
D. 223.258

29. Subtract the following decimals:

23.51 − 20.99 =

A. 3.62
B. 3.49
C. 2.52
D. 2.42

30. Divide the following decimals:

40.896 ÷ 12.78

A. 5.6
B. 4.4
C. 3.6
D. 3.2

31. Change the following percent to a decimal:

9%

A. 0.009
B. 0.09
C. 0.9
D. 9.0

32. Change the following decimal to a percent:

0.32

A. 32%
B. 3.2%
C. 0.32%
D. 0.032%

33. What is 75% of 1250?

A. 937.5
B. 950
C. 975
D. 1,000

34. 25 is what percent of 200?

A. 10%
B. 12%
C. 12.5%
D. 15%

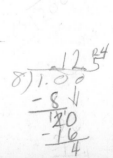

35. Write the following number in scientific notation:

    0.0002392 =

    A. $2,392 \times 10^{-7}$
    B. 23.92×10^{-5}
    C. 23×10^{5}
    D. 2.392×10^{-4}

36. Multiply:

    $(2.3 \times 10^{5}) \times (7.1 \times 10^{-3}) =$

    A. 9.4×10^{-8}
    B. 9.4×10^{8}
    C. 16.33×10^{2}
    D. 16.33×10^{8}

37. What is the square root of 100?

    A. 0.05
    B. 5
    C. 10
    D. 75

38. What is the mean (average) of the following set of numbers?

    12 14 18 22 45 78

    A. 27.5
    B. 31.5
    C. 32.0
    D. 45.5

39. Last month, the librarian at a certain library kept track of all the books checked out. The graph below shows the results by type of book. What percent of all the books checked out last month were travel books?

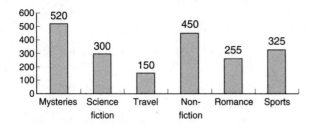

Number of library books checked out of local library

A. 15.3%
B. 15%
C. 8%
D. 7.5%

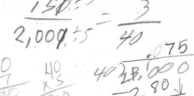

40. How many feet are in 2 miles?

    A. 10,000
    B. 10,560
    C. 11,954
    D. 16,439

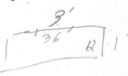

41. How many square inches are in 3 square feet?

    A. 144
    B. 278
    C. 432
    D. 578

42. How many quarts are in 3 gallons?

    A. 3
    B. 9
    C. 12
    D. 16

43. How many meters are in 4 kilometers?

    A. 40
    B. 400
    C. 4,000
    D. 40,000

44. How many grams are in 2.5 kilograms?

    A. 250
    B. 2,500
    C. 25,000
    D. 250,000

45. 4 kilograms is about how many pounds?

    A. 8.8
    B. 9
    C. 9.6
    D. 10.6

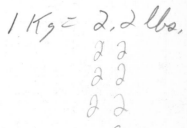

ARITHMETIC REVIEW

The Arithmetic Review will include information on and practice items for the following topics. Working through these sections will help you on the Arithmetic Reasoning and Mathematics Knowledge ASVAB tests.

Topics

Place value	Finding equivalent fractions
Addition	Reducing fractions to lowest terms
Subtraction	Operations with fractions and mixed numbers
Multiplication	Decimals
Division	Operations with decimals
Order of operations	Percent
Rounding	Finding a percent of a number
Positive and negative numbers	Finding the percent of increase or decrease
Absolute value	Exponents
Multiplying and dividing negative numbers	Square roots
Subtracting numbers within parentheses	Scientific notation
Multiplying and dividing by zero	Mean or Average
Factors	Median
Multiples	Mode
Fractions	Graphs
Mixed numbers	Units of Measure

Place Value

In numbers, the *place* is the position held by a digit. *Place value* is the product of the digit multiplied by its place. Here are some examples.

42,657,203.123

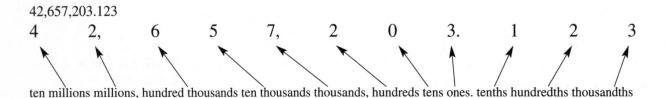

ten millions millions, hundred thousands ten thousands thousands, hundreds tens ones. tenths hundredths thousandths

23,456,789.247

2 (the first 2) is in the ten millions place

3 is in the millions place

4 (the first 4) is in the hundred thousands place

5 is in the ten thousands place

6 is in the thousands place

7 (the first 7) is in the hundreds place

8 is in the tens place

9 is in the ones place

2 is in the tenths place

4 is in the hundredths place

7 is in the thousandths place

Practice Items—Place Value

1. For the number 98,345.47, which number is in the ones place?

2. For the number 77,456,782.09, which number is in the tenths place?

3. For the number 45,234.006, which number is in the thousandths place?

Addition

There are two ways to show addition:

$$234 \quad \text{or} \quad 234 + 123 =$$
$$+\ 123$$

In either case, you need to add the two numbers to get the sum. Many ASVAB problems will require you to add numbers. Practicing this skill will allow you to perform the tasks accurately and quickly.

<u>Practice Items—Addition</u>   Find the answers to the following addition questions.

1.

$$731$$
$$+\ 14$$

2.

$$16,790$$
$$+\ 4,670$$

3.

$$1,677$$
$$+\ 23,999$$

4.

$$18,998$$
$$+\ 78,988$$

5.

$$98,068,459$$
$$+\ 673,899$$

6.

$$3,450,989$$
$$+\ 9,999$$

7.

$$670,369$$
$$+\ 135$$

8.

$$1,700,009,856$$
$$+\ 2,853,990,975$$

9.

$$1,434,209$$
$$+\ 5,478,999$$

10.

$$169,801$$
$$+\ 34,788,976$$

Subtraction

There are also two ways to show subtraction:

$$234 \quad \text{or} \quad 234 - 123 =$$
$$-\ 123$$

Some ASVAB problems will ask you to subtract numbers in order to calculate the correct answer. Practicing subtraction will help you get the correct answer in a short period of time.

Subtraction of Whole Numbers with Renaming

Sometimes you have to "rename" numbers in order to complete a subtraction.

$$731$$
$$-\ 465$$

To subtract the 5 from the 1 in the ones place, "rename" the "31" in the top number as "2 tens and 11 ones." Write "2" above the 3 in the tens place and "11" above the 1 in the ones place. Subtract 5 from 11 to get 6.

$$\begin{array}{r} {}^{2\ 11} \\ 7\cancel{3}\cancel{1} \\ -\ 465 \\ \hline 6 \end{array}$$

Next, you need to subtract the 6 from the (new) 2 in the tens place, so rename "72" as "6 hundreds and 12 tens." Write "6" above the 7 in the hundreds place and "12" above the 3 in the tens place. Subtract 6 from 12 to get 6. Then subtract 4 from 6 in the hundreds place to get 2, completing the subtraction.

$$\begin{array}{r} {}^{6\ 12\ 11} \\ \cancel{7}\cancel{3}\cancel{1} \\ -\ 465 \\ \hline 266 \end{array}$$

<u>Practice Items–Subtraction</u> Find the answers to the following subtraction questions.

1.

$$\begin{array}{r} 890 \\ -\ 78 \\ \hline \end{array}$$

2.

$$\begin{array}{r} 3,456 \\ -\ 961 \\ \hline \end{array}$$

3.

$$\begin{array}{r} 87,589 \\ -\ 65,178 \\ \hline \end{array}$$

4.

$$\begin{array}{r} 89,923 \\ -\ 34,478 \\ \hline \end{array}$$

5.

$$\begin{array}{r} 34,789,909 \\ -\ 23,784,498 \\ \hline \end{array}$$

6.

$$\begin{array}{r} 674,329 \\ -\ 84,498 \\ \hline \end{array}$$

7.

$$\begin{array}{r} 88,320,087 \\ -\ 3,497,698 \\ \hline \end{array}$$

8.

$$\begin{array}{r} 1,000,997 \\ -\ 9,809 \\ \hline \end{array}$$

9.

$$\begin{array}{r} 145,000,045 \\ -\ 14,409 \\ \hline \end{array}$$

10.

$$\begin{array}{r} 1,798 \\ -\ 1,699 \\ \hline \end{array}$$

Multiplication

Multiplication is a bit more complicated in that it can be shown in various ways.

$$10 \times 3 = 30$$
$$10(3) = 30$$
$$(10)(3) = 30$$
$$(10)3 = 30$$

$$\begin{array}{r} 10 \\ \times\ 3 \\ \hline 30 \end{array}$$

Be sure to know your multiplication tables. You should know the answers already for any numbers multiplied up to 12, but the following table is a refresher. Knowing the multiplication tables without any hesitation will help you answer many of the math items quickly and accurately. Knowing this table by heart will give you a bit of extra time to answer the tougher items.

x	0	1	2	3	4	5	6	7	8	9	10	11	12
0	0	0	0	0	0	0	0	0	0	0	0	0	0
1	0	1	2	3	4	5	6	7	8	9	10	11	12
2	0	2	4	6	8	10	12	14	16	18	20	22	24
3	0	3	6	9	12	15	18	21	24	27	30	33	36
4	0	4	8	12	16	20	24	28	32	36	40	44	48
5	0	5	10	15	20	25	30	35	40	45	50	55	60
6	0	6	12	18	24	30	36	42	48	54	60	66	72
7	0	7	14	21	28	35	42	49	56	63	70	77	84
8	0	8	16	24	32	40	48	56	64	72	80	88	96
9	0	9	18	27	36	45	54	63	72	81	90	99	108
10	0	10	20	30	40	50	60	70	80	90	100	110	120
11	0	12	22	33	44	55	66	77	88	99	110	121	132
12	0	12	24	36	48	60	72	84	96	108	120	132	144

<u>Practice Items–Multiplication</u> Calculate the following multiplication items.

1. $(4)(5) =$

2. $(5)(4) =$

3. $9 \times 7 =$

4. $27 \times 65 =$

5. $67 \times 98 =$

6. $899 \times 457 =$

7. $\begin{array}{r} 1,649 \\ \times\ 8,942 \\ \hline \end{array}$

8. $\begin{array}{r} 76,834 \\ \times\ 78,459 \\ \hline \end{array}$

9. $\begin{array}{r} 275,849 \\ \times\ 769,422 \\ \hline \end{array}$

10. $\begin{array}{r} 9,750,439 \\ \times\ 56,893,478 \\ \hline \end{array}$

Division

Division can also be shown in more than one way.

$$12 \div 3 = 4$$
$$12/3 = 4$$
$$\frac{12}{3} = 4$$

Division is important because you will be asked to divide numbers on the ASVAB. Division is also related to the use of fractions and the calculation of percentages.

<u>Practice Items–Division</u> Calculate the following division items.

1. $16 \div 4 =$

2. $48 \div 4 =$

3. $90 \div 45 =$

4. $25,536 \div 56 =$

5. $121,401 \div 123 =$

6. $254,646 \div 987 =$

7. $41,536 \div 1,298 =$

8. $18,895,065 \div 899,765 =$

9. $144 \div 12 =$

10. $1,655 \div 5 =$

Symbols

$=$	is equal to
$\neq$	is not equal to
$<$	is less than
$\leq$	is less than or equal to
$>$	is greater than
$\geq$	is greater than or equal to
$\parallel$	is parallel to
$\cong$	is approximately equal to
$\approx$	is approximately
$\perp$	is perpendicular to
$\mid \mid$	absolute value
$\pm$	plus or minus
$\%$	percent
$a{:}b$	ratio of a to b or $\frac{a}{b}$

<u>Practice Items–Symbols</u> True or false? Write "T" or "F" in the blank to indicate whether each of the following statements is true or false.

1. ____ $9 > 7$

2. ____ $6.99 \cong 7$

3. ____ $47 \geq 47$

4. ____ $89 < 64$

5. ____ 99% is 99 percent

6. ____ $7 \neq 7$

7. ____ $2{:}4 = \frac{2}{4}$

8. ____ $|-7| = 7$

9. ____ $8 = -8$

10. ____ $49 \leq 34$

Order of Operations

If addition, subtraction, multiplication, and division are all in the same mathematical statement, the order of operations (what you do first, second, third, and so on) is

1. Perform operations shown within **P**arentheses.
2. Attend to **E**xponents and square roots.
3. Perform **M**ultiplication or **D**ivision, whichever comes first left to right.
4. Perform **A**ddition or **S**ubtraction, whichever comes first left to right.

Order is important! You almost certainly will get an ASVAB math item that will require you to know order of operations rules. You can use the sentence "**P**lease **E**xcuse **M**y **D**ear **A**unt **S**ally" to help you remember the order of operations.

Examples

$2 + 3 \times 4$
$= 2 + 12$
$= 14$

$3^2 + 4(5 - 2)$
$= 3^2 + 4(3)$
$= 9 + 4(3)$
$= 9 + 12$
$= 21$

$5(10 + 2) + 2 + 3$
$= 5(12) + 2 + 3$
$= 60 + 5$
$= 65$

$3^3(8 + 3) \times (\sqrt{9}) + (9 \times 2) - (298 + 300)$
$= 27(11) \times (3) + (18) - (598)$
$= 297 \times 3 + 18 - 598$
$= 891 + 18 - 598$
$= 909 - 598$
$= 310$

Reminder: Order of Operations

1. Simplify groupings inside parentheses, brackets, and braces first. Work with the innermost pair, moving outward.
2. Simplify the exponents and radicals.
3. Do the multiplication and division in order from left to right.
4. Do the addition and subtraction in order from left to right.

Practice Items–Order of Operations   Calculate the answers to the following.

1. $(17 + 3) + 20 =$

2. $(45 - 43) + (16 + 32) =$

3. $(12 + 3)(2 \times 3) =$

4. $14 \div 2 + 14 =$

5. $6^2 + 3 + 2 =$

6. $12 \times 12 + 2^3 =$

7. $3^2 + 4(5 - 2) =$

8. $(4 + 2)^3 + (3 \times 2) - 2^2 =$

Rounding

Often you will be asked to round to the nearest 10, 100, or 1,000 or to the nearest tenth, hundredth, or thousandth. A good way to do this is to underline the number in the place to which you are rounding. Identify the number immediately to the right. If it is 5 or greater, round up by 1. If it is 4 or less, leave it as is. Change everything to the right of that to zeros.

Examples

Round 123,756 to the nearest thousand.
Underline the number in the thousands place.

123,756

Look at the number in the place immediately to the right.
7 is greater than 5, so round the underlined number to 4 and change the rest to zeros.

Result = 124,000

Round 123,456 to the nearest thousand.
Underline the number in the thousands place.

123,456

Look at the number in the place immediately to the right.
4 is less than 5, so keep the number in the thousands place as it is and change all numbers to the right to zeros.

Result = 123,000

Round 123.456 to the nearest hundredth.
Underline the number in the hundredths place.

123.456

6 is greater than 5, so change the 5 to 6 and make all numbers to the right zeros.

Result = 123.46

Practice Items–Rounding   Answer the following rounding questions.

1. Round the following number to the nearest 100.
   123,456 _____

2. Round the following number to the nearest 1,000.
   123,456 _____

3. Round the following number to the nearest tenth.
   123,456.0996 _____

4. Round the following number to the nearest hundredth.
   123,456.0996 _____

Positive and Negative Numbers

Positive numbers are numbers that are greater than 0, such as +6. Negative numbers are numbers that are less than 0, such as −4.

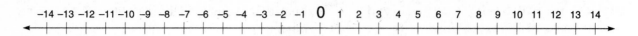

The *absolute value* of a number is the distance of the number from 0 on a number line. For example, the absolute value of +6 is 6. The absolute value of −4 is 4.

Adding Positive and Negative Numbers   *To add numbers with the same sign*, add their absolute values. The sum will have the same sign as the numbers you added.

Examples_____

Add:

$$
\begin{array}{r}
-4 \\
-3 \\
\hline
-7
\end{array}
$$

To add numbers with different signs, first find their absolute values. Subtract the lesser absolute value from the greater absolute value. Give the sum the same sign as the number with the greater absolute value.

Helpful Hint: Know Negative Numbers!

Be sure to practice adding, subtracting, multiplying, and dividing using negative numbers.

Examples_____

Add:

$$
\begin{array}{r}
+4 \\
-3 \\
\hline
+1
\end{array}
$$

Add:

$$
\begin{array}{r}
+4 \\
-6 \\
\hline
-2
\end{array}
$$

Practice Items—Adding Positive and Negative Numbers   Add the following numbers.

1. $4 + (-3) =$ 1

2. $-10 + 3 =$ ⁻7

3. $75 + (-34 - 32) =$

4. $80 + (75 - 25) =$

5. $-64 + 18 - 12 =$

6. $1,000 - (800) =$

7. $1,000 - (800 - 120) =$

8. $200 - 325 =$

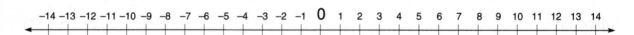

Subtracting Positive and Negative Numbers
Look again at the number line.

- When you subtract a positive number, you move *left* on the number line the distance equal to the absolute value of the number being subtracted.
- When you subtract a negative number, you move *right* on the number line the distance equal to the absolute value of the number being subtracted.

Examples_____

Subtract positive numbers (move *left* on the number line):

$$
\begin{array}{r}
+7 \\
-(+12) \\
\hline
-5
\end{array}
$$

$$
\begin{array}{r}
-7 \\
-(+12) \\
\hline
-19
\end{array}
$$

Subtract negative numbers (move *right* on the number line):

$$\begin{array}{r} 7 \\ -(-12) \\ \hline +19 \end{array}$$

$$\begin{array}{r} -7 \\ -(-12) \\ \hline +5 \end{array}$$

Note: A simple rule is that when you subtract negative numbers, all you really need to do is change the sign of the number being subtracted from negative to positive, and then add.

<u>Practice Items–Subtracting Positive and Negative Numbers</u>   Subtract the following numbers.

1. $12 - (4) =$

2. $12 - (-4) =$

3. $12 - (-8) =$

4. $45 - (12) =$

5. $125 - (-3)^2 =$

6. $500 - (5)^2 =$

7. $1,500 - (-10)^2 =$

8. $1,500 - (10)^2 =$

9. $42 - (45 - 5) - (-60) =$

Absolute Value

A number regardless of its sign (+ or –) is called the *absolute value*. The absolute value of a number is shown as the number placed between two vertical parallel lines; for example, $|-4|$ or $|4|$. In each of these cases, the absolute value of the number is 4. When using absolute values, just ignore the sign.

Examples

$$|-x| = x$$
$$|-5 - 6| = |-11| = 11$$
$$8 + |-9| = 17$$

Multiplying and Dividing Negative Numbers

These operations are easy if you use just one trick. To multiply or divide negative numbers, first treat all the numbers as positive and perform the operation in the normal way.

- If there is an *odd number of negative signs*, the answer will be negative.
- If there is an *even number of negative signs*, the number will be positive.

Examples

$(-5)(+6)(+2) = -60$ This expression has 1 negative sign. Since 1 is an odd number, the result is negative.

$(-5)(-6)(+2) = +60$ This expression has 2 negative signs. Since 2 is an even number, the result is positive.

$\dfrac{-88}{-11} = +8$ This expression has 2 negative signs. Since 2 is an even number, the result is positive.

$\dfrac{-88}{+11} = -8$ This expression has 1 negative sign. Since 1 is an odd number, the result is negative.

<u>Practice Items–Multiplying and Dividing Negative and Positive Numbers</u>   Evaluate the following expressions.

1. $(-2)(-2)(-2) =$

2. $(-2)(-2)(2) =$

3. $(5)(-2)(-4) =$

4. $\dfrac{90}{-45}$

5. $\dfrac{-90}{-45}$

6. $\dfrac{-90}{45}$

7. $(-4)(-5)(-2)(-8) =$

8. $(5)(-5)(2) =$

Subtracting Numbers Within Parentheses

If there is a minus sign in front of numbers in parentheses, change the sign of all the numbers within the parentheses and then add.

Examples

$11 - (+3 - 5 + 2 - 8)$

changes to

$11 + (-3 + 5 - 2 + 8)$
$= 11 + (-5 + 13)$
$= 11 + (+8)$
$= 19$

$20 - (-3 + 5 - 2 + 8)$
$= 20 + (+3 - 5 + 2 - 8)$
$= 20 + (+5 - 13)$
$= 20 + -8$
$= 12$

Practice Items—Subtracting Numbers Within Parentheses   Evaluate the following expressions.

1. $200 - (90 - 10) =$

2. $50 - (45) =$

3. $125 - (45 - 55) =$

4. $575 - (400 - 300) =$

5. $1,000 - (750) =$

6. $22 - (-12 + 15) =$

7. $95 + [34 - (-22)] =$

Multiplying and Dividing by Zero

Any number multiplied by zero equals zero.

Zero divided by any number equals zero.

Dividing by zero is considered to be "undefined."

Examples

$45 \times 0 = 0$

$1,232,456 \times 0 = 0$

$10.45399 \times 0 = 0$

$0 \div 5 = 0$

$0 \div 500 = 0$

$7 \div 0$ is undefined

$32/0$ is undefined

$\dfrac{89}{0}$ is undefined

Practice Items—Multiplying and Dividing by Zero
Evaluate the following expressions.

1. $02316 \times 0 =$

2. $1,457,956,002.234 \times 0 =$

3. $4.78 \times 0 =$

4. $0 \div 6,000 =$

5. $6,000 \div 0 =$

Factors

Factors are numbers that are multiplied together to create another number.

Examples

$2 \times 4 = 8$ (2 and 4 are factors of 8.)
$1 \times 8 = 8$ (1 and 8 are factors of 8.)
So 1, 2, 4, and 8 are all factors of 8.

$1 \times 32 = 32$ (1 and 32 are factors of 32.)
$2 \times 16 = 32$ (2 and 16 are factors of 32.)
$8 \times 4 = 32$ (8 and 4 are factors of 32.)
So 1, 2, 4, 8, 16, and 32 are all factors of 32.

Knowing about factors will be very useful when solving equations.

Common Factors Common factors are factors that are shared by two or more numbers. As shown in the previous examples, 8 and 32 share the common factors 1, 2, 3, and 8.

Multiples

Multiples of a number are found by multiplying the number by 1, 2, 3, 4, 5, 6, 7, 8, and so on. So multiples of 5 are 10, 15, 20, 25, 30, 35, 40, and so on.

Common Multiples Common multiples are multiples that are shared by two or more numbers.

*Example*_____

2	4	6	8	10	12	14	16	18	20	22	24
		⇕			⇕			⇕			⇕
3		6		9	12	15		18		21	24

In this example, 3 and 2 share the common multiples 6, 12, 18, and 24.

Least Common Multiple The least common multiple is the smallest multiple that two numbers share. In the case of the example just given, the number 6 is the least common multiple.

<u>Practice Items–Least Common Multiples</u> What is the least common multiple of the following numbers?

1. ____ 2, 4, 8

2. ____ 3, 4

3. ____ 4, 6

4. ____ 3, 5

Fractions

Fractions have two numbers, a numerator and a denominator. Fractions represent portions of a whole.

$$\frac{3}{6} = \frac{\text{numerator}}{\text{denominator}}$$

The denominator tells how many parts something is divided into. The numerator tells how many of those parts you have. The fraction as a whole tells the *proportion* of the parts you have to the parts there are in all.

So if a pie is divided into 8 pieces and you take 2 of them, the fraction telling the proportion of the pie that you have is 2/8. The denominator (8) tells how many pieces of pie there are in all. The numerator (2) tells how many of those pieces you have.

$$\frac{2}{8} \text{ or a proportion of 2 to 8}$$

Fractions can be positive or negative. A negative fraction is written like this:

$$-\frac{2}{8}$$

Proper Fractions Fractions representing amounts smaller than 1 are called *proper fractions*. Fractions smaller than 1 have numerators that are smaller than their denominators.

*Examples*_____

$$\frac{1}{3} \quad \frac{3}{7} \quad \frac{5}{8} \quad \frac{9}{11} \quad \frac{6}{32} \quad \frac{99}{100}$$

Improper Fractions *Improper fractions* represent amounts greater than 1. The numerator is larger than the denominator.

*Examples*_____

$$\frac{22}{3} \quad \frac{3}{2} \quad \frac{12}{5} \quad \frac{17}{8} \quad \frac{66}{3} \quad \frac{11}{9}$$

Mixed Numbers

Expressions that include both whole numbers and fractions are called *mixed numbers*.

*Examples*_____

$$2\frac{7}{8} \quad 3\frac{1}{2} \quad 9\frac{2}{3} \quad 27\frac{3}{4}$$

Renaming an Improper Fraction as a Mixed Number To rename an improper fraction as a mixed number, simply divide the numerator by the denominator.

Helpful Hint: You'll See These for Sure

You will have items that require you to manipulate fractions and mixed numbers. Don't despair. Be sure to understand the procedures thoroughly and you should have no problem on the ASVAB.

Examples

$$\frac{22}{3} = 22 \div 3 = 7\frac{1}{3}$$

$$\frac{3}{2} = 3 \div 2 = 1\frac{1}{2}$$

$$\frac{12}{5} = 12 \div 5 = 2\frac{2}{5}$$

$$\frac{17}{8} = 17 \div 8 = 2\frac{1}{8}$$

Practice Items—Changing Improper Fractions to Mixed Numbers   Change the following improper fractions into mixed numbers.

1. $\frac{25}{2} = 12\frac{1}{2}$ 4. $\frac{79}{2} = 39\frac{1}{2}$

2. $\frac{7}{3} = 2\frac{1}{3}$ 5. $\frac{84}{5} = 16\frac{4}{5}$

3. $\frac{45}{4} = 11\frac{1}{4}$ 6. $\frac{77}{10} = 10\frac{7}{7}$

Renaming a Mixed Number as a Fraction   To rename a mixed number as an improper fraction, simply multiply the whole number by the denominator and add the numerator. Put that number over the denominator. For example, $2\frac{1}{2}$ would be

$$2 \overset{+}{\underset{\times}{\longleftrightarrow}} \frac{1}{2} \quad \text{or } 2 \times 2 + 1 \text{ over the denominator} = \frac{5}{2}$$

Examples

$$7\frac{1}{3} = 3 \times 7 + 1 = 22$$

Put 22 over the denominator $= \frac{22}{3}$

$$2\frac{2}{5} = 2 \times 5 + 2 = 12$$

Put 12 over the denominator $= \frac{12}{5}$

Practice Items—Renaming a Mixed Number as a Fraction

1. $3\frac{1}{3} =$

2. $6\frac{1}{4} =$

3. $5\frac{11}{12} =$

4. $3\frac{3}{4} =$

5. $7\frac{2}{5} =$

Finding Equivalent Fractions

Two fractions are said to be *equivalent* (the same in value) if they use different numbers but represent the same proportion. For example, the following fractions are equivalent:

$$\frac{1}{2} \quad \frac{4}{8} \quad \frac{3}{6} \quad \frac{5}{10}$$

To change a fraction into an equivalent fraction, multiply or divide the numerator and denominator by the same number.

Examples

$$\frac{2 \times 3 = 6}{4 \times 3 = 12} \text{ so 2/4 is equivalent to 6/12.}$$

$$\frac{9 \div 3 = 3}{12 \div 3 = 4} \text{ so 9/12 is equivalent to 3/4.}$$

Practice Items—Finding Equivalent Fractions   List three equivalent fractions for each of the following.

1. $\frac{1}{3}$

2. $\frac{2}{3}$

3. $\frac{2}{4}$

Reducing Fractions to Lowest Terms

Fractions are commonly shown in their lowest terms, that is, the smallest numbers that still represent the original proportion. When a fraction is not in its lowest terms, you can reduce it to its lowest terms by dividing the numerator and denominator by the largest number that will divide into both evenly.

Examples

$\frac{40}{80}$ can be divided evenly by 40, giving $\frac{1}{2}$

$\frac{9}{15}$ can be divided evenly by 3, giving $\frac{3}{5}$

$\frac{21}{28}$ can be divided evenly by 7, giving $\frac{3}{4}$

Practice Items—Reducing Fractions to Lowest Terms

1. $\dfrac{11}{33} =$

2. $\dfrac{24}{48} =$

3. $\dfrac{16}{64} =$

4. $\dfrac{108}{216} =$

5. $\dfrac{33}{264}$

6. $\dfrac{5}{65} =$

Operations with Fractions and Mixed Numbers

Adding and Subtracting Fractions To add and subtract fractions with *like denominators*, simply add or subtract the numerators. The result is often shown in lowest terms.

Examples

$$\frac{3}{10} + \frac{1}{10} = \frac{4}{10} = \frac{2}{5} \qquad \frac{9}{10} - \frac{1}{10} = \frac{8}{10} = \frac{4}{5}$$

To add and subtract fractions with *unlike denominators*, you first need to find equivalent fractions that all have the same denominator. To do this, you need to find the *least common denominator (LCD)*, the least common multiple of the denominators of all the fractions. Use the LCD to create new fractions equivalent to the original ones. Then add the new numerators.

Examples

$6/8 + 1/2 =$

The least common denominator is 8, so 6/8 does not need to be changed. However, 1/2 is changed to the equivalent fraction 4/8.

$$6/8 + 4/8 = 10/8$$
$$= 1\,2/8$$
$$= 1/4 \text{ (reduced to lowest terms)}$$

$$\frac{1}{3} + \frac{1}{2} + \frac{7}{8} =$$

Find the least common denominator. The least common multiple of 8, 3, and 2 is 24, so 24 is the least common denominator. Use the LCD to create new fractions equivalent to the original ones:

$$1/3 + 1/2 + 7/8 = 8/24 + 12/24 + 21/24$$
$$= 41/24$$
$$= 1\,17/24$$

Use the same approach to add and subtract positive and negative fractions. Refer to the section earlier in this arithmetic review on adding and subtracting positive and negative numbers.

Practice Items—Adding and Subtracting Fractions

1. $\dfrac{1}{3} + \dfrac{6}{12} =$ $\dfrac{4}{12} + \dfrac{6}{12} = \dfrac{10}{12} = \dfrac{5}{6}$

2. $\dfrac{2}{3} + \dfrac{7}{8} =$ $\dfrac{16}{24} + \dfrac{21}{24} = \dfrac{37}{24} = 1\,\dfrac{13}{24}$

3. $\dfrac{3}{4} + \dfrac{7}{8} =$ $\dfrac{6}{8} + \dfrac{7}{8} = \dfrac{13}{8} = 1\dfrac{5}{8}$

4. $\dfrac{8}{10} \,\dfrac{2}{15} =$ $\dfrac{8}{15} + \dfrac{3}{15} = \dfrac{24}{30} - \dfrac{4}{30}$ $\dfrac{20}{30} = \dfrac{2}{3}$

5. $\dfrac{4}{5} \,\dfrac{1}{3} =$ $\dfrac{12}{15} - \dfrac{5}{15} = \dfrac{7}{15}$

Adding and Subtracting Mixed Numbers Add and subtract mixed numbers by following the same rules previously outlined. Change the fractions to equivalent fractions with the least common denominator. Add or subtract the fractions. Add or subtract the whole numbers. If the fractions add up to more than a whole number, add that to the whole numbers.

Example (Addition)

$3\dfrac{3}{4}$	changes to	$3\dfrac{3}{4}$
$+2\dfrac{1}{2}$		$+2\dfrac{2}{4}$

Add $\dfrac{3}{4} + \dfrac{2}{4} = \dfrac{5}{4} = 1\dfrac{1}{4}$

Add 3 and 2 = 5

$5 + 1\dfrac{1}{4} = 6\dfrac{1}{4}$

Examples (Subtraction)

$$3\frac{3}{4}$$ changes to $$3\frac{3}{4}$$
$$-2\frac{1}{2}$$ $$-2\frac{2}{4}$$

$$\frac{3}{4} - \frac{2}{4} = \frac{1}{4}$$

$$3 - 2 = 1$$

$$1 + \frac{1}{4} = 1\frac{1}{4}$$

$$3\frac{3}{4}$$ changes to $$3\frac{3}{4}$$
$$-5\frac{1}{2}$$ $$-5\frac{2}{4}$$

Caution: Remember that subtraction means moving _left_ on the number line. Start at 3 3/4 and move left 52/4 on the number line. The correct answer is –1 3/4.

Practice Items–Adding and Subtracting Mixed Numbers

1. $1\frac{3}{4} + 3\frac{3}{4} =$

2. $6\frac{5}{6} + 9\frac{1}{3} =$

3. $12\frac{1}{3} + \frac{4}{5} =$

4. $8\frac{7}{8} - 4\frac{1}{4} =$

5. $10\frac{2}{3} - 3\frac{1}{9} =$

Multiplying Fractions To multiply fractions, just multiply the numerators and multiply the denominators. Reduce the resulting fraction to lowest terms.

Examples

$$\frac{5}{12} \times \frac{2}{3} =$$

Multiply the numerators: $5 \times 2 = 10$
Multiply the denominators: $12 \times 3 = 36$

Result: $\frac{10}{36} = 5/18$

$$\frac{4}{5} \times \frac{7}{8} =$$

Multiply the numerators: $4 \times 7 = 28$
Multiply the denominators: $5 \times 8 = 40$
Result: $\frac{28}{40} = 7/10$

Helpful Hint: Simplify, Simplify

Sometimes it is possible to simplify terms before performing any math operation. Take the same example that we have already completed:

$$\frac{1}{5} \times \frac{4}{5} \times \frac{7}{8}_{2}$$

Find a number (or greatest common factor) that divides into one of the numerators and one of the denominators. In this example, the number 4 divides into 4 and into 8.

$$\frac{^{1}4}{5} \times \frac{7}{8_{2}}$$

To finish the problem, multiply 1×7 and 5×2, making the final answer

$$\frac{7}{10}$$

Practice Items–Multiplying Fractions

1. $\frac{3}{4} \times \frac{7}{10} =$ $\frac{21}{40}$

2. $\frac{12}{15} \times \frac{1}{5} =$ $\frac{12}{75}$

3. $\frac{2}{7} \times \frac{2}{5} =$ $\frac{4}{35}$

Dividing Fractions To divide fractions, invert the second fraction and multiply. Reduce the result to lowest terms.

Examples

$$\frac{1}{2} \div \frac{1}{3}$$

$$= \frac{1}{2} \times \frac{3}{1}$$

$$= \frac{3}{2} = 1\frac{1}{2}$$

$$\frac{3}{4} \div -\left(\frac{1}{2}\right)$$

$$= \frac{3}{4} \times -\left(\frac{2}{1}\right)$$

$$= -\left(\frac{6}{4}\right)$$

$$= -1\frac{2}{4}$$

$$= -1\frac{1}{2}$$

Reminder: Dividing Fractions

Always remember that when you are dividing fractions, just invert and multiply.

HELPFUL HINT: Dividing Fractions

Sometimes you might see division of fractions in this format:

$$\frac{\frac{1}{2}}{\frac{1}{3}}$$

Treat it the same as

$$\frac{1}{2} \div \frac{1}{3}$$

Reminder: Watch the Signs!

To multiply or divide negative numbers, first treat the numbers and perform the operation in the normal way. Then, if there is an odd number of negative signs, the answer will be a negative. If there is an even number of negative signs, the number will be positive.

Practice Items—Dividing Fractions

1. $\frac{1}{2} \div \frac{2}{4} = \frac{4}{4}$ $\frac{1}{2} \times \frac{4}{2} = \frac{4}{4} = 1$ $12-10=2$

2. $\frac{4}{5} \div \frac{1}{3} =$ $\frac{4}{5} \times \frac{3}{1} = \frac{12}{5} = 2\frac{2}{5}$

3. $\frac{8}{9} \div \frac{1}{3} =$ $\frac{8}{9} \times \frac{3}{1} = \frac{24}{9} = 2\frac{4}{9}$ $24-18$

Multiplying Mixed Numbers To multiply mixed numbers, change each mixed number to a fraction and then multiply as usual. Reduce to lowest terms.

Examples

$$1\frac{1}{4} \times 2\frac{1}{2} = \frac{5}{4} \times \frac{5}{2}$$

$$= \frac{25}{8} = 3\frac{1}{8}$$

$$3\frac{2}{3} \times 9\frac{1}{2} = \frac{11}{3} \times \frac{19}{2}$$

$$= \frac{209}{6} = 34\frac{5}{6}$$

Practice Items—Multiplying Mixed Numbers

1. $2\frac{2}{3} \times 7\frac{2}{5} =$

2. $5\frac{1}{5} \times 4\frac{1}{2} =$

3. $12\frac{2}{3} \times 2\frac{1}{3} =$

Dividing Mixed Numbers To divide mixed numbers, rename the mixed numbers as fractions and then follow the rule for dividing fractions: invert the second fraction and multiply.

Example

$$3\frac{1}{2} \div 1\frac{1}{4} = \frac{7}{2} \div \frac{5}{4}$$

$$= \frac{7}{2} \times \frac{4}{5}$$

$$\frac{28}{10} = 2\frac{8}{10}$$

Simply the fraction.

$$2\frac{4}{5}$$

Reminder: Fractions and Decimals
All proper fractions are less than 1, so the corresponding decimals will be to the right of the decimal point. Numbers to the left of the decimal point will be whole numbers.

Practice Items–Dividing Mixed Numbers

1. $12\frac{2}{3} \div 2\frac{1}{3} =$ 26

2. $6\frac{1}{2} \div \frac{1}{2} =$ $\frac{13}{2} \div \frac{1}{2}$ $\frac{13}{2} \times \frac{2}{1} = \frac{26}{2} = 13$

3. $6\frac{1}{2} \div 2\frac{1}{2} =$ $\frac{13}{2} \div \frac{5}{2}$ $\frac{13}{2} \times \frac{2}{5} = \frac{26}{10} = 10\frac{2}{6}$

Decimals

A decimal is a number with one or more digits to the right of the decimal point. 0.862 and 3.12 are decimals. (Note that a zero is shown to the left of the decimal point when the decimal is between 0 and 1.)

Operations with Decimals

Adding and Subtracting Decimals To add or subtract decimals, line up the decimal points one above the other. Then add or subtract as you would normally. Place a decimal point in the answer beneath the other decimal points.

Examples (Addition) _____

$$
\begin{array}{r}
14.50 \\
200.32 \\
+\ 1{,}245.89 \\
\hline
1{,}460.71
\end{array}
$$

$$
\begin{array}{r}
14.50 \\
200.047 \\
48.0075 \\
+\ 10.6 \\
\end{array}
$$

Add zeros in the blank decimal places to make this problem easier to tackle.

$$
\begin{array}{r}
14.5000 \\
200.0470 \\
48.0075 \\
+\ 10.6000 \\
\hline
273.1545
\end{array}
$$

Examples (Subtraction) _____

$$
\begin{array}{r}
475.89 \\
-\ 62.45 \\
\hline
413.44
\end{array}
$$

$$
\begin{array}{r}
{}^{7\ 14} \\
475.\cancel{84} \\
-\ 62.69 \\
\hline
413.15
\end{array}
$$
Since 9 is larger than 4, rename 84 as 7 tens and 14 ones.

Practice Items–Adding and Subtracting Decimals

1.
$$
\begin{array}{r}
325.45 \\
+\ 221.12
\end{array}
$$

2.
$$
\begin{array}{r}
12{,}456.213 \\
+\ 32{,}114.788
\end{array}
$$

3.
$$
\begin{array}{r}
788.99 \\
+\ 102.12
\end{array}
$$

4.
$$
\begin{array}{r}
788.99 \\
-\ 102.12
\end{array}
$$

5.
$$
\begin{array}{r}
5{,}612.12 \\
-\ 4{,}599.99
\end{array}
$$

6.
$$
\begin{array}{r}
45.00 \\
-\ 12.89
\end{array}
$$

Multiplying Decimals To multiply decimals, follow the usual multiplication rules. Count the number of places to the right of the decimal point in each factor. Add the numbers of places. Put that many decimal places in the answer.

Examples

12.43 (two decimal places)
× 2.4 (one decimal place)

———

29.832 (total of three decimal places in the answer)

6.624 (three decimal places)
× 1.22 (two decimal places)

———

8.08128 (total of five decimal places)

Practice Items–Multiplying Decimals

1. 12.89
    × 2.04
    ———

2. 56.12
    × 2.89
    ———

3. 144.45
    × 16.23
    ———

Dividing Decimals To divide decimals, follow the usual division rules. If the divisor (the number you are dividing by) has decimals, move the decimal point to the right as many places as necessary to make the divisor a whole number. Then move the decimal point of the dividend (the number you are dividing) that same number of places to the right. (You may have to add some zeros to the dividend to make this work.) Put the decimal point in the answer directly above the decimal point in the dividend.

Examples

$$12.76\overline{)58.696} = 1276\overline{)5869.6}^{\,4.6}$$

Note that the decimal point is moved two places to the right in each term. The decimal point in the answer is directly above the decimal point in the dividend.

$$1.25\overline{)50} = 125\overline{)5000}^{\,40}$$

In this example, the decimal point is moved two places to the right in 1.25 to make 125. The dividend 50 can also be expressed as 50.00 (adding zeros), and moving the decimal point the same number of places to the right makes 5,000. No decimal point needs to be shown in the answer because the answer is a whole number.

Practice Items–Dividing Decimals

1. $143.37 \div 12.15 =$

2. $48.88 \div 12.4 =$

3. $62.15 \div 2.2 =$

Changing Decimals to Fractions Read the decimal and then write the fraction. Reduce the fraction to its lowest terms.

Examples

$0.5 = 5$ tenths or 5 over 10: $\frac{5}{10} = \frac{1}{2}$

$0.66 = 66$ hundredths or 66 over 100: $\frac{66}{100} = \frac{33}{50}$

$0.75 = 75$ hundredths or 75 over 100: $\frac{75}{100} = \frac{3}{4}$

$0.006 = 6$ thousandths or 6 over 1,000: $\frac{6}{1,000} = \frac{3}{500}$

$0.0006 = 6$ ten thousandths or 6 over 10,000: $\frac{6}{10,000} = \frac{3}{5,000}$

Practice Items–Changing Decimals to Fractions

1. $0.80 =$

2. $0.\overline{33} =$

3. $0.05 =$

Changing Fractions to Decimals To change a fraction to a decimal, divide the numerator by the denominator.

Examples

$$1/2 = 1 \div 2 = 0.5$$
$$3/4 = 3 \div 4 = 0.75$$
$$6/1,000 = 6 \div 1,000 = 0.006$$
$$2/3 = 2 \div 3 = 0.6\overline{6}$$ (The bar over the final 6 indicates that this is a *repeating decimal*. That means that you could keep on dividing forever and always have the same remainder.)

Practice Items–Changing Fractions to Decimals

1. $\frac{1}{8} =$

2. $\frac{12}{36} =$

3. $\frac{5}{6} =$

Percent

Percent means "out of 100" or "per hundred." For example, "70%" is read as "70 percent," meaning 70 out of 100 equal parts. Percents are useful ways to show parts of a whole. They can also be easily changed into decimals or fractions.

Changing Percents to Decimals Percent means "per 100." So 70% means "70 per 100," which is 70/100 or 70 ÷ 100, which is 0.70. So to change percents to decimals, delete the percent sign and move the decimal point two places to the left. You may need to add zeros.

Examples

$\qquad$ 67% = 0.67
$\qquad$ 6% = 0.06 (A zero was added to the left of the 6.)
$\quad$ 187% = 1.87
$\quad$ 0.14% = 0.0014 (Two zeros were added to the left of the 14.)

Practice Items–Changing Percents to Decimals

1. 78% =

2. 12% =

3. 443% =

Changing Decimals to Percents To change decimals to percents, merely move the decimal point two places to the right and add a percent sign. (You may need to add a zero on the right.)

Examples

$\qquad$ 0.67 = 67%
$\qquad$ 0.4 = 40% (A zero was added to the right of the 4.)
$\quad$ 1.87 = 187%
$\quad$ 28.886 = 2888.6%
$\quad$ 0.0014 = 0.14%

Practice Items–Changing Decimals to Percents

1. 0.75 =

2. 0.225 =

3. 0.4 =

Changing Percents to Fractions A percent is some number over (divided by) 100. So every percent is also a fraction with a denominator of 100. For example, 45% = 45/100.

To change percents to fractions, remove the percent sign and write the number over 100. Reduce the fraction to lowest terms.

Examples

$$50\% = \frac{50}{100} = \frac{5}{10} = \frac{1}{2}$$

$$25\% = \frac{25}{100} = \frac{1}{4}$$

$$30\% = \frac{30}{100} = \frac{3}{10}$$

Practice Items–Changing Percents to Fractions

1. 34% =

2. 57% =

3. 99% =

Changing Fractions to Percents To change fractions to percents, change the fraction to a decimal and then change the decimal to a percent.

Examples

$$\frac{1}{2} = 0.5 = 50\%$$

$$\frac{1}{4} = 0.25 = 25\%$$

$$\frac{1}{10} = 0.10 = 10\%$$

$$\frac{6}{20} = 0.3 = 30\%$$

$$\frac{1}{3} = 0.33\overline{3} = 33\frac{1}{3}\%$$

Memorize the relationships to save calculation time.

Fraction(s)	= Decimal	= Percent (%)
$\frac{1}{100}$	0.01	1%
$\frac{1}{10}$	0.1	10%
$\frac{1}{5} = \frac{2}{10}$	0.2	20%
$\frac{3}{10}$	0.3	30%
$\frac{2}{5} = \frac{4}{10}$	0.4	40%
$\frac{1}{2} = \frac{5}{10}$	0.5	50%
$\frac{3}{5} = \frac{6}{10}$	0.6	60%
$\frac{4}{5} = \frac{8}{10}$	0.8	80%
$\frac{1}{4} = \frac{2}{8} = \frac{25}{100}$	0.25	25%
$\frac{3}{4} = \frac{75}{100}$	0.75	75%
$\frac{1}{3} = \frac{2}{6}$	0.33	$33\frac{1}{3}$%
$\frac{2}{3}$	0.66	$66\frac{2}{3}$%
$\frac{1}{8}$	0.125	12.5%
$\frac{3}{8}$	0.375	37.5%
$\frac{5}{8}$	0.625	62.5%
$\frac{1}{6}$	$0.16\frac{2}{3}$	$16\frac{2}{3}$%
1	1.00	100%
1.5	1.50	150%

<u>Practice Items–Changing Fractions to Percents</u>

1. $\frac{1}{5} =$

2. $\frac{2}{5} =$

3. $\frac{3}{8} =$

Finding a Percent of a Number

The ASVAB Mathematics Knowledge test and Arithmetic Reasoning test frequently include problems that ask you to find a percent of a number. Problems are often worded like this: "What is 25% of 1,000?" There are two ways you can solve this kind of problem. You can start by changing the percent into a fraction, or you can change the percent into a decimal.

If you change 25% into a fraction, solve the problem like this:

$$\frac{25}{100} \times 1,000 = \frac{100}{25,000} = 250$$

If you change 25% into a decimal, solve the problem like this:

$$0.25 \times 1,000 = 250$$

You should use the approach that is easiest and best for you.

Percent problems are sometimes stated in another way. For example, a problem may ask, "25 is what percent of 200?" When you see a problem like this, make it into an equation:

$$25 = x(200) \text{ where } x \text{ is the percent.}$$
$$x = 25/200 = 1/8 = 0.125 = 12.5\%$$

*Example*_____

30 is what percent of 90?

$$30 = x(90)$$
$$30/90 = 1/3 = 0.\overline{33} = 33\tfrac{1}{3}\%$$

There is a third way in which percent problems are sometimes solved. Here is an example: "20 is what percent of 25?"

When you see this kind of question, start by setting up a proportion:

$$\text{Some unknown percent } (x\%) = \frac{20}{25}$$

$x\%$ is really $\frac{x}{100}$. So the proportion becomes $\frac{x}{100} = \frac{20}{25}$.

Reduce the fraction and solve:

$$\frac{x}{100} = \frac{4}{5}$$
$$5x = 400$$
$$x = 80$$

So 20 is 80 percent of 25.

*Example*_____

30 is what percent of 120?

$$\frac{x}{100} = \frac{30}{120}$$
$$\frac{x}{100} = \frac{3}{12}$$
$$12x = 300$$
$$x = \frac{300}{12} = 25$$
$$x = 25\%$$

Practice Items—Finding a Percent of a Number

1. 25% of 125 =

2. 50% of 250 =

3. 80% of 200 =

Finding the Percent of Increase or Decrease

You are likely to also encounter these types of percent problems on the ASVAB. Here is an example: "What is the percent increase in Kim's salary if she gets a raise from $12,000 to $15,000 per year?" Set this up as an equation with the following structure

$$\frac{\text{amount of change}}{\text{original number}} = \text{percent of change}$$

Example Percent of Increase_____

For the problem about Kim's salary, the amount of change is 3,000 because Kim's salary increased by that amount. The original number is 12,000. Plug those numbers into the formula:

$$3,000/12,000 = 3/12 = 0.25 = 25\%$$

Kim's salary increased by 25%.

Example Percent of Decrease_____

A CD player has its price reduced from $250 to $200. What is the percent of decrease?

Use the same process as with the previous problem.

$$\frac{\text{amount of change}}{\text{original number}} = \text{percent of change}$$

The amount of change (decrease) is 50 (250 minus 200). The original number (original price) is $250. Plug these numbers into the formula:

$$\frac{50}{250} = \frac{5}{25} = \frac{1}{5} = .20$$

The CD price decreased by 20%.

Practice Items—Finding the Percent of Increase or Decrease

1. An iPOD went on sale from $500 to $350. What is the percent difference?

2. A house was purchased at $200,000 and sold for $350,000. What is the percent increase?

3. A car that cost $24,000 went on sale for $21,000. What is the percent decrease?

Exponents

An *exponent* is a number that tells how many times another number is multiplied by itself. In the expression 4^3, the 3 is an exponent. It means that 4 is multiplied it by itself three times, or $4 \times 4 \times 4$. So $4^3 = 64$. The expression 4^2 is read "4 to the second power" or "4 squared." The expression 4^3 is read "4 to the third power" or "4 cubed." The expression 4^4 is read "4 to the fourth power." In each of these cases, the exponent is called a *power* of 4. In the expression 5^2 ("5 to the second power" or "5 squared"), the exponent is a power of 5.

Examples

$3^5 = 3 \times 3 \times 3 \times 3 \times 3 = 243$
$6^2 = 6 \times 6 = 36$

Negative Exponents Exponents can also be negative. To interpret negative exponents, follow this pattern:

$$2^{-3} = \frac{1}{2^3} \text{ or } \frac{1}{8}$$

Examples

$3^{-2} = \frac{1}{3^2} = \frac{1}{9}$
$4^{-3} = \frac{1}{4^3} = \frac{1}{64}$

Multiplying Numbers with Exponents To multiply numbers with exponents, multiply out each number and then perform the operation.

Examples

$3^4 \times 2^3 = (3 \times 3 \times 3 \times 3) \times (2 \times 2 \times 2)$
$= 81 \times 8 = 648$

$2^9 \times 12^2 = (2 \times 2 \times 2 \times 2 \times 2 \times 2 \times 2 \times 2 \times 2)$
$\times (12 \times 12)$
$= 512 \times 144 = 73,728$

Practice Items—Multiplying Numbers with Exponents

1. $3^3 \times 6^2 =$
2. $6^2 \times 12^2 =$
3. $8^1 \times 6^3 =$

Square Roots

The *square root* of a number is the number whose square equals the original number. One square root of 4 (written $\sqrt{4}$) is 2, since $2 \times 2 = 4$. –2 is also a square root of 4, since $-2 \times -2 = 4$.

Reminder: Watch the Signs!

Remember that a negative number multiplied by itself results in a positive number.

Examples

$\sqrt{1} = 1$ or –1
$\sqrt{4} = 2$ or –2
$\sqrt{9} = 3$ or –3
$\sqrt{16} = 4$ or –4
$\sqrt{25} = 5$ or –5
$\sqrt{36} = 6$ or –6
$\sqrt{49} = 7$ or –7
$\sqrt{64} = 8$ or –8
$\sqrt{81} = 9$ or –9
$\sqrt{100} = 10$ or –10
$\sqrt{121} = 11$ or –11
$\sqrt{144} = 12$ or – 12
$\sqrt{169} = 13$ or –13
$\sqrt{196} = 14$ or –14
$\sqrt{225} = 15$ or –15

Practice Items—Square Root

1. $= \sqrt{256}$
2. $= \sqrt{400}$
3. $= \sqrt{441}$

Scientific Notation

For convenience, very large or very small numbers are sometimes written in what is called *scientific notation.* In scientific notation, a number is written as the product of two factors. The first factor is a number greater than or equal to 1 but less than 10. The second factor is a power of 10. (Recall that in an expression such as 10^3, which is read "10 cubed" or "10 to the third power," the exponent 3 is a power of 10.)

For example, suppose you need to write the very large number 51,000,000 in scientific notation. This number can also be written 51,000,000.00. Move the decimal point to the left until you have a number between 1 and 10. If you move the decimal point 7 places to the left, you have the number 5.1000000 or 5.1. Since you moved the decimal point 7 places, you would have to multiply 5.1 by 10^7 (a power of 10) to recreate the original number. So in scientific notation, the original number can be written as 5.1×10^7.

For very small numbers, move the decimal point to the right until you have a number between 1 and 10. Then count the decimal places between the new position and the old position. This time, since you moved the decimal point to the right, the power of 10 is negative. That is, the exponent is a negative number.

Examples (Large Numbers)

698,000,000,000 can be written 6.98×10^{11}.
45,000,000 can be written 4.5×10^7.

Examples (Small Numbers)

0.00000006 can be written 6×10^{-8}.
0.0000016 can be written 1.6×10^{-6}.

To change back to the original number from scientific notation, merely move the decimal point the number of places indicated by the "power of 10" number.

Example (Large Numbers)

2.35×10^5 becomes 235,000. The decimal point moved 5 places to the right.
6×10^8 becomes 600,000,000. The decimal point moved 8 places to the right.

Example (Small Numbers)

2.3×10^{-4} becomes 0.00023. The decimal point moved 4 places to the left.
7×10^{-12} becomes 0.000000000007. The decimal point moved 12 places to the left.

Multiplying in Scientific Notation   To multiply numbers written in scientific notation, multiply the numbers and add the powers of 10.

Examples

$$(2 \times 10^8) \times (3.1 \times 10^2) = 6.2 \times 10^{10}$$
$$(3.3 \times 10^{12}) \times (4 \times 10^{-3}) = 13.2 \times 10^9$$

Here you are adding a 12 and a –3, giving you 9 for the power of 10. But remember the rule that the decimal point must be after a number that is between 1 and 9, so you have to move the decimal place one more place to the left to put it after the 1, and you have to increase the power of 10 accordingly. So the final result of the multiplication is 1.32×10^{10}.

Practice Items–Multiplying in Scientific Notation

1. $(3.4 \times 10^2) \times (1.2 \times 10^7) =$

2. $(12.6 \times 10^2) \times (6.6 \times 10^{5)} =$

Dividing in Scientific Notation   To divide in scientific notation, divide the numbers and subtract the powers of 10.

Examples

$$(9 \times 10^7) \div (3 \times 10^3) = 3 \times 10^4$$

Here you divide 9 by 3 (= 3), and you subtract the exponent 3 from the exponent 7 to get the new exponent 4.

$$(1.0 \times 10^4) \div (4 \times 10^{-3}) = 0.25 \times 10^7$$

Since the number in the first position must be between 1 and 9, move the decimal to the right one place and decrease the exponent accordingly, so the final result is 2.5×10^6.

Practice Items–Dividing in Scientific Notation

1. $(2.0 \times 10^4) \div (6 \times 10^{-3}) =$

2. $(4 \times 10^7) \div (4 \times 10^3) =$

Mean or Average

The *mean* of a set of numbers is the average. Add the numbers and divide by the number of numbers.

Examples

What is the mean of the numbers 2, 4, 7, 4, and 5?

The sum is 22. Since there are 5 numbers, divide 22 by 5 to get a mean or average of 4.4.

What is the mean of the numbers 3, 4, 2, 6, 7, 12, 56, and 104?

The sum is 194. There are 8 numbers, so divide 194 by 8 to get 24.25.

Practice Items–Calculating the Mean Calculate the mean of the following numbers.

1. 2, 4, 5, 6, 7, 12, 43, 55, 78, 4, 26 =

2. 44, 67, 80, 10, 23, 23, 23, 77, 88, 100 =

3. 125, 334, 522, 16, 822 =

Median

Order a set of numbers from least to greatest. If there is an odd number of numbers, the *median* is the number in the middle of that sequence of numbers. If there is an even number of numbers, the median is the mean or average of the two middle numbers.

Examples

What is the median of the following numbers?

12, 14, 999, 75, 102, 456, 19

Reorder the numbers from least to greatest: 12, 14, 19, 75, 102, 456, 999

The middle number is 75, so that is the median. What is the median of the following numbers?

15, 765, 65, 890, 12, 1

Reorder the numbers from least to greatest: 1, 12, 15, 65, 765, 890

Since there is an even number of numbers, find the average of the middle two numbers.

$$15 + 65 = 80$$
$$80 \div 2 = 40$$

40 is the median.

Mode

The *mode* of a set of numbers is the number that appears most frequently in that set.

Example

What is the mode of the following set of numbers?

12, 14, 15, 15, 15, 17, 18

The number 15 appears most often in this set, so it is the mode of the set.

Graphs

Often it is helpful to represent numbers in a visual form called a *graph*. The most common types of graphs are circle graphs, bar graphs, and line graphs. You probably won't be asked to construct such graphs on the ASVAB, but you are likely to have to interpret one or more of them on the math and/or science sections of the test.

Circle or Pie Graph This kind of graph uses a circle divided into parts to show fractional or percentage relationships.

Example

In a survey at a local high school, students were asked to name their favorite lunch food. The results of that survey are shown in the circle graph below.

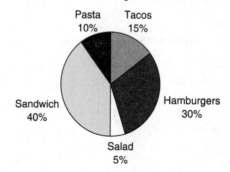

Favorite lunch food of high school students

Questions such as the following are typical.

- Which food was most (or least) popular with the students? (most: sandwich; least: salad)
- Which two food selections of the students make up 50% of the total? (sandwich and pasta: 40% and 10% = 50%)
- What is the ratio of the students who selected sandwiches to the students who selected hamburgers? (4:3)
- If the total number of students surveyed was 2,500, how many chose salad as their favorite lunch? (125; 2,500 × 0.05 = 125)

Practice Items—Pie Graph

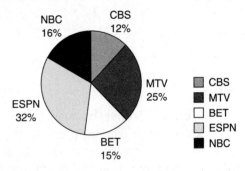

Percent watching various TV stations on monday night

1. Which station was the most watched?
2. What is the ratio of NBC watchers to ESPN watchers?
3. Which was the least-watched station?

Bar Graph This kind of graph uses bars to provide a visual comparison of different quantities.

Example

The following bar graph compares the number of different types of sandwiches sold on Tuesday at a certain sandwich shop.

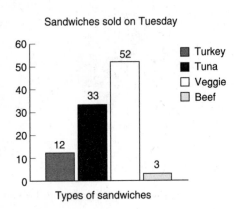

Sandwiches sold on Tuesday

Questions such as the following are typical.

- Which kind of sandwich did the store sell the most of on Tuesday? (veggie)
- How many more tuna sandwiches than turkey sandwiches were sold on Tuesday? (21)
- How many tuna sandwiches and beef sandwiches were sold on Monday? (36)

Practice Items—Bar Graphs

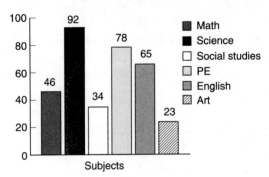

Number of students rating subject as their favorite

1. According to the bar graph, which subject is the favorite of the most students?
2. Which subject is the favorite of the fewest students?
3. What is the total number of students who picked their favorite subject?
4. What is the ratio of students who picked art as their favorite subject to students who picked math?

Line Graph This kind of graph is generally used to show change over time.

Example

The following line graph shows the change in attendance at this year's football games.

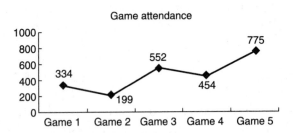

Game attendance

Questions such as the following are typical.

- How many more people attended game 3 than game 2? (353)
- Which game had the highest attendance? (Game 5)
- How many people attended the first game of the year? (334)

<u>Practice Items–Line Graphs</u>

Rainfall in inches in Broadview State Park

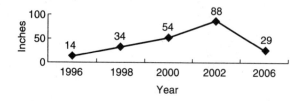

1. Which year had the most rainfall?
2. Which year had the least rainfall?
3. What was the average yearly rainfall in the park during this time period?
4. How many more inches of rain fell in 2000 than in 1996?

Units of Measure

If you don't know the following units of measure, you just need to memorize them.

Units of Measure

Customary System

Length

12 inches (in.) = 1 foot (ft)

3 feet = 1 yard (yd)

36 inches = 1 yard

5,280 feet = 1 mile (mi)

Area

1 square foot (ft²) = 144 square inches (in.²)

9 square feet = 1 square yard (yd²)

Weight

16 ounces (oz) = 1 pound (lb)

2,000 pounds = 1 ton

Liquid Volume

2 cups (c) = 1 pint (pt)

2 pints = 1 quart (qt)

4 quarts = 1 gallon (gal)

Time

7 days = 1 week

4 weeks = 1 month

12 months = 1 year

52 weeks = 1 year

10 years = 1 decade

Metric System

Length

100 centimeters (cm) = 1 meter (m)

1,000 meters = 1 kilometer (km)

Volume

1,000 milliliters (mL) = 1 liter (L)

Mass

1,000 grams (g) = 1 kilogram (kg)

1,000 kilograms = 1 metric ton (t)

Converting between Systems

1 meter ≈ 39.37 inches

1 kilometer ≈ 0.62 mile

1 centimeter ≈ 0.39 inch

1 kilogram ≈ 2.2 pounds

1 liter ≈ 1.057 quarts

1 gram ≈ 0.035 ounce

ARITHMETIC QUIZ–ANSWERS AND CHART

Scoring Your Test

Compare your answer to the correct answer. Mark an X in the column if you got the item correct. Total the number correct.

Item Number	Correct Answer	Mark X if you picked the correct answer
1	C	
2	C	
3	C	
4	A	
5	A	
6	B	
7	A	
8	A	
9	D	
10	C	
11	C	
12	A	
13	B	
14	D	
15	C	
16	B	
17	C	
18	D	
19	C	
20	A	
21	B	
22	B	
23	B	
24	C	
25	D	
26	C	
27	D	
28	C	
29	C	
30	D	
31	B	
32	A	
33	A	
34	C	
35	D	
36	C	
37	C	
38	B	
39	D	
40	B	
41	C	
42	C	
43	C	
44	B	
45	A	
Total Correct		

Gauging Your Level of Performance

In the following chart, find the number of items that you got correct. See the suggestions listed for your performance.

45	This is pretty good work. Rework the items that you got wrong so that you know how to work the problems. This test is a part of the AFQT, and you must do well on it.
44	
43	
42	
41	
40	You are doing OK. Go back and review the lessons on those areas that you got wrong. You should strive to get at least 42 items correct.
39	
38	
37	
36	
35	
34	
33	
32	You need to keep studying and practicing. You should not be satisfied until you can easily work the problems.
31	
30	
29	
28	Spend time working on the math problems in this chapter.
27	
26	
25	Keep working and reworking problems until you are comfortable with the processes. Try the math quiz again.
24	
23	
22	
21	
19	
18	
17	
16	
15	
14	
13	
12	
11	
10	
9	
8	
7	
6	
5	
4	
3	
2	
1	
0	

ANSWERS TO PRACTICE ITEMS

Practice Items—Place Value

1. 5
2. 0
3. 6

Practice Items—Addition

1. 745
2. 21,460
3. 25,676
4. 97,986
5. 98,742,358
6. 3,460,988
7. 670,504
8. 4,554,000,831
9. 6,913,208
10. 34,958,777

Practice Items—Subtraction

1. 812
2. 2,495
3. 22,411
4. 55,445
5. 11,005,411
6. 589,831
7. 84,822,389
8. 991,188
9. 144,985,636
10. 99

Practice Items—Multiplication

1. 20
2. 20
3. 63

4. 1,755
5. 6,566
6. 410,843
7. 14,745,358
8. 6,028,318,806
9. 212,244,289,278
10. 554,736,386,736,842

Practice Items—Division

1. 4
2. 12
3. 2
4. 456
5. 987
6. 258
7. 32
8. 21
9. 12
10. 331

Practice Items—Symbols

1. T
2. T
3. T
4. F
5. T
6. F
7. T
8. T
9. F
10. F

Practice Items—Order of Operations

1. 40
2. 50
3. 90
4. 21
5. 41
6. 152
7. 21
8. 218

Practice Items—Rounding

1. 123,500
2. 123,000
3. 123,456.1
4. 123,456.10

Practice Items—Adding Positive and Negative Numbers

1. 1
2. –7
3. 9
4. 130
5. –58
6. 200
7. 320
8. –125

Practice Items—Subtracting Positive and Negative Numbers

1. 8
2. 16
3. 20
4. 33
5. 116
6. 475

7. 1,400
8. 1,400
9. 62

Practice Items—Multiplying and Dividing Negative Numbers

1. –8
2. +8
3. +40
4. –2
5. +2
6. –2
7. +320
8. –50

Practice Items—Subtracting Numbers Within Parentheses

1. 120
2. 5
3. 135
4. 475
5. 250
6. 19
7. 151

Practice Items—Multiplying and Dividing by Zero

1. 0
2. 0
3. 0
4. 0
5. Undefined

Practice Items—Least Common Multiples

1. 8
2. 12
3. 12
4. 15

Practice Items—Changing Improper Fractions into Mixed Numbers

1. $12\frac{1}{2}$
2. $2\frac{1}{3}$
3. $11\frac{1}{4}$
4. $39\frac{1}{2}$
5. $16\frac{4}{5}$
6. $7\frac{7}{10}$

Practice Items—Renaming a Mixed Number as a Fraction

1. $\frac{10}{3}$
2. $\frac{25}{4}$
3. $\frac{71}{12}$
4. $\frac{15}{4}$
5. $\frac{37}{5}$

Practice Items—Finding Equivalent Fractions

1. $\frac{2}{6}, \frac{3}{9}, \frac{4}{12}$
2. $\frac{4}{6}, \frac{6}{9}, \frac{8}{12}$
3. $\frac{1}{2}, \frac{4}{8}, \frac{6}{12}$

Practice Items—Reducing Fractions to Lowest Terms

1. $\frac{1}{3}$
2. $\frac{1}{2}$
3. $\frac{1}{4}$
4. $\frac{1}{2}$
5. $\frac{1}{8}$
6. $\frac{1}{13}$

Practice Items—Adding and Subtracting Fractions

1. $\frac{5}{6}$
2. $1\frac{13}{24}$
3. $1\frac{5}{8}$
4. $\frac{2}{3}$
5. $\frac{7}{15}$

Practice Items—Adding and Subtracting Mixed Numbers

1. $5\frac{1}{2}$
2. $16\frac{1}{6}$
3. $13\frac{2}{15}$
4. $4\frac{5}{8}$
5. $7\frac{5}{9}$

Practice Items—Multiplying Fractions

1. $\frac{21}{40}$

2. 4/25

3. $\frac{4}{35}$

Practice Items—Dividing Fractions

1. 1

2. $2\frac{2}{5}$

3. $2\frac{2}{3}$

Practice Items—Multiplying Mixed Numbers

1. $19\frac{11}{15}$

2. $23\frac{2}{5}$

3. $29\frac{5}{9}$

Practice Items—Dividing Mixed Numbers

1. $5\frac{3}{7}$

2. 13

3. $2\frac{3}{5}$

Practice Items—Adding and Subtracting Decimals

1. 546.57

2. 44,571.001

3. 891.11

4. 686.87

5. 1,012.13

6. 32.11

Practice Items—Multiplying Decimals

1. 26.2956

2. 162.1868

3. 2344.4235

Practice Items—Dividing Decimals

1. 11.8

2. 3.942

3. 28.25

Practice Items—Changing Decimals to Fractions

1. $\frac{4}{5}$

2. $\frac{1}{3}$

3. $\frac{1}{20}$

Practice Items—Changing Fractions to Decimals

1. 0.125

2. $0.3\overline{3}$

3. $0.8\overline{3}$

Practice Items—Changing Percents to Decimals

1. 0.78

2. 0.12

3. 4.43

Practice Items—Changing Decimals to Percents

1. 75%

2. 22.5%

3. 40%

Practice Items–Changing Percents to Fractions

1. $\frac{17}{50}$

2. $\frac{57}{100}$

3. $\frac{99}{100}$

Practice Items–Changing Fractions to Percents

1. 20%

2. 40%

3. 37.5%

Practice Items–Finding a Percent of a Number

1. 31.25

2. 125

3. 160

Practice Items–Finding the Percent of Increase or Decrease

1. 30%

2. 75%

3. 12.5%

Practice Items–Multiplying Numbers with Exponents

1. 972

2. 5,184

3. 1,728

Practice Items–Square Root

1. 16

2. 20

3. 21

Practice Items–Multiplying in Scientific Notation

1. 4.08×10^9

2. 83.16×10^7

Practice Items–Dividing in Scientific Notation

1. 0.33

2. 1×10^4

Practice Items–Calculating the Mean

1. 22

2. 53.5

3. 363.8

Practice Items–Pie Graph

1. ESPN

2. 1:2

3. CBS

Practice Items–Bar Graph

1. Science

2. Art

3. 338

4. 1:2

Practice Items–Line Graph

1. 2002

2. 1996

3. 43.8

4. 40 inches

SECTION 2: ALGEBRA AND PROBABILITY

READ THIS SECTION TO LEARN:

- **What algebra and probability topics you need to know for the ASVAB**

- **Techniques for solving every kind of ASVAB algebra and probability problem**

- **Tips and strategies to help you raise your ASVAB Arithmetic Reasoning and Mathematics Knowledge scores**

The following pages offer a quick but important overview of the basic algebra and probability that you need to know in order to score well on the ASVAB. Make sure that you carefully review and test yourself on every topic covered in this section. Also make sure that you learn how to use all of the problem-solving methods presented in the examples.

Suggested Review Plan for Algebra and Probability

- Take the Algebra and Probability Quiz.
- Score your quiz.
- Study any problems that you answered incorrectly. Reread the corresponding review section, then try the problem again. Work until you understand how to solve the problem.
- Work through the Algebra and Probability Review at your own pace.

- Pay careful attention to the examples provided.

Remember that while you probably won't get these exact problems on the ASVAB, knowing how to solve them will help you do your best on the actual test.

ALGEBRA AND PROBABILITY QUIZ

Circle the letter that represents the best or correct answer. Check your answers with those on page 170. If any of your answers are wrong, go back and study the relevant section of the algebra review.

1. The phrase "some number plus 20" is the same as

   A. $j + 20$
   B. $j - 20$
   C. $\dfrac{j}{20}$
   D. $j \times 20$

2. Evaluate: $a + 2(b) - (c)$ if $a = 5$, $b = 3$, and $c = 2$

   A. 7
   B. 9
   C. 10
   D. 11

   $5 + 2(\times 3) - 2$
   $5 + 6 = 11 - 2 = 9$

3. Solve for z: $32 + z = 12$

   A. -20
   B. -12
   C. 12
   D. 20

   $32 + z = 12$
   $32 - 32 + z = 12 - 32$
   $z = 20$

4. The proportion "a is to b is as 3 is to 6" can be represented as

   A. $a + b = 3 + 6$
   B. $a \times b = 3 \times 6 + 45$
   C. $a(3) + b(6)$
   D. $\dfrac{a}{b} = \dfrac{3}{6}$

5. Solve for each variable.

   $y + g = 12$ and $2y + 3g = 16$

   A. $g = 15$, $y = -3$
   B. $g = 5$, $y = 7$
   C. $g = 1$, $y = 11$
   D. $g = -8$, $y = 20$

   $y + g = 12$
   $2y + 3g = 16$
   $3y + 4g = 28$

6. Add:

   $45g$
   $-90g$

   A. $-45g$
   B. $45g$
   C. $45g^2$
   D. $135g$

7. Subtract:

   100
   -130
   $\overline{-30}$

   A. -230
   B. -30
   C. 30
   D. 230

8. Multiply: $(g^3)(g^{12})$

   A. g^{-3}
   B. g^{15}
   C. g^{-15}
   D. g^{36}

   12
   $\times\ 3$
   $\overline{36}$

9. Add:

   $g^2 + gh + h^2 + 3g^2 + 4gh + 3h^2 =$

   A. $2g^2 + 3gh + 2h^2$
   B. $2g^2 + 5gh + 4h^2$
   C. $4g^2 + 5gh + 4h^2$
   D. $4g^2 + 3gh + 2h^2$

   $4g^2 + 5gh + 4h^2$

10. Multiply:

    $3h - 2m$
    $\times\ 2h + m$
    $\overline{6h^2 - 2m^2}$

    A. $5h^2 + 3m^2$
    B. $6h^2 - hm - 2m^2$
    C. $6h^2 + 5hm + 2m^2$
    D. $6h^2 + 4hm + 2m^2$

11. Factor: $x^2 + 4x - 12$

   A. $(2x^2 + 1 + 6)(-x^2 + 3x - 2)$
   B. $(x + 6)(x - 2)$ $x^2 + -12$
   C. $(x + 4)(x + 3)$ $x^2 + 4x + 3x + 12$
   D. $(x^2 + 2)(x^{-2} + 4)$

   $(x + 6)(x - 2)$ $x^2 - 12$

12. Reduce to lowest terms:

   $\dfrac{6x - 6}{8x - 8}$ $\dfrac{6x - 3}{8x - 4}$ $\dfrac{3x - 3}{4x - 4}$

   A. $x - 2$

   B. $\dfrac{3x}{4x}$

   C. $\dfrac{6x}{8x}$

   D. $\dfrac{3}{4}$

13. Multiply:

   $\dfrac{j^2}{2j} \times \dfrac{2j}{3g}$ $\dfrac{2j^3}{6jg}$

   A. $\dfrac{3j^2}{6j}$

   B. $\dfrac{2j^3}{6jg}$

   C. $\dfrac{2j^2}{6jg}$

   D. $\dfrac{j^2}{3g}$

14. Divide:

   $\dfrac{8g^3}{15} \div \dfrac{6g^2}{3}$ $\dfrac{8g^3}{15} \div \dfrac{6g^2}{3}$

   A. $\dfrac{48g^5}{45}$

   B. $\dfrac{2g^5}{12}$

   C. $\dfrac{4g}{15}$

   D. $\dfrac{4g^3}{15g^2}$

   $\dfrac{8g^3}{15} \times \dfrac{3}{6g^2} = \dfrac{8g^3 \cdot 1}{15 \cdot 6g^2}$

   $8 \times 6 = 48g^3$

   $15 \times 3 = 45$

15. Which equation is represented by the following graph?

   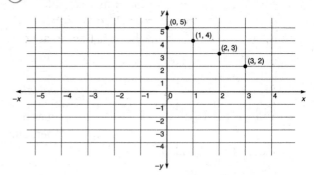

   A. $2x + y = 0$
   B. $x^2 + 1 = 0$
   C. $x + y = 5$
   D. $2x + y = 7$

16. Using a number cube with sides labeled 1 through 6, what is the probability of throwing a 3 or a 4?

   A. 2 in 4
   B. 1 in 3
   C. 2 in 8
   D. 1 in 9

ALGEBRA AND PROBABILITY REVIEW

<table>
<tr><td colspan="2" align="center">Topics</td></tr>
<tr><td>The language of algebra</td><td>Factoring a polynomial</td></tr>
<tr><td>Evaluating expressions</td><td>Solving quadratic equations</td></tr>
<tr><td>Solving equations for one unknown</td><td>Algebraic fractions</td></tr>
<tr><td>Inequalities</td><td>Graphing on a number line</td></tr>
<tr><td>Ratios and proportions</td><td>Graphing on a coordinate plane</td></tr>
<tr><td>Solving equations for two unknowns</td><td>Probability</td></tr>
<tr><td>Monomials, binomials, and polynomials</td><td></td></tr>
</table>

The Language of Algebra

Algebra uses arithmetic functions and processes, but some of the numbers are replaced by letters. The letters merely represent numbers that either are currently unknown or can change in value according to circumstances. In algebra, a letter representing a number that can change in value is called a *variable*.

- The expression $6x$ means "6 times x or x times 6."
- The expression $x + 7$ means "some number, currently unknown, plus 7."

- The expression $x - 12$ means "some number, currently unknown, less 12."
- The expression means "some number, currently unknown, divided by 5" or "the ratio of some number and 5."

Very often verbal expressions in word problems need to be translated into algebraic expressions before the problems can be solved. Below are some examples of verbal expressions and their algebraic counterparts.

Verbal Expression	Algebraic Expression
Some number plus 7	$x + 7$
Some number subtracted from 8	$8 - x$
8 subtracted from some number	$x - 8$
The product of some number and 12	$12x$
The product of 5 and the sum of x and y	$5(x + y)$
Some number divided by 4	$\frac{x}{4}$
The ratio of 6 and some number	$\frac{6}{x}$
9 times some number plus the sum of 5 and y	$9x + (5 + y)$
12 less the sum of 3 and some number	$12 - (3 + x)$

Practice Items–Algebra Language   Write the following using algebraic expressions.

1. Six times some number plus four squared
2. Twelve times the sum of six plus some number
3. The product of x and y times the product of 11 plus the product of x and y.
4. Some number divided by 40 and the product of x and y.
5. Some number squared plus that number times 14 equals minus 21.

Evaluating Expressions

To evaluate an algebraic expression, substitute a given value for the unknown and then perform the arithmetic as indicated.

Examples

Evaluate $a + b + c$ if $a = 2$, $b = 4$, and $c = 3$.

Substitute each value for the corresponding letter and then do the addition as indicated.

$$2 + 4 + 3 = 9$$

Evaluate $2x^2 + 4y + 5$ if $x = 2$ and $y = 3$.

$$2(2)^2 + 4(3) + 5 = 2(4) + 12 + 5$$
$$= 8 + 12 + 5$$
$$= 25$$

Evaluate $\dfrac{a + b}{4} + \dfrac{a}{b + c}$ if $a = 2$, $b = 6$, and $c = 10$

$$\frac{2 + 6}{4} + \frac{2}{6 + 10} = \frac{8}{4} + \frac{2}{16}$$
$$= 2 + \frac{2}{16}$$
$$= 2\frac{1}{8}$$

u can skip $8 = \frac{1}{8}$

Don't Forget:

Order of operations is critical!

- Simplify anything within the parentheses.
- Apply the powers or exponents.
- Multiply and divide in order from left to right.
- Add and subtract in order from left to right.

<u>Practice Items—Evaluating Expressions</u>   Evaluate the following:

1. $x + y + z$ if $x = 2$, $y = 6$, $z = 10$ $= 18$

2. $(x + y)^2 + (y - 1)$ if $x = 8$, $y = 4$ $= 147$

3. $6x + (y + z)^2$ if $x = 5$, $y = 2$, $z = 3$ $= 55$

Solving Equations for One Unknown

An *equation* is a mathematical statement that contains an equal (=) sign. When an equation contains a letter standing for an unknown number, you can use the equation to find the value of that unknown. This is called *solving the equation for the unknown.*

Think of an equation as a balanced scale. Everything to the right of the = sign has to balance with everything on the left side of the = sign.

Because an equation is balanced, it will stay in balance if you do the same thing to the numbers on both sides of the = sign. For example, the equation $10 = 10$ will stay balanced if you add 3 to both sides. The new equation will be $13 = 13$. Similarly, the equation $x + y = x + y$ will stay balanced if you subtract 10 from both sides. The new equation will be $x + y - 10 = x + y - 10$.

Similarly, the equation $x + y = a + b$ will stay balanced if you add 8 to both sides. The new equation will be $x + y + 8 = a + b + 8$.

To solve an equation and find the value of an unknown, you need to get the *unknown on one side of the equation* and all the other terms on the other side of the equation. Consider this example.

Solve: $y - 4 = 20$

Add 4 to both sides:

$$y - 4 + 4 = 20 + 4$$
$$y = 20 + 4$$
$$y = 24$$

Another Way to Think About It

Here is a simple way to think about using addition or subtraction to solve an equation: just move the number you are adding or subtracting from one side of the = sign to the other and change its sign (either − to + or + to −). So in the equation shown, move the − 4 to the other side of the = sign and make it + 4. This makes the equation $y = 20 + 4$ or 24.

An equation will also stay balanced if you multiply or divide both sides by the same number. So you can also use these operations to solve equations.

Example (Division)

Solve: $3x = 18$

You want to get x all alone on the left side of the equation, so divide $3x$ by 3. Since $3/3 = 1$, $3x/3 = x$. To maintain the balance, divide the right side of the equation by 3 as well: $\dfrac{18}{3} = 6$. So $x = 6$.

Another Way to Think About It

Here is another way to think about using division to solve an equation: in a problem such as $3x = 18$, instead of trying to divide both sides by 3, simply move the 3 across the $=$ sign and make it the denominator of the other side of the equation:

$$3x = 18$$
$$x = \frac{18}{3}$$
$$x = 6$$

Example (Multiplication)

$$\frac{x}{3} = 12$$

Multiply both sides by 3:

$$3\frac{x}{3} = 33(12)$$
$$x = 3(12)$$
$$x = 36$$

Another Way to Think About It

Here is another way to think about using multiplication to solve an equation: in a problem such as $x/2 = 20$, move the denominator 2 across the $=$ sign and make it the multiplier on the other side.

$$x/2 = 20$$
$$x = 2(20)$$
$$x = 40$$

Examples

Solve for z:

$$16 + z = 24$$

Subtract 16 from both sides.

$$z = 24 - 16 = 8$$

Solve for x:

$$\frac{x}{5} - 4 = 2$$

Add 4 to both sides.

$$\frac{x}{5} = 2 + 4$$
$$\frac{x}{5} = 6$$

Multiply each side by 5 to isolate x on the left side.

$$x = 5(6) = 30$$

Solve for a:

$$\frac{2}{3}a - 5 = 9$$

Add 5 to both sides.

$$\frac{2}{3}a = 9 + 5$$
$$\frac{2}{3}a = 14$$

Multiply each side by $\frac{3}{2}$.

$$a = 14(\frac{3}{2})$$
$$a = \frac{42}{2} = 21$$

Divide Out Common Factors

Another way to do this final step is to divide out common factors.

$$\frac{\overset{7}{\cancel{14}}}{1} \times \frac{3}{\underset{1}{\cancel{2}}} = 21$$

Solve for y:

$$7y = 3y - 12$$
$$7y - 3y = -12$$
$$4y = -12$$
$$y = -\frac{12}{4}$$
$$y = -3$$

Practice Items—Solving Equations for One Unknown
Solve for the unknown in each equation.

1. $20 + z = 32$ $= 10$

2. $\frac{x}{10} - 5 = 25$ $= 255$

3. $\frac{x}{3} - 15$ $(?)$

4. $y - 12 = -20$ -8

Inequalities

Unlike equations, inequalities are statements that show that certain relationships between selected variables and numbers are *not* equal. Instead of using the equal sign, you use the "greater than" sign (>) or the "less than" sign (<). At times you may see signs for "greater than or equal to" ( ) or "less than or equal to" ( ).

Examples

$x > 13$ means that the value of x is greater than 13.

$y < 45$ means that the value of y is less than 45.

$x - y < 33$ means that when y is subtracted from x, the result is less than 33.

$\frac{x}{5}$ z means that when x divided by 5, the result is greater than or equal to the value of z.

Solving Inequalities If you work problems with inequalities, you can treat them much like equations. If you multiply or divide both sides by a negative number, you must reverse the sign.

Examples

Solve for x:

$$3x + 5 > 8$$
$$3x + 5 - 5 > 8 - 5 \text{ Subtract 5 from both sides.}$$
$$3x > 3 \text{ Divide each side by 3.}$$
$$x > 1$$

Solve for x:

$$5 - 2x > 9$$
$$5 - 5 - 2x > 9 - 5 \text{ Subtract 5 from both sides.}$$
$$-2x > 4 \text{ Divide by } -2 \text{ (Be sure to reverse the sign, since you are dividing by a negative number.)}$$
$$x < 2$$

Practice Items–Solving Inequalities   Solve for each unknown.

1. $15 - 2x > 9$ $x < 3$

2. $33 + 3y < 12$ $y < 6\frac{3}{6}$

Ratios and Proportions

A *ratio* is a comparison of one number to another. A ratio can be represented by a fraction.

Example

On a certain road, there are 6 cars for every 4 trucks. The ratio is $\frac{6}{4}$ or $\frac{3}{2}$.

A *proportion* is an equation stating that two ratios are equivalent. Ratios are equivalent if they can be represented by equivalent fractions. A proportion may be written

$$\frac{a}{b} = \frac{c}{d}$$

where *a/b* and *c/d* are equivalent fractions. This proportion can be read "*a* is to *b* as *c* is to *d*."

Like any other equation, a proportion can be solved for an unknown by isolating that unknown on one side of the equation. In this case, to solve for *a*, multiply both sides by *b*:

$$(b)\frac{a}{b} = (b)\frac{c}{d}$$
$$a = \frac{bc}{d}$$

Examples

Solve for p:

$$\frac{c}{p} = \frac{h}{j}$$

Multiply both sides by *p*.

$$(p)\frac{c}{p} = (p)\frac{h}{j}$$
$$c = \frac{ph}{j}$$

Solve for a:

$$\frac{a}{4} = \frac{3}{6}$$
$$(4)\frac{a}{4} = (4)\frac{3}{6}$$
$$a = \frac{12}{6}$$
$$a = 2$$

Another Way to Solve It

Another way to solve proportion problems is to find the cross products.

Solve for *a*:

$$a/4 = 3/6$$

Cross-multiply:

$$a \times 6 = 4 \times 3$$
$$6a = 12$$
$$a = 2$$

Solve for k:

$$\frac{2}{5} = \frac{8}{k}$$

$$2k = 40$$

$$k = 20$$

Practice Items—Ratios and Proportions

1. Solve for m: $\dfrac{2}{5} = \dfrac{16}{m}$ $m = 40$

2. Solve for q: $\dfrac{2}{5} = \dfrac{q}{16}$ $q = 6\frac{2}{5}$

3. Solve for d: $\dfrac{a}{b} = \dfrac{c}{d}$ $d =$

Solving Equations for Two Unknowns

An equation may have two unknowns. An example is $3a + 3b = 9$. If you are given two equations with the same unknowns, you can solve for each unknown. Here is how this process works.

Solve for a and b:

$$3a + 4b = 9$$
$$2a + 2b = 6$$

Follow these steps:

Step 1. Multiply one or both equations by a number that makes the number in front of one of the unknowns the same in both equations.

Multiply the second equation by 2 to make $4b$ in each equation.

$$2(2a + 2b = 6)$$
$$4a + 4b = 12$$

Step 2. Add or subtract the two equations to eliminate one unknown. Then solve for the remaining unknown.

$$\begin{array}{r} 3a + 4b = 9 \\ 2a + 2b = 6 \\ \hline -a \quad\quad = -3 \\ a \quad\quad = 3 \end{array}$$

Step 3. Insert the value for the unknown that you have found into one of the two equations. Then solve for the other unknown.

$$3a + 4b = 9$$
$$3(3) + 4b = 9$$
$$9 + 4b = 9$$
$$4b = 0$$
$$b = 0$$

Answer: $a = 3$, $b = 0$

Examples

Solve for j and k:

$$j + k = 7$$
$$j - k = 3$$

You can skip Step 1 of the solution process because the number in front of each of the unknowns is understood to be 1.

Step 2. Add the equations.

$$\begin{array}{r} j + k = 7 \\ j - k = 3 \\ \hline 2j \quad = 10 \\ j \quad = 5 \end{array}$$

Step 3. Substitute the solution for j into one of the equations and solve for k.

$$5 + k = 7$$
$$k = 7 - 5$$
$$k = 2$$

Solve for c and d:

$$3c + 4d = 2$$
$$6c + 6d = 0$$

Step 1. Multiply the first equation by 2.

$$2(3c + 4d = 2)$$
$$6c + 8d = 4$$

Step 2. Subtract the two equations and solve for one unknown.

$$\begin{array}{r} 6c + 8d = 4 \\ 6c + 6d = 0 \\ \hline 2d \quad = 4 \\ d \quad = 2 \end{array}$$

Step 3. Substitute the solution for *d* into one of the equations and solve for *c*.

$$3c + 4(2) = 2$$
$$3c + 8 = 2$$
$$3c = -6$$
$$c = -2$$

Answer: $d = 2$, $c = -2$

Practice Items–Solving Equations for Two Unknowns
Solve for *a* and *b*:

1. $3a + 4b = 12$
   $2a + 2b = 6$

2. $6a + 8b = 20$
   $4a - 4b = 4$

Monomials, Binomials, and Polynomials

You can guess by the prefix *mono-* that a monomial has something to do with "one." A *monomial* is a mathematical expression consisting of only one term. Examples include $12x$, $3a^2$, and $9abc$.

A *binomial* (the prefix *bi-* means "two") has exactly two terms: $12z + j$.

A *polynomial*, as indicated by the prefix *poly-*, meaning "many," has two or more terms. Examples include $x + y$, $x + y + z$, and $y^2 - 2z + 12$.

Adding and Subtracting Monomials If the variables are the same, just add or subtract the numbers.

Examples

Add:

$$\begin{array}{r} 9y \\ +11y \\ \hline 20y \end{array}$$

Subtract:

$$\begin{array}{r} 30b \\ -15b \\ \hline 15b \end{array}$$

Add:

$$\begin{array}{r} 12a^2bc \\ + 4a^2bc \\ \hline 16a^2bc \end{array}$$

Subtract:

$$\begin{array}{r} 12a^2bc \\ - 4a^2bc \\ \hline 8a^2bc \end{array}$$

Multiplying Monomials When multiplying monomials, multiply any numbers, then multiply unknowns. Add any exponents. Keep in mind that in a term like *x* or $2x$, the *x* is understood to have the exponent 1 even though the 1 is not shown.

Examples

$$(2k)(k) = 2k^2$$
$$(3x)(2y) = 6xy$$
$$(k^2)(k^3) = k^5$$
$$(j^3k)(j^2k^3) = j^5k^4$$
$$-5(b^4c)(-3b^3c^5) = 15b^7c^6$$

Dividing Monomials To divide monomials, divide the numbers and subtract any exponents (the exponent of the divisor from the exponent of the number being divided).

Examples

$$\frac{2g^5}{6g^3} = \frac{1}{3}g^2$$

$$3\frac{g^5}{g^3} = 3g^2$$

$$\frac{12a^6b^2}{3a^3b} = 4a^3b$$

$$m^5/m^8 = m^{-3} = 1/m^3$$

$$\frac{-5(ab)(ab^2)}{ab} =$$

This example can be handled in two ways. One way is to simplify the numerator:

$$\frac{-5a^2b^3}{ab} = -5ab^2$$

Another way is to divide out similar terms:

$$\frac{-5(\cancel{ab})(ab^2)}{\cancel{ab}} = -5ab^2$$

Either way works just fine and will give you the correct answer.

<u>Practice Items–Monomials</u>

1. Add:

$$6a^2bc$$
$$+3a^2bc$$

2. Subtract:

$$12a^2bc$$
$$-16a^2bc$$

3. Multiply:

$$5(g^4c)\,(-3g^3c^5)$$

4. Divide:

$$\frac{3x^3y^5}{xy^2}$$

Adding and Subtracting Polynomials Arrange the expressions in columns with like terms in the same column. Add or subtract like terms.

Examples (Addition)

Add:

$$j^2 + jk + k^2$$
$$+\ 3j^2 + 4jk - 2k^2$$
$$\overline{\ \ 4j^2 + 5jk - k^2}$$

Add:

$$3p^3 + 2pq + p^2 + r^3$$
$$+\ 2p^3 - 6pq + 2p^2 + 3r^3$$
$$+\ -p3 + pq + 3p2 - 6r3$$
$$\overline{\ \ 4p^3 - 3pq + 6p^2 - 2r^3}$$

Examples (Subtraction)

Remember that when you subtract negative terms, you change the sign and add.

Subtract:

$$j^2 + jk + k^2$$
$$-3j^2 + 4jk - 2k^2$$ (Change this last term to $+2k^2$ and add k^2 terms.)

$$\overline{-2j^2 - 3jk + 3k^2}$$

Subtract:

$$9pq^3 + 3ab - 12m^2$$
$$-3pq^3 + 2ab - 15m^2$$
$$\overline{\ \ 6pq^3 + ab + 3m^2}$$

Multiplying Polynomials To multiply polynomials, multiply each term in the first polynomial by each term in the second polynomial. The process is just like regular multiplication. For example, if you multiply 43 times 12, the problem looks like this:

$$43$$
$$\times 12$$
$$\overline{86}$$ Multiply 2×3 and 2×4 to make 86.
$$\underline{43}$$ Then multiply 1×3 and 1×4 to make 43.
$$516$$ Add the results.

Using polynomials, the process is just the same.

Examples

Multiply:

$$2g - 2h$$
$$\times\ 3g + h$$

$$2gh - 2h^2$$ Multiply $h \times 2g$ and $h \times -2h$ to make $2gh - 2h^2$.
$$6g^2 - 6gh$$ Multiply $3g \times 2g$ and $3g \times -2h$ to make $+6g^2 - 6gh$.

$$\overline{6g^2 - 4gh - 2h^2}$$ Add.

Multiply:

$$3b + a$$
$$2b - 2a$$

$$-6ab - 2a^2$$ Multiply $-2a \times 3b$ and $-2a \times a$ to make $-6ab - 2a^2$.
$$6b^2 + 2ab$$ Multiply $2b \times 3b$ and $2b \times a$ to make $6b^2 + 2ab$.

$$\overline{6b^2 - 4ab - 2a^2}$$ Add.

Dividing a Polynomial by a Monomial Just divide the monomial into each term of the polynomial.

Examples

Divide:

$$\frac{8b^2+2b}{2b} = \frac{8b^2}{2b} + \frac{2b}{2b}$$

$$= 4b + 1$$

Divide:

$$\frac{9c^3+6c^2+3c}{3c} = \frac{9c^3}{3c} + \frac{6c^2}{3c} + \frac{3c}{3c}$$

$$= 3c^2 + 2c + 1$$

Dividing a Polynomial by a Polynomial To divide a polynomial by another polynomial, first make sure that the terms in each polynomial are in descending order (i.e., cube→square→first power).

For example, $6c + 3c^2 + 9$ should be written $3c^2 + 6c + 9$.

$10 + 2c + 5c^2$ should be written $5c^2 + 2c + 10$.

Then use long division to solve the problem.

Example

Divide $(a^2 + 18a + 45)$ by $(a + 3)$.

$$a + 3 \overline{)a^2 + 18a + 45}$$

$$\begin{array}{r} a + 15 \\ a + 3 \overline{)a^2 + 18a + 45} \end{array}$$

$a^2 + 3a$ Multiply a times $a + 3$ and subtract the result, leaving $15a$.

_____

$+15a + 45$ Bring down the 45 and continue by dividing a into $15a$.

$+15a + 45$

_____ Subtracting $15a + 45$ from $15a + 45$ gives zero.

0

Check your work by multiplying $(a + 3)(a + 15)$ to get $a^2 + 18a + 45$.

> **A Faster Way?**
>
> If you run into a problem like this one on the ASVAB, it might be quicker to multiply the divisor (in this case, $a + 3$) by each answer choice to see which choice produces the dividend (in this case. $a^2 + 18a + 45$).

Practice Items—Adding, Subtracting, Multiplying, and Dividing Polynomials

1. Add:

    $-2s^3 + 8sq + 12s^2 + r^3$
    $2s^3 - 6sq + 2s^2 + 3r^3$
    $-s^3 + sq + 3s^2 - 8r^3$
    _____

2. Subtract:

    $9pq^3 + 3xy - 5r^2$
    $-3pq3 + 2xy - 15r^2$
    _____

3. Multiply:

    $3g + 5a$
    $2g - 2a$
    _____

4. Multiply:

    $3h + 9j + 3$
    $\underline{ 2j + 2}$

5. Divide:

    $$\frac{16j^2 + 4j}{4j}$$

6. Divide:

    Divide $(a^2 + 18a + 32)$ by $(a + 2)$

Factoring a Polynomial

A *factor* is a number that is multiplied to give a product. *Factoring* a mathematical expression is the process of finding out which numbers when multiplied together produce the expression.

To factor a polynomial, follow these two steps:

- Find the largest common monomial in the polynomial. This is the first factor.

- Divide the polynomial by that monomial. The result will be the second factor.

Examples

Factor the following expression:

$$5y^2 + 3y$$

y is the largest common monomial.

$$(5y^2 + 3y)/y = 5y + 3$$

y and $5y + 3$ are the two factors.

Factor the following expression:

$$8x^3 + 2x^2$$

$2x^2$ is the largest common monomial.

$$(8x^3 + 2x^2)/2x^2 = 4x + 1$$

$2x^2$ and $4x + 1$ are the two factors.

To check your work, multiply the two factors. The result should be the original expression.

$$\begin{array}{r} 4x + 1 \\ 2x^2 \\ \hline 8x^3 + 2x^2 \end{array}$$

Special Case: Factoring the Difference between Two Squares
Sometimes you may be asked to factor an expression in which each term is a perfect square.

Examples

Factor the following expression:

$$y^2 - 100$$

In this expression, each term is a perfect square; that is, each one has a real-number square root. The square root of y^2 is y, and the square root of 100 is 10.

When an expression is the difference between two squares, its factors are the sum of the squares $(y + 10)$ and the difference of the squares $(y - 10)$. Multiplying the plus sign and the minus sign in the factors gives the minus sign in the original expression.

> **Remember the Rules for Multiplying Positive and Negative Terms.**
>
> Don't forget that the product of a positive term $(+)$ and a negative term $(-)$ is a negative term $(-)$.

Factoring Polynomials in the Form $ax^2 + bx + c$, where a, b, and c Are Numbers
Remember that you want to find two factors that when multiplied together produce the original expression.

Examples

Factor the expression:

$$x^2 + 5x + 6$$

First, you know that x times x will give x^2, so it is likely that each factor is going to start with x.

$$(x)\,(x)$$

Now you need to find two factors of 6 that, when added together, give the middle term of 5. Some options are 1 and 6 and 2 and 3. 2 and 3 add to 5, so add those numbers to your factors. Now you have

$$(x\ 2)\,(x\ 3)$$

Finally, deal with the sign. Since the original expression is all positive, both signs in the factors must be positive. So the two factors must be

$$(x + 2)\,(x + 3)$$

Check your work by multiplying the two factors to see if you come up with the original expression.

$$(x + 2)\,(x + 3) = x^2 + 5x + 6$$

Factor the expression:

$$6x^2 + 8x - 8$$

$6x^2$ can be factored into either $(6x)(x)$ or $(2x)(3x)$. Using the latter, the first terms in our factors are as follows:

$$(2x)\,(3x)$$

Now let's consider the -8. Factors of 8 can be $(8)(1)$ or $(2)(4)$. Let's try 2 and 4, so our factors are now

$$(2x\ 2)(3x\ 4)$$

Now for the signs. In order to get a -8 in the original expression, one of the numbers must be a negative and the other a positive. Let's try making the 4 negative, making the factors

$$(2x + 2)(3x - 4) = 6x^2 - 2x - 8$$

That's close, but the original expression was $6x^2 + 8x - 8$, not $6x^2 - 2x - 8$. What if we switched the numbers 2 and 4?

$$(2x + 4)(3x - 2) = 6x^2 + 8x - 8$$

Now the factors give the original expression when multiplied together, so this is the correct answer.

It Helps to Practice

Don't worry about factoring. Factoring is a little bit of intuition and a lot of practice. Once you do a lot of these kinds of problems, factoring will become almost second nature.

Practice Items–Factoring Polynomials Factor the following expressions:

1. $6y^2 + 2y$

2. $2x^2 + 11x + 12$

3. $6x^2 - 7x - 20$

4. $4x^2 + 5x + 1$

5. $7x^2 - 20x - 3$

Solving Quadratic Equations

A quadratic equation is one that is written in the form $ax^2 + bx + c$, where a, b, and c are numbers.

To solve an equation in this form for x, set the expression equal to zero. x will have more than one value.

There are several steps necessary to solve these equations.

- Put all the terms of the expression on one side of the = sign and set the expression equal to zero.
- Factor the equation.
- Set each factor equal to zero.
- Solve the equations.

Examples

Solve:

$$x^2 + 7x = -10$$
$$x^2 + 7x + 10 = 0$$

Add 10 to both sides in order to get all the terms on one side of the = sign. Now the expression is equal to 0.

$(x + 5)(x + 2) = 0$ Factor the equation.
$x + 5 = 0; x + 2 = 0$ Set each factor equal to zero.
$x = -5; x = -2$ Solve the equations.

Check your answer by substituting each value back into the original equation.

$$x^2 + 7x = -10$$
$$(-5)^2 + 7(-5) = -10$$
$$25 - 35 = -10$$
$$(-2)^2 + 7(-2) = -10$$
$$4 - 14 = -10$$

Solve for y:

$$y^2 - 4y = 12$$
$y^2 - 4y - 12 = 0$ Move all terms to one side and set the equation equal to zero.
$(y - 6)(y + 2) = 0$ Factor.
$y - 6 = 0; y + 2 = 0$ Set each factor equal to zero.
$y = 6; y = -2$ Solve the equations.

Practice Items–Solving Quadratic Equations

1. Solve for y: $y^2 - 16 = 0$

2. Solve for x: $x^2 - 6x = 27$

3. Solve for y: $y^2 - 6y = 27$

4. Solve for g: $g^2 - 10g = -21$

Algebraic Fractions

An algebraic fraction is a fraction containing one or more unknowns.

Reducing Algebraic Fractions to Lowest Terms To reduce an algebraic fraction to lowest terms, factor the numerator and denominator. Cancel out or divide out common factors.

Examples

Reduce to lowest terms:

$\dfrac{3y-3}{4y-4} = \dfrac{3\,(y-1)}{4\,(y-1)}$ Factor each expression.

$= \dfrac{3\,(y\!\!-\!\!1)}{4\,(y\!\!-\!\!1)}$ Divide out common terms.

$= \dfrac{3}{4}$ Reduce the fraction to lowest terms.

Division Reminder

Don't divide out common terms from a term that includes an addition or subtraction sign.

For example, in a term such as , $\dfrac{x+2}{2}$ you cannot divide out the 2s.

WRONG: $\dfrac{x+\cancel{2}}{\cancel{2}}$

$\dfrac{k^2 + 2k + 1}{3k + 3}$

$= \dfrac{(k+1)\,(k+1)}{3\,(k+1)}$ Factor each expression.

$= \dfrac{(k+1)\,(k\!\!-\!\!1)}{3\,(k\!\!-\!\!1)}$ Divide out common terms.

$= \dfrac{k+1}{3}$

Practice Items–Reducing Algebraic Fractions to Lowest Terms   Reduce to lowest terms:

1. $\dfrac{6y-6}{4y-4}$

2. $\dfrac{k^2 + 2k + 1}{3k + 3}$

3. $\dfrac{2x^2 + 11x + 12}{x + 4}$

Adding or Subtracting Algebraic Fractions with a Common Denominator
To add or subtract algebraic functions that have a common denominator, combine the numerators and keep the result over the denominator. Reduce to lowest terms where possible.

Examples

$\dfrac{3y + 9y}{m} = \dfrac{12y}{m}$

$\dfrac{9y - 8}{z} - \dfrac{6y - 6}{z}$

$= \dfrac{9y - 8 - 6y - (-6)}{3k + 3}$

$= \dfrac{9y - 6y - 8 + 6}{3k + 3}$

$= \dfrac{3y - 2}{z}$

Practice Items–Adding or Subtracting Algebraic Fractions with a Common Denominator

1. $\dfrac{10g - 2}{h} - \dfrac{g + 4}{h}$

2. $\dfrac{12j + 2}{m} - \dfrac{22j - 16}{m}$

Adding or Subtracting Algebraic Fractions with Different Denominators
To add or subtract algebraic fractions that have different denominators, examine the denominators and find the least common denominator. Then change each fraction to the equivalent fraction with that least common denominator. Combine the numerators as shown in the previous section. If needed, reduce the result to lowest terms.

Examples

$7/a + 12/b = 7b/ab + 12a/ab$ Note that ab is the least common denominator.

$= (12a + 7b)/ab$

$\dfrac{g + 2}{4x} + \dfrac{g - 5}{6x}$ In this example, $12x$ is the least common denominator, as $4x$ and $6x$ both divide into it

$= \dfrac{3}{3} \times \dfrac{g+2}{4x} + \dfrac{2}{2} \times \dfrac{g-5}{6x}$ Note that you have to multiply in order to make each term contain the least common denominator

$= \dfrac{3g+6}{12x} + \dfrac{2g+10}{12x}$

$= \dfrac{3g+6+2g-10}{12x}$

$= \dfrac{5g-4}{12x}$

<u>Practice Items–Adding or Subtracting Algebraic Fractions with Different Denominators</u>

1. $\dfrac{k+4}{4x} + \dfrac{k-5}{2x}$

2. $\dfrac{x+2}{3x} - \dfrac{x-3}{6x}$

Multiplying Algebraic Fractions When multiplying algebraic fractions, factor any numerator and denominator polynomials. Divide out common terms where possible. Multiply the remaining terms in the numerator and denominator together. Be sure that the result is in lowest terms.

Examples

Multiply the following fractions:

$\dfrac{y^2}{2j} \times \dfrac{2j}{3y} = \dfrac{2y^2 j}{6yj}$

$= \dfrac{2\cancel{y^2}\cancel{j}}{6\cancel{y}j} = \dfrac{1y}{3} = \dfrac{y}{3}$ Divide out common terms, then multiply. Reduce to lowest terms.

Multiply the following fractions:

$\dfrac{6}{x+1} \times \dfrac{3x+3}{6}$

$= \dfrac{6}{x+1} \times \dfrac{3\,(x+1)}{6}$ Factor where possible.

$= \dfrac{\cancel{6}}{\cancel{x+1}} \times \dfrac{3\,(\cancel{x+1})}{\cancel{6}} =$ Divide out common terms and multiply.

$= 3$

<u>Practice Items–Multiplying Algebraic Fractions</u>

1. $\dfrac{9}{x+1} \times \dfrac{3x+3}{3}$

2. $\left(\dfrac{5}{h+1}\right)\left(\dfrac{3h+3}{6}\right)$

Dividing Algebraic Fractions To divide algebraic fractions, follow the same process used to divide regular fractions: invert one fraction and multiply.

Examples

Divide the following fractions:

$\dfrac{3k^2}{5} \div \dfrac{2k}{z}$

$= \dfrac{3k^2}{5} \times \dfrac{z}{2k}$ Invert the second fraction and multiply.

$= \dfrac{3\cancel{k^2}}{5} \times \dfrac{z}{2\cancel{k}}$ Simplify where possible.

$= \dfrac{3kz}{10}$

Divide the following fractions.

$\dfrac{8m^3}{15} \div \dfrac{6m^2}{3}$

$= \dfrac{8m^3}{15} \times \dfrac{3}{6m^2}$ Invert and multiply.

$= \dfrac{\cancel{8}m^3}{\cancel{15}} \times \dfrac{\cancel{3}}{\cancel{6}m^2}$ Simplify where possible.

$= \dfrac{4m}{5} \times \dfrac{1}{3} = \dfrac{4m}{15}$

<u>Practice Items–Dividing Algebraic Fractions</u>

1. $\dfrac{4p^3}{15} \div \dfrac{2p^2}{3}$

2. $\dfrac{p^2}{5} \div p^2$

Graphing on a Number Line

You can represent a number as a point on a number line, as shown in the following examples. Representing a number on a number line is called *graphing*. Note that whole numbers on the line are equally spaced. Note too that in these examples, both positive and negative numbers are represented.

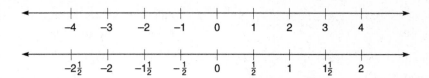

On the number line, positive numbers are shown to the right of zero. Negative numbers are shown to the left of zero. The positive number $+3$ is three units to the right of zero. The negative number -2 is two units to the left of zero.

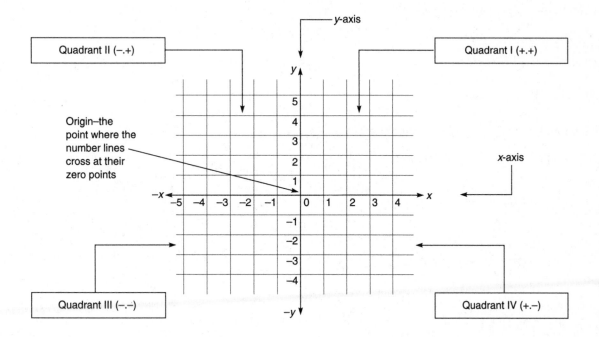

Graphing on a Coordinate Plane

A coordinate plane is based on an x axis (horizontal number line) and a y axis (vertical number line). The axes intersect at their zero points. This point of intersection is called the *origin*. Every point on the plane has both an x coordinate and a y coordinate.

The x coordinate tells the number of units to the right of the origin (for positive numbers) or to the left of the origin (for negative numbers). The y coordinate tells the number of units above the origin (for positive numbers) or below the origin (for negative numbers).

The coordinates of each point are often shown in what is called an *ordered pair* of numbers. An ordered pair looks like this: (2,3). In every ordered pair, the first number is the x coordinate and the second number is the y coordinate. So the ordered pair (2,3) identifies a point with an x coordinate of 2 and a y coordinate of 3. The point is located at the intersection of the vertical line that is 2 units to the right of the origin ($x = +2$) and the horizontal line that is 3 units above the origin ($y = +3$). The point $(2,-3)$ is located at the intersection of the vertical line that is 2 units to the right of the origin ($x = +2$) and the horizontal line that is 3 units below the origin ($y = -3$). The origin is identified by the ordered pair (0,0).

The *x* and *y* axes separate the graph into four parts called quadrants.

- Points in Quadrant I have positive numbers for both the *x* and the *y* coordinates.
- Points in Quadrant II have a negative number for the *x* coordinate but a positive number for the *y* coordinate.
- Points in Quadrant III have negative numbers for both the *x* and the *y* coordinates.
- Points in Quadrant IV have a positive number for the *x* coordinate but a negative number for the *y* coordinate.

Examples

The graph below shows the following points:

(2,3), (–3,2), (–4,–4), and (0,–2)

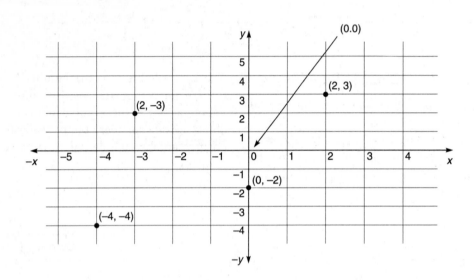

The graph below shows the following points:

A (4,–2), B (–1,1), C (3,3), and D (–4,–3)

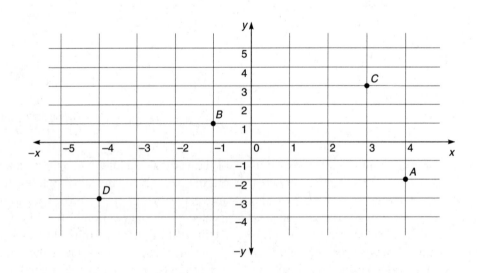

Graphing Equations on the Coordinate Plane
An equation with two variables x and y can be graphed on a coordinate plane. Start by plugging in values for either x or y. Then solve the equation to find the value of the other variable. The x and y values make ordered pairs that you can plot on the graph.

Examples

Graph the equation $x + y = 4$.
   Solving for x, the equation becomes $x = 4 - y$.

If $y = 1$, then $x = 3$.

If $y = 2$, then $x = 2$.

If $y = 3$, then $x = 1$.

If $y = 4$, then $x = 0$.

Use a Function Machine to Generate Ordered Pairs!

For $x = 4 - y$, plug in numbers for y to get x.
If $y = $ ___, then $x = $ ___.

Function Machine

x	y
3	1
2	2
1	3
0	4

Plot the ordered pairs $(3,1)$, $(2,2)$, $(1,3)$, and $(0,4)$ on a graph. If you connect the points, you will see that the result is a straight line.

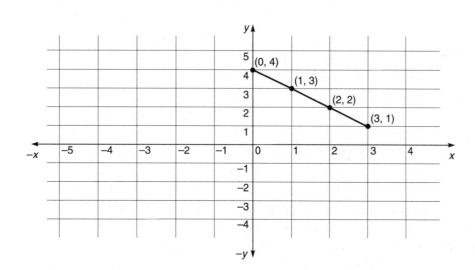

Graph the equation $y - x^2 = 2$
$$y = 2 + x^2$$
If $x = 0$, then $y = 2$.

If $x = 1$, then $y = 3$.

If $x = 2$, then $y = 6$.

If $x = 3$, then $y = 11$.

If $x = 4$, then $y = 18$.

If $x = -1$, then $y = 3$

If $x = -2$, then $y = 6$

If $x = -3$, then $y = 11$

If $x = -4$, then $y = 18$

Graph these points and connect the points with a line. Note that when you connect the points, you get a curved line.

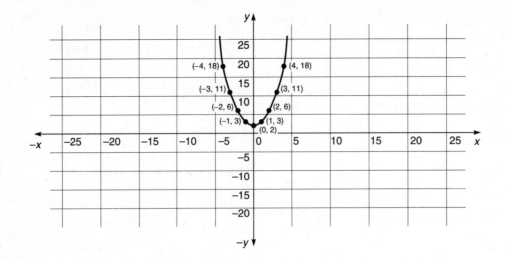

Practice Items—Graphing Equations   Graph the following equations.

1. $y = x^2 + 1$

2. $x + 6 = y$

Probability

When every event in a set of possible events has an equal chance of occurring, probability is the chance that a particular event (or "outcome") will occur. Probability is represented by the formula

$$\text{Probability} = \frac{\text{number of positive outcomes}}{\text{number of possible outcomes}}$$

Let's say you have a spinner with an arrow that spins around a circle that is divided into six equal parts. The parts are labeled from 1 to 6. When you spin the arrow, what is the probability that it will land on the part labeled 4? Following the formula,

$$\text{Probability} = \frac{\text{number of positive outcomes}}{\text{number of possible outcomes}}$$

$$\text{Probability} = \frac{1}{6} \text{ or 1 in 6}$$

Let's take that same spinner. What is the probability that the arrow will land on the number 2 or the number 3 when spun? Using the formula,

$$\text{Probability} = \frac{\text{number of positive outcomes}}{\text{number of possible outcomes}}$$

$$\text{Probability} = \frac{2}{6} = \frac{1}{3} \text{ or 1 in 3}$$

Examples

Solve: The National Fruit Growers' Association is conducting a random survey asking people to tell their favorite fruit. The chart shows the results so far.

Favorite Fruit	Number of People
Apples	236
Peaches	389
Oranges	250
Pears	125

What is the probability that the next randomly selected person will say that pears are his or her favorite fruit?

To solve probability problems, follow this word problem solution procedure.

Procedure

What must you find? The probability that a certain event will occur

What are the units? Fraction or decimal or percent

What do you know? The number of people selecting each fruit as their favorite.

Create an equation and solve.

$$\text{Probability} = \frac{\text{number of positive outcomes}}{\text{number of possible outcomes}}$$

Substitute values and solve.

Number of positive outcomes = 125 people who named pears as their favorite fruit

Number of possible outcomes = all people surveyed = $236 + 389 + 250 + 125 = 1,000$

Probability = $125/1,000 = 1/8 = 1{:}8 = 0.125 = 12.5\%$

Solve: A box is filled with 25 black balls, 50 white balls, and 75 red balls. If Wendell reaches into the box and picks a ball without looking, what is the probability that he will pick a black or a white ball?

Procedure

What must you find? The probability that either of two events will occur

What are the units? Fraction, decimal, or percent

What do you know? How many of each kind of ball are in the box

Create an equation and solve.

$$\text{Probability} = \frac{\text{number of positive outcomes}}{\text{number of possible outcomes}}$$

Substitute values and solve.

Number of positive outcomes = number of black balls + number of white balls = $25 + 50 = 75$

Number of possible outcomes = $25 + 50 + 75 = 150$

Probability = $\dfrac{75}{150} = \dfrac{1}{2} = 1{:}2 = 0.5 = 50\%$

Practice Items–Probability

1. The local travel bureau is conducting a random survey asking people to indicate how they will spend their next vacation. The chart shows the results so far.

Type of Vacation	Number of People
Spending time at the beach	56
Cruising the islands	89
Hiking in the mountains	50
Scuba diving	40
Visiting museums	67
Reading and relaxing	98
Total number of people surveyed	**400**

What is the probability that the next randomly selected person will say that hiking in the mountains will be how he or she will spend his or her vacation?

2. A box is filled with 50 black balls, 75 white balls, and 25 red balls. If Marty reaches into the box and picks a ball without looking, what is the probability that he will pick a black or a red ball?

ALGEBRA AND PROBABILITY QUIZ — ANSWERS AND CHART

Scoring Your Test

Compare your answer to the correct answer. Mark an X in the column if you got the item correct. Total the number correct.

Gauging Your Level of Performance

In the following chart, find the number of items that you got correct. See the suggestions listed for your performance.

Item Number	Correct Answer	Mark X if you picked the correct answer
1	A	✓
2	B	✓
3	A	X
4	D	✓
5	D	✓
6	A	✓
7	B	✓
8	B	✓
9	C	X
10	B	✓
11	B	✓
12	D	X
13	D	X
14	C	X
15	C	X
16	B	✓
Total Correct		

16	This is pretty good work. Rework the items that you got wrong so that you know how to work the problems.
15	
14	You are doing OK. Go back and review the lessons on those areas that you got wrong.
13	
12	You need to keep studying and practicing. You should not be satisfied until you can easily work the problems.
11	
10	Spend time working on the algebra problems in this chapter.
9	
8	
7	Keep working and reworking problems until you are comfortable with the processes. Try the algebra quiz again to determine your improvement.
6	
5	
4	
3	
2	
1	
0	

ANSWERS TO PRACTICE ITEMS

Practice Items—Algebra Language

1. $6x + (4)^2$

2. $12(6 + x)$

3. $(xy)(11 + xy)$

4. $\dfrac{g}{40 + xy}$

5. $x^2 + 14x = -21$

Practice Items—Evaluating Expressions

1. 18

2. 147

3. 55

Practice Items—Solving Equations for One Unknown

1. $z = 12$

2. $x = 300$

3. $x = -45$

4. $y = -8$

Practice Items—Solving Inequalities

1. $x > 3$

2. $y < -7$

Practice Items—Ratios and Proportions

1. $m = 40$

2. $q = 6\frac{2}{5}$

3. $d = \dfrac{cb}{a}$

Practice Items—Solving Equations for Two Unknowns

1. $a = 0, b = 3$

2. $a = 2, b = 1$

Practice Items—Monomials

1. $9a^2bc$

2. $-4a^2bc$

3. $-15g^7c^6$

4. $3x^2y^3$

Practice Items—Adding, Subtracting, Multiplying, and Dividing Polynomials

1. $-s^3 + 3sq + 17s^2 - 4r^3$

2. $12pq^3 + xy + 10r^2$

3. $6g^2 + 4ga - 10a^2$

4. $6hj + 18j^2 + 6h + 24j + 6$

5. $4j + 1$

6. $a + 16$

Practice Items—Factoring Polynomials

1. $2y(3y + 1)$

2. $(2x + 3)(x + 4)$

3. $(3x + 4)(2x - 5)$

4. $(4x + 1)(x + 1)$

5. $(7x + 1)(x - 3)$

Practice Items—Solving Quadratic Equations

1. $y = +4$

2. $x = -3; x = 9$

3. $y = -3; y = 9$

4. $g = 3; g = 7$

Practice Items—Reducing Algebraic Fractions to Lowest Terms

1. $1\frac{1}{2}$

2. $\dfrac{k + 1}{6}$

3. $2x + 3$

Practice Items–Adding or Subtracting Algebraic Fractions with a Common Denominator

1. $\dfrac{9g - 6}{h}$

2. $\dfrac{34j - 12}{m}$

Practice Items–Adding or Subtracting Algebraic Fractions with Different Denominators

1. $\dfrac{3k - 6}{4x}$

2. $\dfrac{x + 7}{6x}$

Practice Items–Multiplying Algebraic Fractions

1. 9

2. 21/2

Practice Items–Dividing Algebraic Fractions

1. $\dfrac{2p}{5}$

2. $\dfrac{1}{5}$

Practice Items–Graphing Equations

1.

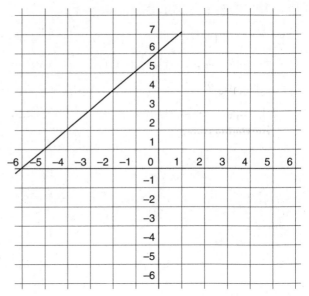

2.

$x + 6 = y$

x	y
0	6
1	7
−1	5
−2	4
−3	3
−4	2
−5	1
−6	0

Practice Items–Probability

1. $\dfrac{1}{8}$

2. 1/2

SECTION 3: GEOMETRY

READ THIS SECTION TO LEARN:

- **What geometry topics you need to know for the ASVAB**

- **Techniques for solving every kind of ASVAB geometry problem**

- **Tips and strategies to help you raise your ASVAB Arithmetic Reasoning and Mathematics Knowledge scores**

INTRODUCTION: GEOMETRY ON THE ASVAB

Along with problems in algebra and probability, the ASVAB mathematics tests also include problems in geometry. To do well, you'll need to know the basic geometry concepts taught in middle school and high school math courses. Topics tested include classifying angles, identifying different kinds of triangles and parallelograms, calculating perimeter and area, finding the circumference and area of circles, identifying different kinds of solid figures, and calculating the volume of different shapes.

The following pages offer a quick but important overview of the basic geometry you need to know in order to score well on the ASVAB. Make sure that you carefully review and test yourself on every topic covered in this section. Also make sure that you learn how to use all of the problem-solving methods presented in the examples. If you master the core information presented in this chapter, you will be able to answer ASVAB geometry questions with relative ease.

Suggested Review Plan for Geometry

- Take the Geometry Quiz.
- Score your quiz.
- Study any problems that you answered incorrectly. Reread the corresponding review section, then try the problem again. Work until you understand how to solve the problem.

- Work through the geometry review at your own pace.
- Pay careful attention to the examples provided.

Remember that while you probably won't get these exact problems on the ASVAB, knowing how to solve them will help you do your best on the actual test.

GEOMETRY QUIZ

1. The endpoint shared by two rays that form an angle is called a

   A. line segment
   B. degree
   C. vertex
   D. straight line

2. A right angle is an angle that measures

   A. exactly 90°
   B. greater than 90°
   C. less than 90°
   D. 45°

3. An acute angle is an angle that measures

   A. exactly 90°
   B. greater than 90°
   C. less than 90°
   D. exactly 180°

4. An obtuse angle is an angle that measures

   A. exactly 90°
   B. between 90° and 180°
   C. exactly 180°
   D. greater than 180°

5. In the figure shown, if angle 1 measures 65°, what is the measure of angle 2?

   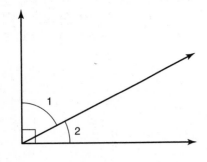

   A. 120°
   B. 90°
   C. 25°
   D. 10°

6. In the figure shown, if angle 1 measures 35°, what is the measure of angle 2?

   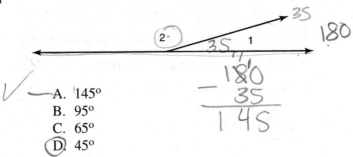

   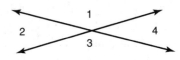

   A. 145°
   B. 95°
   C. 65°
   D. 45°

7. In the figure shown, if angle 2 measures 45°, what is the measure of angle 4?

   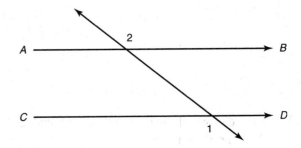

   A. 135°
   B. 75°
   C. 45°
   D. 35°

8. In the figure shown, lines *AB* and *CD* are parallel and angle 1 measures 120°. What is the measure of angle 2?

   A. 60°
   B. 90°
   C. 120°
   D. 180°

9. A certain triangle has exactly two congruent (equal) sides, and the angles opposite those sides are also congruent. This triangle is a(n)

   A. isosceles triangle
   B. scalene triangle
   C. equilateral triangle
   D. right triangle

10. In the equilateral triangle shown, what is the measure of each angle?

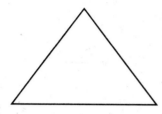

A. 60°
B. 90°
C. 120°
D. 180°

11. In the triangle shown, *ACB* measures 55° and *CAB* measures 65°. What is the measure of *CBA*?

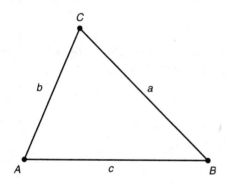

A. 50°
B. 60°
C. 80°
D. 90°

12. In the triangle shown, side *a* is 5 in. long and side *b* is 6 in. long. How long is side *c*?

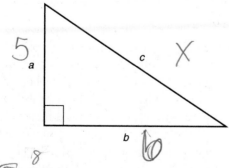

8

A. 7.81 in. ·
B. 8.51 in. 8.5
C. 9.11 in. 9²
D. 10.71 in. 10²

$a^2 + b^2 = c^2$
$5^2 + 6^2$
$25 + 36 = \sqrt{61}$

13. In the rectangle shown, side *a* measures 13 cm and side *b* measures 36 cm. What is the perimeter of the rectangle?

$2l + 2w$

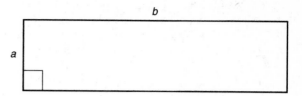

A. 49 cm
B. 98 cm
C. 469 cm
D. 512 cm

$2(13) + 2(36)$
$26 + 72 = 98$

14. In the triangle shown, side *a* is 4 ft long, side *b* is 6 ft long, and side *c* is 8 ft long. What is the area of the triangle?

$\frac{1}{2}bh$

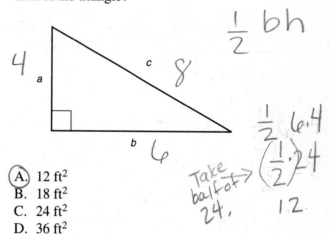

A. 12 ft²
B. 18 ft²
C. 24 ft²
D. 36 ft²

$\frac{1}{2}(6 \cdot 4)$

Take half of → $(\frac{1}{2} \cdot 24$
24.   12

15. In which of the following circles is the line segment a diameter?

A.

B.

C.

D.

16. The circle shown has a diameter of 12 m. What is the area of the circle?

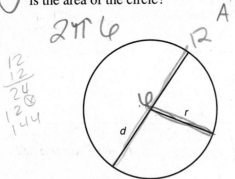

$A = \pi r^2$

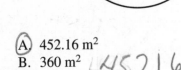

A. 452.16 m²
B. 360 m²
C. 144 m²
D. 113.04 m²

17. In the trapezoid shown, $b_1 = 4$ ft, $b_2 = 8$ ft, and $h = 5$ ft. What is the area of the trapezoid?

$A = \frac{1}{2}(b_1 + b_2)h$ or $A = \frac{(b_1 + b_2)h}{2}$

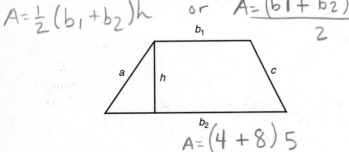

$A = \frac{(4+8)5}{2}$

$\frac{12 \times 5}{2} = \frac{60}{2}$

A. 16 ft²
B. 30 ft²
C. 90 ft²
D. 160 ft²

18. Figure WXYZ is a parallelogram. Which of the following is *not* necessarily true?

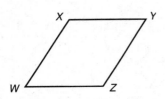

A. Side WX is parallel to side ZY.
B. Side XY is parallel to side WZ.
C. ∠W has the same measure as ∠Y.
D. Side WX is the same length as side XY.

19. Which of the following figures contains line segments that are perpendicular?

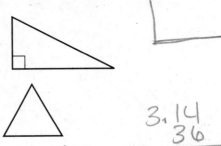

A.

B.

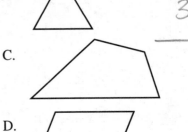

C.

D.

20. What is the ratio of the length of a side of an equilateral triangle to its perimeter?

A. 1:1
B. 1:2
C. 1:3
D. 3:1

$a^2 + b^2 = c^2$

21. Jules needs to purchase a ladder that just reaches the top of a 16-foot building. If the bottom of the ladder will be placed 12 feet from the base of the building, how long should Jules's ladder be?

A. 18 ft
B. 20 ft
C. 25 ft
D. 30 ft

$256 + 144 =$
$\sqrt{400} =$
$20 \cdot 20 = 4$

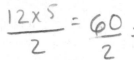

$16^2 + 12^2 = C$

22. Kai must buy canvas to make a sail for his sailboat. The sail will have the shape of a right triangle. It will be as tall as the mast (the vertical pole) and as wide at the bottom as the boom (the horizontal pole). If the mast measures 18 meters and the boom measures 9 meters, about how much canvas does Kai need to buy?

A. 27 m²
B. 61 m²
C. 81 m²
D. 103 m²

23. Renee wants to carpet her living room. If the room measures 15 feet × 18 feet, how many square yards of carpet must she purchase?

   A. 20 yd²
   B. 30 yd²
   C. 32 yd²
   D. 35 yd²

24. Saul wants to wallpaper one wall in his dining room. The wall is 11 ft high and 14 ft long. It has a window that measures 3 ft by 4 ft. About how many square feet of wallpaper must Saul buy?

   A. 25 ft²
   B. 32 ft²
   C. 112 ft²
   D. 142 ft²

25. In the following figure, line *AB* intersects two parallel lines. If angle 1 measures 35 °, what is the measure of angle 4?

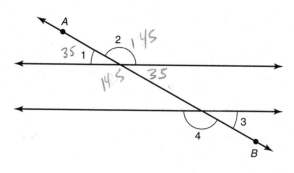

   A. 35º
   B. 55º
   C. 90º
   D. 145º

26. The Lakeville skating rink is a perfect circle. If the diameter of the rink is 50 ft, which of the following best represents its area? (Use p = 3.14)

   A. 78.5 ft²
   B. 157 ft²
   C. 1,962 ft²
   D. 7,850 ft²

27. A tomato paste can has a diameter of 8 cm and a height of 20 cm. Which of the following tells about how much tomato paste it will hold?

   A. 4,019 cm³
   B. 1,005 cm³
   C. 201 cm³
   D. 50 cm³

28. In the figure shown, what is the area of the rectangle if the radius of each circle is 6 cm?

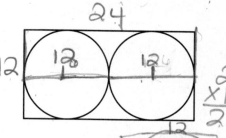

   A. 72 cm²
   B. 112 cm²
   C. 288 cm²
   D. 310 cm²

29. A square garden is doubled in length and 4 feet is added to its width. Which of the following expressions represents the new area of the garden?

   A. 2x(x + 4)
   B. 4x²
   C. 4x + 4
   D. (2x)(4x)

30. A rectangular garden is 40 yards long and 15 yards wide. Darryl runs once around the edge of the garden. How far does Darryl run?

   A. 55 yards
   B. 80 yards
   C. 100 yards
   D. 110 yards

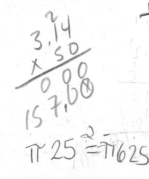

GEOMETRY REVIEW

Topics	
Points, lines, and angles	Quadrilaterals
Classifying angles	Circles
Classifying pairs of lines	Perimeter and area
Classifying pairs of angles	Finding the perimeter of a polygon
Identifying congruent (equal) angles	Finding the area of a polygon
Solving angle problems	Finding the circumference and area of a circle
Triangles	Three-dimensional (solid) figures
Base and height of a triangle	Finding the volume of solid figures
Median of a triangle	

Points, Lines, and Angles

To work with geometry, you need to understand points, lines, and angles.

- A *point* is an exact location in space. It is represented by a dot and a capital letter.
- A *line* is a set of points that form a straight path extending in either direction without end. A line that includes points *B* and *D* is represented as follows: $\overleftrightarrow{BD}$.
- A *ray* is a part of a line that has one endpoint and continues without end in the opposite direction. A ray that ends at point *A* and includes point *B* is represented as follows: $\overrightarrow{AB}$.
- A *line segment* is a part of a ray or a line that connects two points. A line connecting points *A* and *B* is represented as follows: $\overline{AB}$.

An *angle* is a figure formed by two rays that have the same endpoint. That endpoint is called the *vertex* (plural: *vertices*) of the angle. An example is shown below.

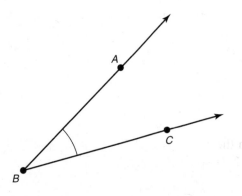

In this example, rays *BA* and *BC* have the same endpoint, which is point *B*. So point *B* is the vertex of the angle. The two line segments *BA* and *BC* are called the sides of the angle. The symbol is ∠ used to indicate an angle.

An angle can be labeled or identified in several different ways:

- By the vertex: ∠*B*
- By the letters of the three points that form it: ∠*ABC* or ∠*CBA*. (The vertex is always the middle of the three letters.)

The measure of the size of an angle is expressed in *degrees* (°).

> **Helpful Hint**
>
> You will see the word *bisect* used in some geometry problems. To *bisect* merely means to split into two equal parts.

Classifying Angles

There are three types of angles that you should know for the ASVAB test. They are right angles, acute angles, and obtuse angles. A straight line is called a *Straight angle*.

Right Angles A *right angle* measures exactly 90°. Right angles are found in squares, rectangles, and certain triangles. ∠*ABC* in the figure below is a right angle.

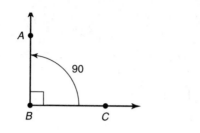

Examples

The angles below are both right angles.

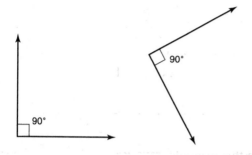

Acute Angles An angle that measures less than 90°
is called an *acute angle*. *ABC* in the figure below is
an acute angle.

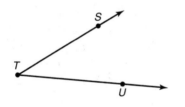

Examples

The angles below are all acute angles.

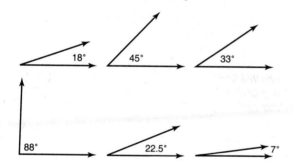

Obtuse Angles An angle with a measure that is
greater than 90° but less than 180° is called an
obtuse angle. ∠*DEF* is an obtuse angle.

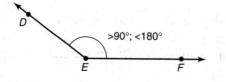

Examples

The angles below are all obtuse angles.

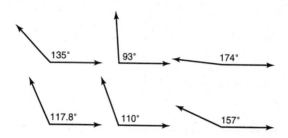

Straight Angles A *straight angle* is one that measures exactly 180°. This kind of angle forms a
straight line. ∠*ABC* in the figure below is a straight
angle.

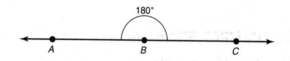

Classifying Pairs of Lines

Intersecting Lines *Intersecting lines* are lines that
meet or cross each other.

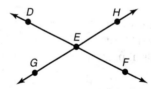

In the figure above, line *DF* intersects line *GH* at
point *E*.

Parallel Lines *Parallel lines* are lines in a plane
that never intersect.

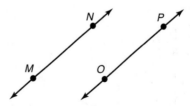

In the figure above, line *MN* is parallel to line
OP. In symbols, *MN* ∥ *OP*.

Perpendicular Lines *Perpendicular lines* intersect to form right angles.

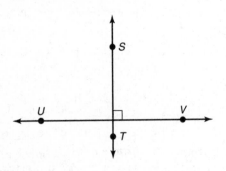

In the figure above, line *ST* is perpendicular to line *UV*. In symbols, *ST* ⊥ *UV*.

Classifying Pairs of Angles

Adjacent Angles *Adjacent angles* have the same vertex and share one side. ∠*ABC* and ∠*CBD* in the figure below are adjacent angles.

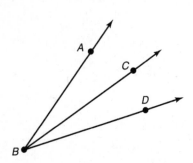

Complementary Angles Two adjacent angles whose measures total 90° are called *complementary angles*. ∠1 and ∠2 are complementary. Their measures total exactly 90°.

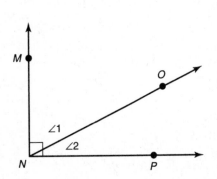

Example

The two angles in the figure below are complementary. Together they measure 90°.

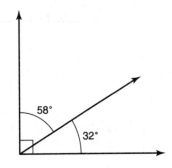

Supplementary Angles Two adjacent angles whose measures total 180° are called *supplementary angles*. Together they make a straight line. ∠*KHG* and ∠*GHJ* in the figure below are supplementary because together they add to 180°, or a straight line.

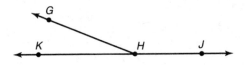

Example

The two angles shown here are supplementary. Together they measure 180° and form a straight line.

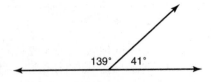

Vertical Angles Two angles formed by intersecting lines are called *vertical angles* if they are not adjacent. In the figure that follows, ∠*AED* and ∠*BEC* are vertical angles. ∠*AEB* and ∠*DEC* are also vertical angles. Vertical angles are often said to be "opposite" to each other as shown in the figure.

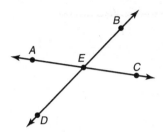

Vertical angles are *congruent*. That is, their measures are the same. $\angle AED = \angle BEC$ and $\angle AEB = \angle DEC$.

*Example*_____

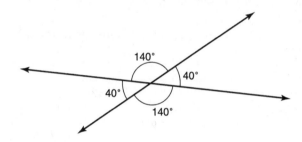

Identifying Congruent (Equal) Angles

In the figure that follows, lines *AC* and *DF* are parallel. They are intersected by a third line *GH*. This third line is called a *transversal*.

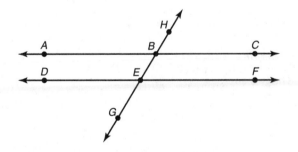

This intersection creates eight angles. There are four pairs of vertical congruent angles:

$$\angle ABH = \angle EBC$$
$$\angle ABE = \angle HBC$$
$$\angle DEB = \angle GEF$$
$$\angle DEG = \angle BEF$$

Alternate Interior Angles In addition, four of these angles make two pairs of *alternate interior angles*. These are angles that are on opposite sides of the transversal, are between the two parallel lines, and are not adjacent. When parallel lines are intersected by a transversal, alternate interior angles are congruent. The two pairs are

$$\angle ABE = \angle BEF$$
$$\angle DEB = \angle EBC$$

Alternate Exterior Angles Four of the angles also make two pairs of *alternate exterior angles*. These are angles that are on opposite sides of the transversal, are outside the two parallel lines, and are not adjacent. When parallel lines are intersected by a transversal, alternate exterior angles are congruent. The two pairs are

$$\angle ABH = \angle GEF$$
$$\angle HBC = \angle DEG$$

Corresponding Angles The eight angles also make four pairs of *corresponding angles*. These are angles that are in corresponding positions. When parallel lines are intersected by a transversal, corresponding angles are congruent. The four pairs are

$$\angle ABH = \angle DEB$$
$$\angle HBC = \angle BEF$$
$$\angle ABE = \angle DEG$$
$$\angle EBC = \angle GEF$$

> **Watch Out! Angles Count!**
>
> Pay attention to these angle relationships! They are almost certain to appear in some form on the ASVAB.

Solving Angle Problems

On the ASVAB, you will most likely be asked to use what you know about angles and angle relationships to solve problems. You may be asked to tell which angles in a figure are congruent. Or you may be given the measure of one angle and asked for the measure of an adjacent angle or some related angle in a figure.

Examples

In the following diagram, parallel lines *MO* and *RT* are intersected by transversal *WV*.

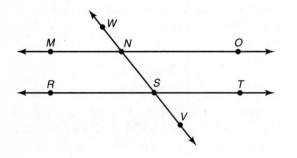

Which angle is congruent to ∠*MNW*?

    A. ∠*MNS*
    B. ∠*WNO*
    C. ∠*RSV*
    D. ∠*VST*

Of the choices, the only one that is congruent to *MNW* is *VST* because *MNW* and *VST* are alternate exterior angles.

Which angle is congruent to *MNS*?

    A. ∠*RSV*
    B. ∠*SNO*
    C. ∠*VST*
    D. ∠*MNW*

Of the choices, the only one that is congruent to ∠*MNS* is ∠*RSV* because ∠*MNS* and ∠*RSV* are corresponding angles.

If *RSN* measures 50°, what is the measure of ∠*RSV*?

    A. 90°
    B. 110°
    C. 130°
    D. 150°

∠*RSN* and ∠*RSV* are supplementary angles. That is, together they form a straight line and their measures add up to 180°. So if ∠*RSN* measures 50°, then ∠*RSV* measures 180 − 50 = 130°.

Practice Items—Angles

1. Which of the following is an obtuse angle?

    A.

    B.

    C.

    D.

2. A straight angle has how many degrees?

3. What is the measure of ∠*A* in the figure below?

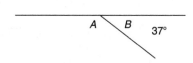

4. If ∠*ABC* is a right angle, what is the measure of ∠*ABD*?

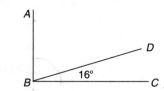

5. In the figure below, if ∠*AEB* measures 24°, what is the measure of ∠*CED*?

6. In the figure above, if ∠*AEB* measures 24°, what is the measure of ∠*AEC*?

7. In the figure below, if ∠IHK measures 43°, what is the measure of ∠JBA?

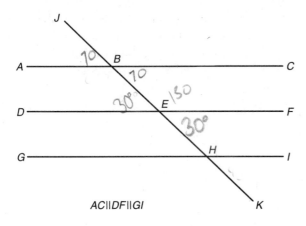

ACIIDFIIGI

8. In the figure above, if ∠FEH measures 40°, what is the measure of ∠ABE?

9. In the figure above, if ∠FEH measures 30°, what is the measure of ∠JBC?

10. In the figure above, if ∠JBC measures 110°, what is the measure of ∠DEH?

Triangles

A *polygon* is a closed figure that can be drawn without lifting the pencil. It is made up of line segments (sides) that do not cross. A *triangle* is a polygon with three sides. Every triangle has three angles that total 180°.

Hint: Look for Tick Marks and Arcs

When sides of a polygon are congruent (equal), they may be marked with an equal number of tick marks. When angles are congruent, they may be marked with an equal number of arcs.

Example

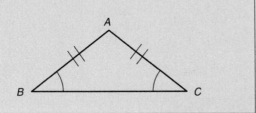

The tick marks indicate that sides *AB* and *AC* have the same length. The arcs indicate that ∠ABC has the same measure as ∠ACB.

If sides have different numbers of tick marks, they are not congruent. If angles have different numbers of arcs, they are not congruent.

Reminder

All triangles have angles that total 180°.

Identifying the Longest Side of a Triangle The longest side of a triangle is always opposite the largest angle. So, if a triangle has angles of 45°, 55°, and 80°, the side opposite the 80° angle is the longest.

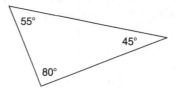

There are four main types of triangles. They are equilateral, isosceles, scalene, and right. Each has special characteristics that you should know.

Equilateral Triangle This kind of triangle has three congruent (equal) sides and three congruent (equal) angles. In an equilateral triangle, each angle measures 60°.

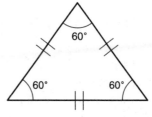

Isosceles Triangle This type of triangle has at least two congruent sides, and the angles opposite the congruent sides are also congruent. In the isosceles triangle shown here, sides *AB* and *BC* are congruent. ∠BAC and ∠BCA are also congruent. In an isosceles triangle, if you know the measure of any one angle, you can calculate the measures of the other two.

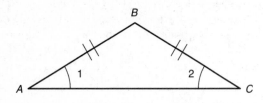

Examples

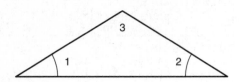

In this isosceles triangle, if ∠1 measures 30°, what is the measure of ∠3?

Since ∠1 and ∠2 are congruent, ∠2 must also measure 30°. Together, ∠1 and ∠2 add up to 60°. Since the sum of all three angles in any triangle is 180°, 3 must be 180 − 60 = 120°.

If ∠3 measures 100°, what are the measures of ∠1 and ∠2?

Since the sum of all three angles in any triangle is 180°, the sum of the measures of ∠1 and ∠2 must be 180 − 100 = 80°. Since angles 1 and 2 are congruent, each one must measure 80° ≡ 2 = 40°.

Scalene Triangle This kind of triangle has no equal sides or angles.

Right Triangle This kind of triangle has one angle that measures 90°. This angle is the *right angle*. It is identified in the figure by the little "box." Since the sum of all three angles in any triangle is 180°, the sum of the two remaining angles in a right triangle is 180 − 90 = 90°.

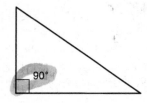

In a right triangle, there is a special relationship among the lengths of the three sides. This relationship is described by the *Pythagorean theorem*.

In the right triangle shown here, ∠C is the right angle. The side opposite the right angle is called the *hypotenuse* (c). It is always the longest side. The other two sides (a and b) are called *legs*.

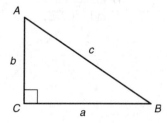

According to the Pythagorean theorem, in any right triangle, the sum of the squares of the legs equals the square of the hypotenuse. In symbols:

$$a^2 + b^2 = c^2$$

So if you know the lengths of any two sides of a right triangle, you can calculate the length of the third side.

Examples

If $a = 2$ and $b = 3$, what is c?
Following the Pythagorean theorem,

$$2^2 + 3^2 = c^2$$
$$4 + 9 = c^2$$
$$13 = c^2$$
$$\sqrt{13} = c$$

If $a = 3$ and $b = 4$, what is c?

$$3^2 + 4^2 = c^2$$
$$9 + 16 = c^2$$
$$25 = c^2$$
$$5 = c$$

If $a = 6$ and $c = 10$, what is b?

$$6^2 + b^2 = 10^2$$
$$36 + b^2 = 100$$
$$b^2 = 100 - 36$$
$$b^2 = 64$$
$$b = \sqrt{64}$$
$$b = 8$$

Base and Height of a Triangle

Any side of a triangle can be called the *base*. The *height* is the length of a line segment that connects a base to the vertex opposite that base and is perpendicular to it.

Look at the triangle that follows. Dashed line *CD* is the height. Line *CD* is perpendicular to the base *AB*. Where line *CD* meets base *AB*, it creates two right angles, ∠*CDA* and ∠*CDB*.

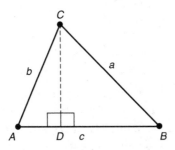

Helpful Hint

Sometimes you will see the word *perpendicular* represented by the symbol ⊥. So in the triangle shown, $\overline{CD} \perp \overline{AB}$.

Median of a Triangle

A *median* of a triangle is a line drawn from any vertex to the middle of the opposite side. This line splits the opposite side into two equal lengths.

*Example*_____

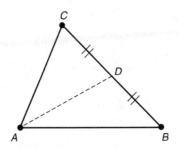

Dashed line *AD* is a median of triangle *ABC*. It splits side *BC* into two equal lengths, $\overline{CD}$ and $\overline{BD}$.

Practice Items—Triangles

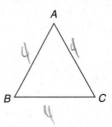

1. The triangle above is an equilateral triangle. What is the measure of ∠*ACB*?

2. In the triangle above, if line *AC* measures 4 inches, what is the length of line *BC*?

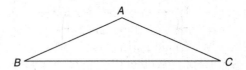

3. If the triangle above is an isosceles triangle and ∠*ABC* measures 100°, what is the measure of ∠*BAC*?

4. In the triangle above, if line *AB* measures 15 cm, what is the length of line *BC*?

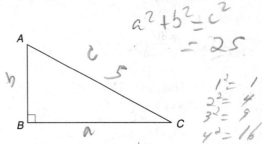

5. In the triangle above, if ∠*ACB* measures 30°, what is the measure of ∠*CAB*?

6. In the triangle above, which side is the longest?

7. In the triangle above, if side *AC* measures 5 cm, what are the lengths of sides *AB* and *BC*?

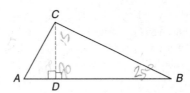

8. In the figure above, if ∠*CBD* measures 25°, what is the measure of ∠*CAD*?

Quadrilaterals

A *quadrilateral* is a polygon with four sides and four angles. The sum of the four angles is always 360°.

There are several different kinds of quadrilaterals. Each type is classified according to the relationships among its sides and angles. The square, rectangle, parallelogram, and rhombus are all types of quadrilaterals.

Parallelogram A *parallelogram* is a quadrilateral with both pairs of opposite sides parallel and congruent. The opposite angles are also congruent. Around the edge of the parallelogram, each pair of consecutive angles is supplementary; that is, their sum is 180°. Diagonal lines drawn from opposite vertices *bisect* each other (divide each other exactly in half), but the diagonals themselves are not equal in length.

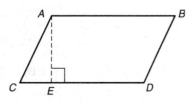

$$\angle A = \angle D$$
$$\angle C = \angle B$$
$$\angle A + \angle B = 180°$$
$$\angle B + \angle D = 180°$$
$$\angle D + \angle C = 180°$$
$$\angle C + \angle A = 180°$$

Reminder

Consecutive angles are angles that are next to each other. *Supplementary* means that the angles add to 180°.

Like triangles, quadrilaterals have bases and height. Any side of a parallelogram can be a base. The *height* is a line originating at a vertex and drawn

perpendicular to the opposite base. The height forms two right angles where it meets the base.

Rhombus A *rhombus* is a parallelogram with four congruent sides. Opposite angles are also congruent.

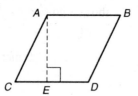

Rectangle A *rectangle* is a parallelogram with four right angles. Diagonal lines drawn from opposite vertices of a rectangle bisect each other (divide each other exactly in half) and are equal in length.

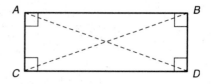

Square A *square* is a rectangle with four congruent sides. Diagonal lines drawn from opposite vertices of a rectangle bisect each other (divide each other exactly in half) and are equal in length.

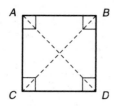

Trapezoid A *trapezoid* is a quadrilateral with only one pair of parallel sides. Like other quadrilaterals, it has bases and height. In the example that follows, dashed line *CE* is the height. Sides *AB* and *CD* are parallel, but sides *AC* and *BD* are not parallel.

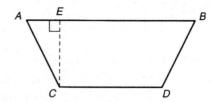

Practice Items—Quadrilaterals

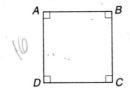

1. In the square above, what is the sum of all four angles?

2. In the square above, if side *AD* measures 16 inches, what is the length of side *DC*?

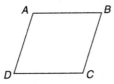

3. In the rhombus above, what is the sum of all four angles?

4. In the rhombus above, if ∠*ADC* measures 60°, what is the measure of ∠*ABC*?

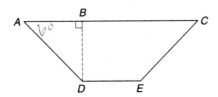

5. In the trapezoid above, what is the measure of ∠*CBD*?

Circles

A circle is a closed figure having all points the same distance from a *center*. A circle with its center at point *A* is called circle *A*.

Parts of a Circle A *chord* is a line segment that has endpoints on a circle. A *diameter* is a chord that passes through the center of a circle. A *radius* is a line segment that connects the center of a circle and a point on the circle. Its length equals half the length of the diameter. In the figure that follows, *A* is the center of the circle. *EF* is a chord. *BC* is a diameter of the circle. *AC*, *AB*, and *AD* are each a radius of the circle.

An *arc* is two points on a circle and the part of the circle between the two points. In the figure

below, *CD* is an arc of the circle. A *central angle* is an angle whose vertex is the center of a circle. In the figure below, ∠*CAD* is a central angle. Its measure is 50°. The sum of the measures of the central angles in a circle is 360°.

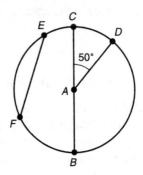

Perimeter and Area

The *perimeter* is the distance around a closed two-dimensional figure. The *area* is the amount of surface a two-dimensional figure covers. Area is measured in square units, such as square inches (in.^{2}) or square centimeters (cm^2). A square inch is the area of a square with sides 1 inch long.

Finding the Perimeter of a Polygon

To find the perimeter of a polygon, just add the length of each side to find the total.

*Example*_____

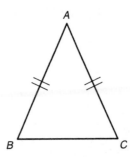

△*ABC* is an isosceles triangle. If side *AB* has a length of 25 cm and side *BC* has a length of 15 cm, what is the perimeter?

Since △*ABC* is an isosceles triangle, side *AB* = side *AC*. So if side *AB* has a length of 25 cm, side *AC* also has a length of 25 cm. Thus the perimeter is $25 + 25 + 15 = 65$ cm.

Helpful Hint

Watch out for ASVAB questions that use parallelograms, rhombuses, or trapezoids, but involve the Pythagorean theorem. In the trapezoid, for example, you might be asked to calculate the hypotenuse by knowing the length of $\overline{CE}$ and $\overline{AE}$.

Finding the Area of a Polygon

There are special formulas you can use to calculate the areas of various types of polygons. You will want to memorize these, as you will almost certainly be asked a question about area on the ASVAB.

Area of a Triangle The area (A) of a triangle is one-half the base (b) multiplied by the height (h), or $A = \frac{1}{2} bh$.

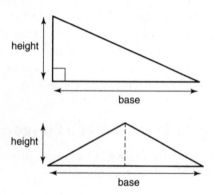

Example

If a triangle has a height that measures 30 cm and a base that measures 50 cm, what is its area?

$b = 50$ cm
$h = 30$ cm
$A = \frac{1}{2} bh$
$A = \frac{1}{2} (50)(30)$
$A = \frac{1}{2} (1,500)$
$A = 750$ cm^2

Reminder

Anytime you see units squared, you are dealing with area. Examples: square inches (in.^{2}), square centimeters (cm^2), square yards (yd^2), and so on.

Area of a Square or Rectangle The area (A) of a square or rectangle is its length (l) multiplied by its width (w), or $A = lw$.

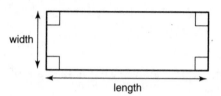

Example

If this rectangle is 10 miles long and 6 miles wide, what is its area?

$A = lw$
$A = (10)(6)$
$A = 60$ square miles (60 mi^2)

Area of a Parallelogram (including the Rhombus) The area (A) of a parallelogram is its base (b) multiplied by its height (h), or $A = bh$.

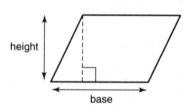

Example

If a parallelogram has a base of 6 meters and a height of 4 meters, what is the area?

$A = bh$
$A = (6)(4)$
$A = 24$ square meters (24 m^2)

Area of a Trapezoid The area (A) of a trapezoid is one-half the height (h) multiplied by the sum of the two bases (b_1 and b_2), or $A = 1/2 \, (b_1 + b_2)h$

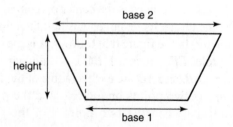

Example

If a trapezoid has one base of 30 meters and another base of 60 meters, and its height is 20 meters, what is the area?

$A = (30 + 60)(20)$
$A = (90)(20)$
$A = (1,800)$
$A = 900$ square meters (900 m²)

Practice Items–Perimeter and Area

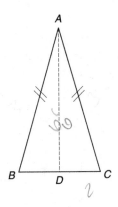

1. In the triangle above, if side *AB* measures 3 inches and side *BC* measures 2 inches, what is the perimeter of the triangle?

2. In the triangle above, if line *AD* measures 6 inches and side *BC* measures 2 inches, what is the area of the triangle?

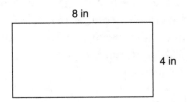

3. What is the perimeter of the rectangle above?

 4. What is the area of the rectangle above?

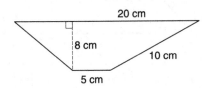

5. What is the perimeter of the trapezoid above?

6. What is the area of the trapezoid above?

Finding the Circumference and Area of a Circle

The *circumference* of a circle is the distance around the circle. The circumference (*C*) divided by the diameter (*d*) always equals the number π (pi). Pi is an irrational number—a nonterminating and nonrepeating decimal. When you use it to solve problems, you can approximate π as 3.14 or 22/7.

To find the circumference of a circle, use the formula $C = \pi d$.

Example

If a circle has a radius of 3 inches, what is the circumference?

Since the diameter is twice the radius (2*r*), the diameter is 6 inches.

$C = \pi d$
$C \approx 3.14(d)$
$C \approx 3.14(6)$
$C \approx 18.84$ in.

To find the area of a circle, multiply π times the square of the radius: $A = \pi r^2$.

Helpful Hint

If you prefer working with fractions, then $\pi = \frac{22}{7}$.

Example

If a circle has a radius of 4 centimeters, what is its area?

$A = \pi r^2$
$A = 3.14(4)^2$
$A = 3.14(16)$
$A = 50.24$ cm²

Practice Items–Circles: Circumference and Area

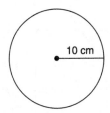

1. What is the circumference of the circle above?

2. What is the area of the circle above?

Three-Dimensional (Solid) Figures

A figure is *two-dimensional* if all the points on the figure are in the same plane. A square and a triangle are two-dimensional figures. A figure is *three-dimensional* (solid) if all of its points do not exist in the same plane.

On solid figures, the flat surfaces are called *faces*. *Edges* are line segments where two faces meet. A point where three or more edges intersect is called a *vertex*.

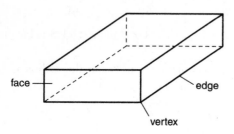

On the ASVAB, you may see problems related to these solid figures: rectangular solid (prism), cube, cylinder, and sphere.

Rectangular Solid (Prism)

On a *rectangular solid* (also called a *prism*), all of the faces are rectangular. The top and bottom faces are called bases. All opposite faces on a rectangular solid are parallel and congruent.

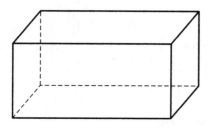

Cube

A *cube* is a rectangular solid on which every face is a square. All faces of a cube are congruent squares.

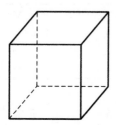

Cylinder

A *cylinder* is a solid figure with two parallel congruent circular bases and a curved surface connecting the boundaries of the two faces.

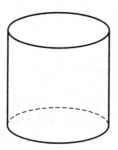

Sphere

A *sphere* is a solid figure that is the set of all points that are the same distance from a given point, called the center. The distance from the center to the curved surafce is the radius (*r*) of the sphere.

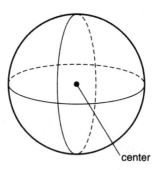

Finding the Volume of Solid Figures

Volume is the amount of space within a three-dimensional figure. Volume is measured in cubic units, such as cubic inches (in.^{3}) or cubic centimeters (cm^3). A cubic inch is the volume of a cube with edges 1 inch long.

Volume of a Rectangular Solid

To find the volume (*V*) of a rectangular solid, multiply the length (*l*) times the width (*w*) times the height (*h*). The formula is $V = lwh$.

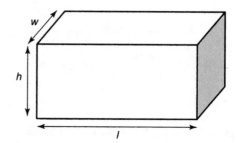

Example

If a rectangular solid has a length of 3 yards, a height of 1.5 yards, and a width of 1.5 yards, what is its volume?

$V = lwh$
$V = (3)(1.5)(1.5)$
$V = 6.75$ cubic yards (6.75 yd^3)

Volume of a Cube On a cube, the length, width, and height are all the same: each one equals 1 side (s). To find the volume (V) of a cube, multiply the length × width × height. This is the same as multiplying side × side × side. The formula is $V = s \times s \times s = s^3$.

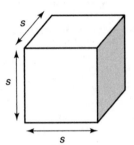

Example

If each side of a cube measures 9 feet, what is its volume?

$V = s^3$
$V = (9)^3$
$V = 729$ cubic feet (729 ft^3)

Volume of a Cylinder To find the volume (V) of a cylinder, first find the area of the circular base by using the formula: $A = \pi r^2$. Then multiply the result times the height (h) of the cylinder. The formula is $V = (\pi r^2)\, h$.

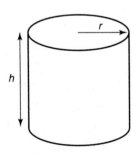

Example

If a cylinder has a height of 7 meters and a radius of 2 meters, what is its volume?

$V = (\pi r^2)\, h$
$V = 3.14(2)^2(7)$
$V = 3.14(4)(7)$
$V = 87.92$ cubic meters (87.92 m^3)

Volume of a Sphere To find the volume of a sphere, multiply 4/3 times π times the radius cubed. The formula is $V = \frac{4}{3}\pi r^3$.

Example

If the radius of a sphere measures 12 inches, what is its volume?

$$V = \frac{4}{3}\pi r^3$$

$$V = \frac{4}{3}\pi(12)^3$$

$$V = \frac{4}{3}(3.14)(1,728)$$

$$V = \frac{4}{3}(5,425.92)$$

$$V = 7,234.56 \text{ cubic inches } (7,234.56 \text{ in.}^3)$$

Practice Items–Volume

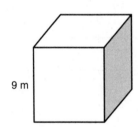

1. What is the volume of the cube above?

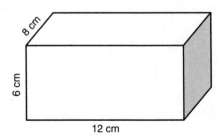

2. What is the volume of the rectangular solid above?

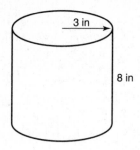

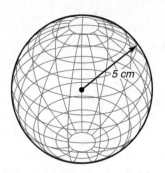

3. What is the volume of the cylinder above?

4. What is the volume of the sphere above?

Shapes and Formulas: Summary

Shapes	Formulas
	Triangle Area = 1/2 the base × the height $A = 1/2\ bh$ Perimeter = $a + b + c$
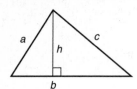	**Square** Area = length × width $A = lw$ Perimeter = side + side + side + side $P = 4s$
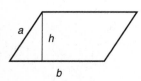	**Rectangle** Area = length × width $A = lw$ Perimeter = 2 × length + 2 × width $P = 2l + 2w$
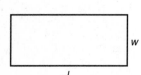	**Parallelogram and Rhombus** Area = base × height $A = bh$ Perimeter = 2 × length + 2 × width $P = 2l + 2w$
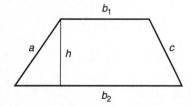	**Trapezoid** Area = the sum of the two bases divided by 2 × height Perimeter = $a + b_1 + b_2 + c$ $P = a + b_1 + b_2 + c$

Shapes	**Formulas**

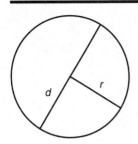

Circle
The distance around the circle is its circumference (*C*).
The length of a line segment passing through the center
with endpoints on the circle is the diameter (*d*). The
length of a line segment connecting the center to a
point on the circle is the radius (*r*). The diameter is
twice the length of the radius ($d = 2r$).

$C = \pi d = 2\pi r$
$A = \pi r^2$
$\pi = 3.14$ or $22/7$

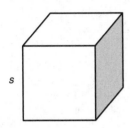

Cube
Volume = side × side × side
$V = s^3$

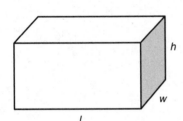

Rectangular Solid
Volume = length × width × height
$V = lwh$

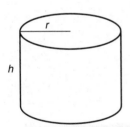

Cylinder
Volume = πr^2 × height
$V = \pi r^2 h$

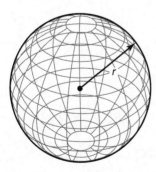

Sphere
Volume = 4/3 πr^3
$V = 4/3\ \pi r^3$

GEOMETRY QUIZ— ANSWERS AND CHART

Scoring Your Test

Compare your answer to the correct answer. Mark an X in the column if you got the item correct. Total the number correct.

Gauging Your Level of Performance

In the following chart, find the number of items that you got correct. See the suggestions listed for your performance.

Item Number	Correct Answer	Mark X if You Picked the Correct Answer
1	C	✓
2	A	✓
3	C	✓
4	B	✓
5	C	✓
6	A	X
7	C	✓
8	C	✓
9	A	X
10	A	✓
11	B	✓
12	A	✓
13	B	✓
14	A	✓
15	A	✓
16	D	X
17	B	✓
18	D	✓
19	A	X
20	C	✓
21	B	✓
22	C	✓
23	B	
24	D	✓
25	D	✓
26	C	X
27	B	X
28	C	
29	A	X
30	D	
Total Correct		

30	This is pretty good work. Rework the items that you got wrong so that you can improve your score. This test is a part of the AFQT, and you must do well on it.
29	
28	
27	You are doing OK. Go back and review the lessons on those areas that you got wrong. You should strive to get at least 28 items correct.
26	
25	
24	You need to keep studying and practicing. You should not be satisfied until you can easily work the problems. Spend time working on the geometry problems in this chapter. Keep working and reworking problems until you are comfortable with the processes. Try the geometry quiz again.
23	
22	
21	
20	
19	
18	
17	
16	
15	
14	
13	
12	
11	
10	
9	
8	
7	
6	
5	
4	
3	
2	
1	
0	

ANSWERS TO PRACTICE ITEMS
Practice Items—Angles

1. B
2. 180°
3. 143°
4. 74°
5. 24°
6. 156°
7. 43°
8. 140°
9. 150°
10. 110°

Practice Items—Triangles

1. 60°
2. 4 in.
3. 40°
4. 15 cm
5. 60°
6. b
7. 2 cm; 3 cm
8. 65°

Practice Items—Quadrilaterals

1. 360°
2. 16 in.
3. 360°
4. 60°
5. 90°

Practice Items—Perimeter and Area

1. 8 in.
2. 6 in.^{2}
3. 24 in.
4. 32 in.^{2}
5. 45 cm
6. 100 cm^2

Practice Items—Circles: Circumference and Area

1. 162.8 cm
2. 314 cm^2

Practice Items—Volume

1. 729 m^3
2. 576 cm^3
3. 226.08 in.^{3}
4. 532.33 cm^3

Chapter 9

Sharpen Your Word Problem Skills

READ THIS SECTION TO LEARN:

- **What kinds of word problems appear on the ASVAB Arithmetic Reasoning test**

- **Techniques for solving every kind of ASVAB word problem**

- **Tips and strategies to help you raise your ASVAB Arithmetic Reasoning score**

INTRODUCTION: ASVAB WORD PROBLEMS

What is a word problem? Basically it is a description of a real-life situation that requires a mathematical solution. To solve a word problem, you need to translate the situation into mathematical terms and then calculate the answer.

All of the questions on the ASVAB Arithmetic Reasoning test are word problems. To do well,

you need to learn good word problem–solving skills. The following pages will show you many different kinds of arithmetic word problems. For each kind, you'll learn how to translate the facts of the problem into mathematical terms. Then you'll see how to use those terms to set up an equation. Finally, you'll see how to solve that equation for the missing piece of information that you're looking for.

Suggested Review Plan for Word Problems

- Take the Word Problems Quiz and score it.
- Mark those problems that you got wrong and those that you were not sure of.
- Study any problems that you answered incorrectly or were hesitant about.
- Reread the corresponding review section.
- Pay special attention to the examples.
- Work until you understand how to solve the example problems given.

- Complete the practice items.
- Work the Word Problems Quiz again.

Remember that while you probably won't get these exact problems on the ASVAB, knowing how to solve them will help you do your best on the actual test. The answers are found on page 208.

WORD PROBLEMS QUIZ

1. The U.S. Treasury Department spends 3.5 cents to manufacture every quarter. 3.5 cents is what percent of the value of the coin?

   A. 3%
   B. 7%
   C. 12%
   D. 14%

2. A person's recommended weight can be calculated using the following formula:

   $w = \dfrac{11(h - 40)}{2}$ where w = weight and h = height in inches

   If Stuart is 5 feet 10 inches tall, what is his recommended weight?

   A. 135 lb
   B. 155 lb
   C. 165 lb
   D. 167 lb

3. It takes 200 lb of sugar cane to produce 5 lb of refined sugar. How many pounds of sugar cane does it take to produce 200 lb of refined sugar?

   A. 2,500 lb
   B. 7,500 lb
   C. 7,700 lb
   D. 8,000 lb

4. Rudy is training for a race. On Monday he ran 2 km. On Tuesday he ran 15% farther than on Monday. If he increases his running distance by the same percentage each day, on which day will he first run more than 4 km?

   A. Wednesday
   B. Thursday
   C. Friday
   D. Saturday

5. Julie's salary is $600 per month, but after taxes and insurance are deducted, her monthly paycheck is $444. What percent of her monthly salary goes for taxes and insurance?

   A. 15%
   B. 26%
   C. 33%
   D. 34%

6. Keisha worked 75 hours during July at a pay rate of $12.50/hour. What were her total earnings for the month before taxes and insurance were deducted?

   A. $447.50
   B. $937.50
   C. $1,447.50
   D. $1,667.50

7. Debbie is walking to raise money for her favorite charity. She is being sponsored by Sally at 10 cents per mile, by Lucie at 12 cents per mile, and by Kelsey at 14 cents per mile. If she walks 8 miles, how much money will she raise?

   A. $2.88
   B. $3.12
   C. $5.25
   D. $10.75

8. Mark has saved 150 quarters in a jar. Of that total, 25 were minted before 1970, 35 were minted between 1970 and 1980, and the remaining quarters were minted after 1980. If Mark picks a quarter out of the jar without looking, what is the probability that he will pick a quarter minted after 1980?

   A. 3:5
   B. 1:2
   C. 7:8
   D. 9:5

9. The bar graph shows the results of a survey asking workers in a company to tell what means of transportation they use to get to work. Based on the graph, what percent of all

the workers surveyed said that they take the bus to work?

How Workers Get to Work

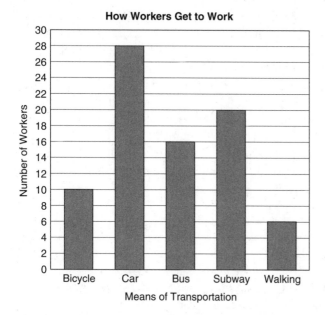

A. 16%
B. 20%
C. 31%
D. 35%

10. Jennifer was elected state senator with 60% of the vote. Which of the following represents that percent as a fraction in simplest form?

A. $\frac{60}{100}$

B. $\frac{6}{10}$

C. $\frac{3}{5}$

D. $\frac{3}{2}$

11. Samuel's current salary is $30,000. He has been promised a raise to $31,500 next year. His raise will be what percent increase over his current salary?

A. 3%
B. 3.5%
C. 4%
D. 5%

12. Phillip deposited $450 in an account that earns 5% interest, compounded yearly. If he makes no further deposits, how much will be in the account after 2 years?

A. $472.50
B. $491.14
C. $496.13
D. $512.24

13. If Kevin saves $4.75 per week, how many weeks will it take him to save $266?

A. 27
B. 34
C. 51
D. 56

14. If an airplane flies at an average speed of 320 miles per hour, how long will it take to fly 1,200 miles?

A. 2.50 hours
B. 3.25 hours
C. 3.75 hours
D. 4.5 hours

15. What is the difference between 2 meters and 180 centimeters?

A. 2 cm
B. 12 cm
C. 18 cm
D. 20 cm

HOW TO TACKLE WORD PROBLEMS

Here are some helpful suggestions for dealing with word problems.

- Read the problem all the way through before you start making any calculations. That way, you will better understand what the problem is about and what you are supposed to find out.
- Be sure you understand what the problem is asking. Are you supposed to find a distance? How fast something is moving? When someone will arrive at point *A*? How much something costs? How many items you can buy if you have a certain amount of money? How much older Kim is than Kay? Draw a picture if that helps.

- List the information that the problem gives you. Note any units of measure (meters, pounds, feet per second, and the like).
- Look for key words in the problem that define relationships or indicate what mathematical operation you need to use. (See the list of key words that follows.)
- Figure out what unit of measure you must use to express your answer. Cubic meters? Centimeters per second? Dollars? Minutes? Number of items?
- Weed out unnecessary information that will not help you solve the problem.
- Use the information you have gathered to create an equation to help you solve the problem.
- Solve the equation.

Key Words

Many word problems contain key words that tell you what mathematical operation you need to use to solve the problem. It pays to know these key words, so be sure you study the following list.

Key Words	Example Phrases
	These key words tell you to *add*.
Increased by	If the temperature is increased by
More than	If the bicycle costs $75 more than
Sum	If the sum of the paychecks is
Total	The total number of payments equals
Added	If *a* is added to *b*
Plus	If the interest plus the principal is
Combined	If the volume of the cube is combined with
In all	How many pounds in all
Successive	The cost of eight successive phone bills
	These key words tell you to *subtract*.
Less than	The interest payment was less than
Difference	The difference between the time it takes to
Are left	How many pieces of pie are left if
Fewer than	If there are 15 fewer scholarships this year than
Minus	Some number minus 36
Reduced by	If the federal budget is reduced by
	These key words tell you to *multiply*.
Times	There are three times as many red tiles as blue tiles
Product	The product of *a* and *b* is
Increased by a factor of	If the speed is increased by a factor of
Decreased by a factor of	If the temperature is decreased by a factor of
At	If you buy 12 cameras at $249 each
Per	If a ferry can carry 20 cars per trip, how many cars can it carry in 6 trips?
Total	If you spend $10 a week on movies for a total of five weeks
Twice	The house covers twice as many square feet as

Key Words	Example Phrases
	These key words tell you to *divide*.
Quotient	What is the quotient if the numerator is 500?
Divided equally among	If 115 tickets are divided equally among five groups
Divided into equal groups	If the students were divided into six equal groups
Ratio of	If the ratio of oxygen to hydrogen is
Per	If a ferry can carry 24 cars per trip, how many trips will it take to carry 144 cars?
Percent	What percent of 100 is 30?
Half	If half the profits go to charity, then how much
	These key words tell you to use an *equal sign*.
Is	If the total bill is $19.35
Sells for	If the car sells for $26,000
Gives	If multiplying a^2 and b^2 gives c^2

Practice Items—Key Words

For each of the following phrases, indicate what operation is appropriate.

1. How many are left? _____

2. What is the ratio of 6 to 3? _____

3. What is the total? _____

4. How much is twice the amount? _____

5. If it sells for _____

Setting Up an Equation and Solving for an Unknown

Before you start tackling word problems, you need to know how to set up an equation and solve for an unknown. For each problem, you will be given certain pieces of information ("what you know"). You first need to translate this information into mathematical terms. Then you can use those terms to set up an equation. An *equation* is nothing more than a mathematical expression that indicates that one mathematical term is equal to another. The terms in an equation are shown on opposite sides of an equal sign. The missing piece of information that you are looking for ("what you need to find") is called the *unknown*. In your equation, you can represent an unknown by a letter, such as x or a.

In the pages that follow, you will see how to set up equations for many different kinds of word problems. The process of solving an equation for an

unknown is pretty simple. Work through these examples until you get perfectly comfortable with the process.

Examples

Solve for x.

$$25x = 200$$

This equation is read, "25 times some unknown number x equals 200." Your task is to determine what number x is. Here is how to solve this equation.

Divide both sides of the equation by 25:

$$\frac{25x}{25} = \frac{200}{25}$$

$$x = 200/25$$

$$x = 8$$

Solve for x:

$$\frac{x}{3} = \frac{5}{45}$$

To solve this type of problem, cross multiply (45 times x and 3 times 5).

$$45x = 15$$

$$x = 15/45 = 1/3 = 0.33$$

Solve for x:

$$\frac{10}{x} = \frac{50}{350}$$

To solve this problem, cross multiply (10 times 350 and 50 times x).

$$50x = 3,500$$
$$x = 70$$

To check your answer, merely substitute 70 back into the equation and see if it works.

$$\frac{10}{70} = \frac{50}{350}$$

You can reduce the fractions to $\frac{1}{7} = \frac{1}{7}$ or you can cross multiply (10 times 350 and 70 times 50), making $3,500 = 3,500$. Either way, you are correct.

Arithmetic Word Problem Types

Simple interest

Compound interest

Ratio and proportion

Motion

Percent

Percent change

Numbers and number relationships

Age

Measurement

TYPES OF ASVAB ARITHMETIC WORD PROBLEMS

In the pages that follow, you will learn about many different kinds of word problems that you are likely to see on the ASVAB Arithmetic Reasoning test. For each kind, you will see how to use the information you are given to set up an equation. Then you will see how to solve the equation for the unknown that is the answer to the problem. The following chart shows the different kinds of word problems discussed in this chapter.

Simple Interest

Interest is an amount paid for the use of money. The *interest rate* is the percent paid per year or some other period. The *principal* is the amount of money on which interest is paid. *Simple interest* is interest that is computed based only on the principal, the interest rate, and the time. To calculate simple interest, use this formula:

$$\text{Interest} = \text{principal} \times \text{rate} \times \text{time.}$$
$$I = prt$$

Examples

Martina has $300 in a savings account that pays simple interest at a rate of 3% per year. How much interest will she earn on that $300 if she keeps it in the account for 5 years?

Procedure
What must you find? The amount of simple interest
What are the units? Dollars
What do you know? Rate = 3% per year; time = 5 years; principal = $300
Create an equation and solve.

$$I = (\$300)(0.03)(5)$$
$$I = \$45$$

Five years ago, Robin deposited $500 in a savings account that pays simple interest. She made no further deposits, and today the account is worth $750. What is the rate of interest?

Procedure
What must you find? The rate of simple interest
What are the units? Percent per year
What do you know? Interest = $250 ($750 − $500); principal = $500; time = 5 years
Write an equation and solve.

$$250 = (500)(x)(5)$$
$$250 = 2,500x$$
$$\frac{250}{2,500} = x$$
$$x = \frac{250}{2,500} = 0.10 \text{ or } 10\%$$

Practice Items–Simple Interest

1. Sheena has $500 in a savings account that pays simple interest at a rate of 2% per year. How much interest will she earn on that $500 if she keeps it in the account for 5 years?
2. Five years ago, Kevin deposited $1,000 in a savings account that pays simple interest. He made no further deposits, and today the account is worth $1,250. What is the rate of interest?
3. Two years ago, Peggy borrowed $5,000 to purchase a car. The interest rate is 2.5%. After two years, how much interest has she paid?

Compound Interest

Compound interest is interest that is paid on the principal and also on any interest that has already been paid. To calculate compound interest, you can use the formula $I = prt$, but you must calculate the interest for each time period and then combine them for a total.

Example

Ricardo bought a $1,000 savings bond that earns 5% interest compounded annually. How much interest will he earn in two years?

Procedure

What must you find? The amount of compound interest

What are the units? Dollars

What do you know? Principal = $1,000; rate = 5%; time = 2 years

Create an equation and solve.

To find the compound interest, calculate the amount earned in the first year. Add that amount to the principal, then calculate the interest earned in the second year. Total the amount of interest earned in the two years.

Year 1:

$$I = prt$$
$$I = (\$1,000)(0.05)(1)$$
$$I = \$50$$

New principal = $1,050.

Year 2:

$$I = prt$$
$$I = (\$1,050)(0.05)(1)$$
$$I = \$52.50$$

So the total compound interest paid in two years is $50 + $52.50 = $102.50.

Practice Items–Compound Interest

1. Kerry bought a $500 savings bond that earns 8% interest compounded annually. How much will the bond be worth in two years?
2. Leo invested $5,000 in a savings account that earned 3.5% annually. How much will the account be worth in three years?

Ratio and Proportion

On the ASVAB, you will almost certainly encounter word problems that that will require you to work with ratios and proportions.

Examples

Kim reads an average of 150 pages per week. At that rate, how many weeks will it take him to read 1,800 pages?

Procedure

What must you find? How long it will take to read 1,800 pages.

What are the units? Weeks

What do you know? 150 pages read each week; 1,800 pages to be read

Set up a proportion and solve.

$$\frac{\text{Number of pages}}{1 \text{ week}} = \frac{\text{number of pages}}{x \text{ weeks}}$$

Substitute values into the equation.

$$\frac{150 \text{ pages}}{1 \text{ week}} = \frac{1800 \text{ pages}}{x \text{ weeks}}$$

Cross multiply:

$$150x = 1,800$$
$$x = 12 \text{ weeks}$$

It takes 8 hours to fill a swimming pool that holds 3,500 gallons of water. At that rate, how many hours will it take to fill a pool that holds 8,750 gallons?

Procedure

What must you find? How long it will take to fill the 8,750-gallon pool

What are the units? Hours

What do you know? Number of hours for 3,500 gallons

Set up a proportion and solve.

$$\frac{\text{Number of gallons}}{\text{Number of hours}} = \frac{\text{number of gallons}}{\text{number of hours}}$$

$$\frac{3,500 \text{ gallons}}{8 \text{ hours}} = \frac{8,750 \text{ gallons}}{x \text{ hours}}$$

Cross multiply:

$$3,500x = (8)(8,750)$$
$$x = 20 \text{ hours}$$

An airplane travels the 1,700 miles from Phoenix to Nashville in 2.5 hours. Flying at the same speed, the plane could travel the 2,550 miles from Phoenix to Boston in how many hours?

Procedure

What must you find? The time it would take to fly 2,550 miles

What are the units? Hours

What do you know? The plane traveled 1,700 miles in 2.5 hours

Set up a proportion and solve.

$$\frac{\text{Number of miles}}{\text{Number of hours}} = \frac{\text{number of miles}}{\text{number of hours}}$$

Substitute values.

$$\frac{1,700 \text{ miles}}{2.5 \text{ hours}} = \frac{2,550 \text{ miles}}{x \text{ hours}}$$

Cross multiply:

$$1,700x = (2.5)(2,550)$$
$$1,700x = 6,375$$
$$x = 3.75 \text{ hours}$$

Practice Items—Ratio and Proportion

1. Jerry reads an average of 75 pages per week. At that rate, how many weeks will it take him to read 1,000 pages?
2. It takes 2 minutes to fill a balloon that holds 4,000 units of helium. At that rate, how many minutes

will it take to fill a balloon that holds 6,000 units of helium?

3. An empty swimming pool can hold 5,000 gallons of water. If a hose can fill the pool at 250 gallons every 1/2 hour, how long will it take to fill the pool?

Motion

Motion problems deal with how long it will take to get from point *a* to point *b* if you are traveling at a certain steady rate. To solve them, use this formula:

$$\text{Distance} = \text{rate} \times \text{time or } d = rt$$

Example

If a racing boat travels at a steady rate of 80 miles per hour, how many miles could it travel in 3.5 hours?

Procedure

What must you find? Distance traveled in 3.5 hours

What are the units? Miles

What do you know? Rate = 80 miles per hour; time = 3.5 hours

Create an equation and solve.

$$d = rt$$

Substitute values into the formula:

$$d = (80)(3.5)$$
$$d = 280 \text{ miles}$$

Practice Items—Motion

1. If a motorcycle travels at a steady rate of 40 miles per hour, how many miles could it travel in 4.5 hours?
2. If a jet travels at 450 miles per hour, how long will it take for the jet to travel 5,940 miles?

Percent

There are likely to be word problems involving percent on both the Arithmetic Reasoning and the Mathematics Knowledge tests of the ASVAB.

Examples

Lilly's bill at a restaurant is $22.00, and she wants to leave a 15% tip. How much should her tip be?

Procedure

What must you find? The amount of the tip

What are the units? Dollars and cents

What do you know? Total bill = $22.00; percent of tip = 15
Create an equation and solve.

Tip = 15% × 22.00

Substitute and solve.

$t = (0.15)(22.00)$
$t = \$3.30$

Frederick earns $1,500 per month at his job, but 28% of that amount is deducted for taxes. What is his monthly take-home pay?

Procedure

What must you find? Monthly take-home pay
What are the units? Dollars and cents
What do you know? Monthly pay before taxes = $1,500; percent deducted = 28%
Create an equation and solve.

Take-home pay is 1,500 minus 28% × 1,500.

$T = 1,500 - (1,500 \times 0.28)$
$T = 1,500 - (420)$
$T = \$1,080$

40 is 80% of what number?

Procedure

What must you find? The number of which 40 is 80%
What are the units? Numbers
What do you know? 40 is 80% of some larger number
Create an equation and solve.

$40 = 0.8x$
$0.8x = 40$
$x = \dfrac{40}{.8}$
$x = 50$

Practice Items—Percent

1. If your gross monthly pay is $3,000 and 32% is removed for taxes and insurance, what is your net pay?
2. If you invest $1,000 in a mutual fund that has a 0.5% fee, how much is the fee?

Percent Change

Some ASVAB word problems ask you to calculate the percent of change from one number or amount to another.

Examples

Samantha now earns $300 per month working at a cosmetics store, but starting next month her monthly salary will be $375. Her raise will be what percent increase over her current salary?

Procedure

What must you find? Percent change from current salary
What are the units? Percent
What do you know? Current pay = $300/month; pay after the raise = $375/month
Create an equation and solve.

$$\text{Percent change} = \frac{\text{amount of change}}{\text{starting point}}$$

Substitute values and solve:

$$\text{Percent change} = \frac{(375 - 300)}{300}$$

$$\text{Percent change} = \frac{75}{300}$$

Percent change = 0.25 or 25%

On his sixteenth birthday, Brad was 60 inches tall. On his seventeenth birthday, he was 65 inches tall. What was the percent increase in Brad's height to the nearest whole number during the year?

Procedure

What must you find? Percent change in height
What are the units? Percent
What do you know? Starting height = 60 inches; height after a year = 65 inches
Create an equation and solve.

$$\text{Percent change} = \frac{\text{amount of change}}{\text{starting point}}$$

Substitute values and solve.

$$\text{Percent change} = \frac{5 \text{ inches}}{60 \text{ inches}}$$

Perscent change = 0.08 or 8%

At a certain store, every item is discounted by 15% off the original price. If Kevin buys a CD originally priced at $15.00 and a baseball cap originally priced at $11.50, how much money to the nearest cent will he save?

Procedure

What must you find? Total amount saved
What are the units? Dollars and cents

What do you know? Percent change = 15%; original price for two items = $15.00 + $11.50 = $26.50
Create an equation and solve.

$$\text{Percent change} = \frac{\text{amount of change}}{\text{starting point}}$$

Substitute values and solve.

$$0.15 = \frac{x}{26.50}$$
$$x = 0.15(26.50)$$
$$x = \$3.98$$

Practice Items—Percent Change

1. A company has reduced its subscription price from $15.00 per month to $13.00 per month. What is the percent reduction to the nearest whole number?
2. The tuition for college was increased from $10,000 per year to $12,500 per year. What is the percent increase?
3. A car went on a 12% "end of the year" sale. The car's original price was $25,000. What is the sale price?

Numbers and Number Relationships

Pay attention to the key words in this type pf word problem.

Examples

If the sum of two numbers is 45 and one number is 5 more than the other, what are the two numbers?

Procedure

What must you find? The value of each number
What are the units? Numbers
What do you know? Sum of two numbers is 45; one number is 5 more than the other
Create an equation and solve.

Let x be the smaller number.

$$x + (x + 5) = 45$$

Solve for x:

$$x + x + 5 = 45$$
$$2x = 40$$
$$x = 20$$

So the two numbers are 20 and 20 + 5 = 25.

One number is twice the size of another and the two numbers together total 150. What are the two numbers?

Procedure

What must you find? The value of each number
What are the units? Numbers
What do you know? One number is twice the size of the other; the sum of the numbers is 150
Create an equation and solve.

Let x be the smaller number.

$$x + 2x = 150$$
$$3x = 150$$
$$x = 50$$

So the smaller number is 50 and the larger number is 100.

Age

Some word problems ask you to calculate a person's age given certain facts.

Example

Jessica is 26 years old. Two years ago she was twice as old as her brother Ned. How old is Ned now?

Procedure

What must you find? Ned's age now
What are the units? Years
What do you know? When Jessica was 24, she was 2 times as old as Ned
Create an equation and solve.

Prepare an equation that shows the relationship.
Let x = Ned's age two years ago.

$$2x = 24$$
$$x = 12$$

Ned's age two years later = 12 + 2 = 14 years.

Practice Items—Numbers and Number Relationships

1. One number is three times another number less 12. If the first number is 108, what is the second number?
2. Aaron is 30 years old. If his sister Angela is half his age plus 2 years, how old is Angela?

Measurement

Some word problems will ask you to use what you know about units of measure to solve problems. If necessary, review the table of units of measure in Chapter 8.

Example

How many cups of milk are in 5 pints of milk?

Procedure

What must you find? The number of cups of milk in 5 pints

What are the units? Cups

What do you know? According to the chart in Chapter 8, there are 2 cups in 1 pint

Create an equation and solve.

Let x = the number of cups in 5 pints.

$$5 \text{ pints} = x \text{ cups}$$
$$1 \text{ pint} = 2 \text{ cups}$$
$$5 \times 1 \text{ pint} = 5 \times 2 \text{ cups} \text{ (Multiply both sides of}$$
$$\text{the equation by 5)}$$
$$5 \text{ pints} = 10 \text{ cups} = x \text{ cups}$$
$$x = 10$$

So there are 10 cups in 5 pints.

Practice Items – Measurement

1. If Candice lives 2 miles from Thomas, how many feet is the distance?
2. A football field is 100 yards. If a ship is 4 football fields long, how many feet long is the ship?

ASVAB GEOMETRY WORD PROBLEMS

Word problems on the ASVAB may also deal with geometry concepts, such as perimeter, area, and volume. To solve these problems, you may also need to use information about different units of measure. To review units of measure, see Chapter 8.

Just as with other kinds of word problems, you can solve geometry problems by following a specific procedure. In the examples that follow, pay special attention to the procedure outlined in each solution. Follow this same procedure whenever you need to solve this kind of word problem.

Examples

Sally is buying wood to make a rectangular picture frame measuring 11 in. × 14 in. The wood costs 25 cents per inch. How much will Sally have to pay for the wood?

Procedure

What must you find? The cost of the wood for the frame

What are the units? Dollars and cents

What do you know? The cost of the wood per inch; the shape of the frame; the measure of the frame

Create an equation and solve.

Length of wood needed for rectangular frame = $2l + 2w$

Substitute values and solve:

Length of wood = $2(14) + 2(11)$
Length of wood = $28 + 22 = 50$ in.

If each inch costs 0.25, then $0.25 \times 50 = \$12.50$.

Sergei is planting rosebushes in a rectangular garden measuring 12 ft × 20 ft. Each rosebush needs 8 ft^2 of space. How many rosebushes can Sergei plant in the garden?

Procedure

What must you find? The number of rosebushes that can be planted in the garden

What are the units? Numbers

What do you know? The shape of the garden; the garden length and width; the amount of area needed for each rosebush

Create an equation and solve.

$$A = lw$$

Substitute values and solve.

$$A = 12 \times 20 = 240 \text{ ft}^2$$

Each rosebush needs 8 ft^2.

$$240 \div 8 = 30$$

Sergei can plant 30 rosebushes in the garden.

Practice Items–Geometry

1. A floor is 10 feet long and 12 feet wide. Chris wants to lay tiles that are 10 inches square on the floor. How many whole tiles will he need?
2. Ian has a front lawn that is 300 feet by 120 feet. If 1 pound of fertilizer is needed for every 600 square feet, how many pounds of fertilizer are needed?
3. Gerry wants to inflate an exercise ball. The ball has a radius of 15 inches. If a pump can push 5 cubic inches of air every second, how many seconds will it take to inflate the ball?
4. A gray wolf needs 10.75 square miles of land to live. If a national park measures 20 miles by 60 miles of land, about how many grey wolves can be supported?
5. A garden is shaped like a triangle with a base of 40 feet and a height of 25 feet. If Ralph wants to plant lemon trees, each of which requires about 15 square feet of growing space, what is the maximum number of trees he can plant?

WORD PROBLEMS QUIZ—ANSWERS AND CHART

Scoring Your Test

Compare your answer to the correct answer. Mark an X in the column if you got the item correct. Total the number correct.

Gauging Your Level of Performance

In the following chart, find the number of items that you got correct. See the suggestions listed for your performance.

Item Number	Correct Answer	Mark X if You Picked the Correct Answer
1	D	
2	C	
3	D	
4	D	
5	B	
6	B	
7	A	
8	A	
9	B	
10	C	
11	D	
12	C	
13	D	
14	C	
15	D	
Total correct		

15	This is pretty good work. Rework the items that you got wrong so that you know how to work the problems.
14	
13	You are doing OK. Go back and review the lessons on those areas that you got wrong.
12	
11	You need to keep studying and practicing. You should not be satisfied until you can easily work the problems.
10	
9	Spend time working on the word problems in this chapter.
8	
7	
6	Keep working and reworking problems until you are comfortable with the processes. Try the word problems quiz again to determine your improvement.
5	
4	
3	
2	
1	
0	

ANSWERS TO PRACTICE ITEMS
Practice Items—Key Words

1. Subtract
2. Divide
3. Add
4. Multiply
5. Equals

Practice Items—Simple Interest

1. $50
2. 5%
3. $250

Practice Items—Compound Interest

1. $583.20
2. $5,938.43

Practice Items—Ratio and Proportion

1. 13.33 weeks
2. 3 minutes
3. 20 1/2 hours or 10 hours

Practice Items—Motion

1. 180 miles
2. 13.2 hours

Practice Items—Percent

1. $2,040.00
2. $5.00

Practice Items—Percent Change

1. About 13%
2. 25%
3. $22,000

Practice Items—Numbers and Number Relationships

1. 40
2. 17

Practice Items—Measurement

1. 10,560 feet
2. 1,200 feet

Practice Items—Geometry

1. 173 tiles
2. 60 pounds
3. 2,826 seconds
4. About 112 wolves
5. 33 trees

Part 3

TWO AFQT
PRACTICE
TEST FORMS

AFQT Practice Test Form 1

The following practice test form is designed to be just like the real AFQT portion of the ASVAB test. It matches the actual test in content coverage and level of difficulty. The test is in four parts: Arithmetic Reasoning, Word Knowledge, Paragraph Comprehension, and Mathematics Knowledge.

On this test, the parts are numbered from 2 through 5. (When you take the real ASVAB, Part 1 will be a test of General Science. It is not included here because it isn't a part of the AFQT.)

This Practice Test Form will be an accurate reflection of how you'll do on test day if you treat it as if it were the real examination. Here are some hints on how to take the test under conditions similar to those of the actual exam:

- Find a quiet place to work and set aside a period of approximately an hour and a half when you will not be disturbed.
- Work on only one part at a time, and use your watch or a timer to keep track of the time limits for each test part.
- Tear out your answer sheet and mark your answers by filling in the ovals for each question. On the computer adaptive version of the test you will mark your answers by clicking on ovals on a computer screen.
- Become familiar with the directions for each part of the test. You'll save time on the actual test day by already being familiar with this information.

At the end of the test, you'll find answer keys for each part and explanations for every question. After you check your answers against the keys, you can complete self-scoring charts that will show you how you did on each part of the test and what test topics you might need to study more. Then review the explanations, paying particular attention to the ones for the questions that you answered incorrectly.

GENERAL DIRECTIONS

IF YOU ARE TAKING THE PAPER-AND-PENCIL VERSION OF THE ASVAB, THE TEST ADMINISTRATOR WILL READ THE FOLLOWING ALOUD TO YOU:

DO NOT WRITE YOUR NAME OR MAKE ANY MARKS in this booklet. Mark your answers on the separate answer sheet. Use the scratch paper which was given to you for any figuring you need to do. Return this scratch paper with your other papers when you finish the test.

If you need another pencil while taking this test, hold your pencil above your head. A proctor will bring you another one.

This booklet contains eight tests. *[Note: This practice test form for the AFQT contains only four of the eight tests.]* Each test has its own instructions and time limit. When you finish a test, you may check your work in that test ONLY. Do not go on to the next test until the examiner tells you to do so. Do not turn back to a previous test at any time.

For each question, be sure to pick the BEST ONE of the possible answers listed. Each test has its own instructions and time limit. When you have decided which one of the choices given is the best answer to the question, blacken the space on your answer sheet that has the same number and letter as your choice. Mark only in the answer space. BE CAREFUL NOT TO MAKE ANY STRAY MARKS ON YOUR ANSWER SHEET. Each test has a separate section on the answer sheet. Be sure you mark your answers for each test in the section that belongs to that test.

Here is an example of correct marking on an answer sheet.

S1   A triangle has

    A. 2 sides
    B. 3 sides
    C. 4 sides
    D. 5 sides

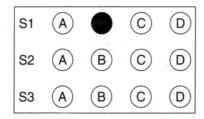

S1. [oval A] [oval B, blackened] [oval C] [oval D]

The correct answer to Sample Question S1 is B.

Next to the item, note how space B opposite number S1 has been blackened. Your marks should look just like this and be placed in the space with the same number and letter as the correct answer to the question. Remember, there is only ONE BEST ANSWER for each question. If you are not sure of the answer, make the BEST GUESS you can. If you want to change your answer, COMPLETELY ERASE your first answer mark.

Answer as many questions as possible. Do not spend too much time on any one question. Work QUICKLY, but work ACCURATELY. DO NOT TURN THE PAGE UNTIL TOLD TO DO SO. Are there any questions?

AFQT PRACTICE TEST FORM 1

Answer Sheet

Note: When you take the real ASVAB, Part 1 will be a test of General Science. This test is *not* part of the AFQT and is *not* included here.

PART 2-AR	PART 3-WK	PART 4-PC	PART 5-MK
1 (A)(B)(C)(D)	1 (A)(B)(C)(D)	1 (A)(B)(C)(D)	1 (A)(B)(C)(D)
2 (A)(B)(C)(D)	2 (A)(B)(C)(D)	2 (A)(B)(C)(D)	2 (A)(B)(C)(D)
3 (A)(B)(C)(D)	3 (A)(B)(C)(D)	3 (A)(B)(C)(D)	3 (A)(B)(C)(D)
4 (A)(B)(C)(D)	4 (A)(B)(C)(D)	4 (A)(B)(C)(D)	4 (A)(B)(C)(D)
5 (A)(B)(C)(D)	5 (A)(B)(C)(D)	5 (A)(B)(C)(D)	5 (A)(B)(C)(D)
6 (A)(B)(C)(D)	6 (A)(B)(C)(D)	6 (A)(B)(C)(D)	6 (A)(B)(C)(D)
7 (A)(B)(C)(D)	7 (A)(B)(C)(D)	7 (A)(B)(C)(D)	7 (A)(B)(C)(D)
8 (A)(B)(C)(D)	8 (A)(B)(C)(D)	8 (A)(B)(C)(D)	8 (A)(B)(C)(D)
9 (A)(B)(C)(D)	9 (A)(B)(C)(D)	9 (A)(B)(C)(D)	9 (A)(B)(C)(D)
10 (A)(B)(C)(D)	10 (A)(B)(C)(D)	10 (A)(B)(C)(D)	10 (A)(B)(C)(D)
11 (A)(B)(C)(D)	11 (A)(B)(C)(D)	11 (A)(B)(C)(D)	11 (A)(B)(C)(D)
12 (A)(B)(C)(D)	12 (A)(B)(C)(D)	12 (A)(B)(C)(D)	12 (A)(B)(C)(D)
13 (A)(B)(C)(D)	13 (A)(B)(C)(D)	13 (A)(B)(C)(D)	13 (A)(B)(C)(D)
14 (A)(B)(C)(D)	14 (A)(B)(C)(D)	14 (A)(B)(C)(D)	14 (A)(B)(C)(D)
15 (A)(B)(C)(D)	15 (A)(B)(C)(D)	15 (A)(B)(C)(D)	15 (A)(B)(C)(D)
16 (A)(B)(C)(D)	16 (A)(B)(C)(D)		16 (A)(B)(C)(D)
17 (A)(B)(C)(D)	17 (A)(B)(C)(D)		17 (A)(B)(C)(D)
18 (A)(B)(C)(D)	18 (A)(B)(C)(D)		18 (A)(B)(C)(D)
19 (A)(B)(C)(D)	19 (A)(B)(C)(D)		19 (A)(B)(C)(D)
20 (A)(B)(C)(D)	20 (A)(B)(C)(D)		20 (A)(B)(C)(D)
21 (A)(B)(C)(D)	21 (A)(B)(C)(D)		21 (A)(B)(C)(D)
22 (A)(B)(C)(D)	22 (A)(B)(C)(D)		22 (A)(B)(C)(D)
23 (A)(B)(C)(D)	23 (A)(B)(C)(D)		23 (A)(B)(C)(D)
24 (A)(B)(C)(D)	24 (A)(B)(C)(D)		24 (A)(B)(C)(D)
25 (A)(B)(C)(D)	25 (A)(B)(C)(D)		25 (A)(B)(C)(D)
26 (A)(B)(C)(D)	26 (A)(B)(C)(D)		
27 (A)(B)(C)(D)	27 (A)(B)(C)(D)		
28 (A)(B)(C)(D)	28 (A)(B)(C)(D)		
29 (A)(B)(C)(D)	29 (A)(B)(C)(D)		
30 (A)(B)(C)(D)	30 (A)(B)(C)(D)		
	31 (A)(B)(C)(D)		
	32 (A)(B)(C)(D)		
	33 (A)(B)(C)(D)		
	34 (A)(B)(C)(D)		
	35 (A)(B)(C)(D)		

PART 2. ARITHMETIC REASONING

THE TEST ADMINISTRATOR WILL READ THE FOLLOWING ALOUD TO YOU:

Turn to Part 2 and read the directions for Arithmetic Reasoning silently while I read them aloud.

This is a test of arithmetic word problems. Each question is followed by four possible answers. Decide which answer is CORRECT, and then blacken the space on your answer sheet that has the same number and letter as your choice. Use your scratch paper for any figuring you wish to do.

Here is a sample question. DO NOT MARK your answer sheet for this or any further sample questions.

S1   A student buys a sandwich for 80 cents, milk for 20 cents, and pie for 30 cents. How much did the meal cost?

    A. $1.00
    B. $1.20
    C. $1.30
    D. $1.40

The total cost is $1.30; therefore, C is the right answer. Your score on this test will be based on the number of questions you answer correctly. You should try to answer every question. DO NOT SPEND TOO MUCH TIME on any one question. If you finish before time is called, go back and check your work in this part ONLY.

Now find the section of your answer sheet that is marked PART 2. When you are told to begin, start with question number 1 in Part 2 of your test booklet and answer space number 1 in Part 2 on your separate answer sheet.

DO NOT TURN THIS PAGE UNTIL TOLD TO DO SO. You will have 36 minutes for the 30 questions. Are there any questions?

Begin.

1. Louisa went to the grocery store and bought a package of hamburger patties for $6.16, a package of buns for $2.10, a container of mustard for $1.78, a jar of relish for $2.16, and a bag of charcoal for $5.35. What was her total bill?

   A. $12.64
   B. $14.74
   C. $16.15
   D. $17.55

2. Lance bought a shirt for $27.16, slacks for $38.19, socks for $4.45, and a belt for $12.14. If he hands the clerk a $100 bill, what is his change?

   A. $ 0.55
   B. $11.25
   C. $18.06
   D. $20.26

3. Cassidy answered 45 questions correctly on a test with 75 items. What percent did she answer correctly?

   A. 60%
   B. 72%
   C. 84%
   D. 89%

4. Bobby's test scores for Social Studies are 93, 76, 91, 83, and 72. What is his average score?

   A. 83
   B. 87
   C. 91
   D. 93

5. A box of chocolates has 45 pieces. If 9 pieces have nuts in them, what percentage of the chocolates are without nuts?

   A. 20%
   B. 45%
   C. 79%
   D. 80%

6. In the Northshore Swimming Club, 6 of 48 members are female. What is the ratio of females to total members?

   A. $\dfrac{3}{16}$

   B. $\dfrac{1}{15}$

   C. $\dfrac{1}{4}$

   D. $\dfrac{1}{8}$

7. A teacher has assigned 315 pages of reading. If Jessica starts reading on Monday and reads 65 pages each day, on what day will she complete the assignment?

   A. Wednesday
   B. Thursday
   C. Friday
   D. Saturday

8. Jack has been saving coins in a jar so that he can purchase a video game. He has saved 150 pennies, 56 nickels, 98 quarters, and 46 dimes. If he reaches into the jar to pick one coin at random, what is the probability that he will pick a penny?

   A. $\dfrac{1}{2}$

   B. $\dfrac{2}{3}$

   C. $\dfrac{3}{7}$

   D. $\dfrac{112}{138}$

9. Renee deposits $4,000 in a savings account that earns 2% simple interest per year. How much interest will she earn after 1 year?

   A. $60
   B. $80
   C. $95
   D. $120

10. Rachel flies 5,200 miles in 9 hours. What is the average speed of her airplane?

    A. 472.73 miles/hour
    B. 499.17 miles/hour
    C. 577.77 miles/hour
    D. 687.43 miles/hour

11. The Washington High School Science Club has 250 members. In 90 days it hopes to have a membership of 376 by using a Web-based membership campaign. On average, how many new members does it need to sign up each day to reach that goal?

    A. 1
    B. 1.4
    C. 1.5
    D. 2.2

12. Paul has a garden that is 4 meters by 7 meters. If he needs 2 ounces of fertilizer per square meter for the garden to flourish, how many ounces must he use?

    A. 21 oz
    B. 42 oz
    C. 44 oz
    D. 56 oz

13. The local electronics store is holding a 25%-off sale on all its products. Marla selects two CDs at the original price of $14.99 each. What is the price of the two CDs after the 25% discount?

    A. $15.99
    B. $22.48
    C. $25.78
    D. $27.18

14. The Berkeley Athletic Store is running a special back-to-school sale on running shoes. A pair of shoes costs $67.50. In six weeks the price will increase to $87.75. What percent will the price increase?

    A. 15%
    B. 20%
    C. 24%
    D. 30%

15. Two numbers together add to 375. One number is twice the size of the other. What are the two numbers?

    A. 25; 50
    B. 50; 100
    C. 75; 150
    D. 125; 250

16. Patrick is making a frame for a mirror. The mirror is 18 inches by 24 inches. If the wood for the frame costs 50 cents an inch, how much will the wood for the frame cost?

    A. $19.00
    B. $22.00
    C. $42.00
    D. $45.00

17. The distance across a circular track running through its center is 75 yards. What is the distance around the track?

    A. 145.5 yd
    B. 215.5 yd
    C. 235.5 yd
    D. 315.5 yd

18. Jake spent one-fifth of his life in school. If he is now 55, how many years did he spend in school?

    A. 9
    B. 11
    C. 13
    D. 15

19. Paula plays tennis with Lindsey, who is two years younger than Paula. If Paula is 17, how old is Lindsey?

    A. 15
    B. 17
    C. 19
    D. 21

20. Al has three times as much money as Bill. Bill has two times as much money as Charlie. If Charlie has $12.55, how much money does Al have?

    A. $33.75
    B. $75.30
    C. $85.20
    D. $96.35

21. The car owned by Alex gets an average of 26 miles per gallon of gas on the highway. If he recently took a trip of 858 miles, how many gallons of gas did he use?

    A. 33 gallons
    B. 57 gallons
    C. 78 gallons
    D. 84 gallons

22. A swimming pool is 6 feet deep, 44 feet long, and 26 feet wide. What is the volume of the pool?

    A. 2,016 ft^3
    B. 3,966 ft^3
    C. 5,014 ft^3
    D. 6,864 ft^3

23. Josh wants to put a fence around his rectangular garden. The garden is 12 feet by 30 feet. How much fencing must he purchase?

    A. 84 feet
    B. 89 feet
    C. 92 feet
    D. 94 feet

24. In a recent election, Jim received 32% of the votes, Rebecca received 14% of the votes, Peter received 42% of the votes, and Keith received 12% of the votes. If 7,000 votes were cast, how many votes did Rebecca receive?

    A. 680
    B. 980
    C. 1,080
    D. 1,220

25. A circular pool is 3.5 meters deep and has a radius of 9 meters. What is the volume?

    A. 450.2 m^3
    B. 575.9 m^3
    C. 890.2 m^3
    D. 974.4 m^3

26. The diameter of an asteroid is 8,000 miles. What is its circumference?

    A. 19,412 miles
    B. 20,889 miles
    C. 25,120 miles
    D. 28,475 miles

27. Will has $12,444.12 in his checking account. He writes checks for $8,204.94 and $890.99. How much is left in Will's account?

    A. $989.65
    B. $2,259.30
    C. $2,867.30
    D. $3,348.19

28. A club collected $1,085.00. If 75% of that came from membership dues, how much money came from sources other than membership?

    A. $271.25
    B. $338.75
    C. $365.75
    D. $425.05

29. Danny buys a computer originally priced at $750.00, software programs originally priced at $398.75, a printer originally priced at $149.98, and a case of paper originally priced at $24.99. All items are on sale for 15% off. How much will Danny save because of the sale?

    A. $124.94
    B. $198.56
    C. $236.24
    D. $264.74

30. A ladder is placed against a building. If the ladder makes a 65° angle with the ground, what is the measure of the angle that the ladder makes with the building?

    A. 25°
    B. 30°
    C. 35°
    D. 40°

STOP! DO NOT TURN THIS PAGE UNTIL TIME IS UP FOR THIS TEST. IF YOU FINISH BEFORE TIME IS UP, CHECK OVER YOUR WORK ON THIS TEST ONLY.

PART 3. WORD KNOWLEDGE

THE TEST ADMINISTRATOR WILL READ THE FOLLOWING ALOUD TO YOU:

Now turn to Part 3 and read the directions for Word Knowledge silently while I read aloud.

This is a test of your knowledge of word meanings. These questions consist of a sentence or phrase with a word or phrase underlined. From the four choices given, you are to decide which one MEANS THE SAME OR MOST NEARLY THE SAME as the underlined word or phrase. Once you have made your choice, mark the space on your answer sheet that has the same number and letter as your choice.

Look at the sample question.

S1   The weather in this geographic area tends to be <u>moderate</u>.

    A. severe
    B. warm
    C. mild
    D. windy

The correct answer is "mild," which is choice C. Therefore, you would have blackened in space C on your answer sheet.

Your score on this test will be based on the number of questions you answer correctly. You should try to answer every question. DO NOT SPEND TOO MUCH TIME on any one question. If you finish before time is called, go back and check your work in this part <u>ONLY</u>.

Now find the section of your answer sheet that is marked PART 3. When you are told to begin, start with question number 1 in Part 3 of your test booklet and answer space number 1 in Part 3 on your separate answer sheet.

DO NOT TURN THE PAGE UNTIL TOLD TO DO SO. You will have 11 minutes to complete the 35 questions in this part. Are there any questions?

Begin.

1. She <u>yearned</u> for the "good old days," even though her life then had been difficult.

   A. feared
   B. longed
   C. danced
   D. seethed

2. She looked <u>regal</u> in her ball gown.

   A. dowdy
   B. foolish
   C. royal
   D. trivial

3. It was only his <u>persistence</u> that allowed him to reach the other side of the raging river.

   A. termination
   B. resolve
   C. physique
   D. height

4. The danger of the situation <u>pervaded</u> all their thoughts.

   A. permeated
   B. erased
   C. scrambled
   D. eased

5. <u>Indignant</u> most nearly means

   A. splendid
   B. superior
   C. angry
   D. strange

6. <u>Inimitable</u> most nearly means

   A. common
   B. peerless
   C. intimidated
   D. friendly

7. The family was overwhelmed by the veritable <u>onslaught</u> of warm wishes.

   A. attack
   B. removal
   C. lack
   D. list

8. Winning the lottery made them <u>jubilant</u>.

   A. upset
   B. frightened
   C. suspicious
   D. joyous

9. As much as she tried to play grown up like her older sister, her actions were <u>maladroit</u>.

   A. graceful
   B. clumsy
   C. punctual
   D. ridiculous

10. Sal was usually quite supportive of all his friends, but this recent action was quite <u>despicable</u>.

    A. humorous
    B. successful
    C. unexpected
    D. wicked

11. Lance, who wanted to study physics, was distraught to learn that he had to take <u>compulsory</u> English composition courses.

    A. required
    B. optional
    C. important
    D. easy

12. The debate team found the statement to be <u>extraneous</u> to the principal logic of the argument.

    A. poignant
    B. unrelated
    C. critical
    D. useful

13. Even though his grades were barely passing, when Rob walked across the stage at graduation, his pride was not <u>diminished</u>.

    A. acceptable
    B. suppressed
    C. appropriate
    D. acknowledged

14. The conversation was so heated that Gina felt she needed to <u>placate</u> the person who was most angry.

    A. pacify
    B. recognize
    C. oust
    D. chastise

15. Jimmy was so confused by the legal document that he asked his friend for a <u>clarification</u>.

    A. translation
    B. rejection
    C. explanation
    D. conference

16. <u>Massive</u> most nearly means

    A. mischievous
    B. faulty
    C. gigantic
    D. likely

17. The scholars were <u>deluded</u> in their thinking because the documents they were studying were fakes.

    A. enhanced
    B. sharpened
    C. explained
    D. misled

18. The addition of the herbs and spices <u>enhanced</u> the flavor of the ethnic dish.

    A. subdued
    B. magnified
    C. ruined
    D. reflected

19. The building was <u>engulfed</u> in flames before the first responders could reach the scene.

    A. immersed
    B. withdrawn
    C. affected
    D. destroyed

20. Jordan's ego was <u>inflated</u> by the applause he received for his performance in the play.

    A. supported
    B. acknowledged
    C. magnified
    D. mystified

21. The club members <u>ratified</u> the mission statement of the organization in a democratic vote of the entire membership.

    A. rejected
    B. accepted
    C. revised
    D. endorsed

22. <u>Meager</u> most nearly means

    A. sparse
    B. lonely
    C. plentiful
    D. outrageous

23. The witness provided evidence to the <u>detriment</u> of Sara's case.

    A. advantage
    B. closure
    C. damage
    D. protection

24. The family's decision to vacation in Florida was <u>capricious</u>.

    A. predictable
    B. whimsical
    C. logical
    D. pretentious

25. The annual tuition for the training program was <u>exorbitant</u>, so the student found it difficult to justify enrolling.

    A. confusing
    B. excessive
    C. fair
    D. difficult

26. It took a day at the beach to <u>reinvigorate</u> Jasmine after a hard week at the office.

    A. refresh
    B. depress
    C. excite
    D. exhaust

27. The <u>impromptu</u> celebration took place after Kevin learned that he had been promoted.

    A. extravagant
    B. boisterous
    C. spontaneous
    D. planned

28. The gravity of the crime was <u>implicit</u> in the severity of the jail sentence.

    A. specified
    B. understood
    C. stated
    D. described

29. Saul was <u>negligent</u> in paying his rent on time, so the eviction was not a surprise.

    A. punctual
    B. inattentive
    C. furious
    D. welcome

30. To the relief of his friends, the paramedics reported that Kevin came out of the accident <u>unscathed</u>.

    A. scared
    B. injured
    C. intact
    D. relieved

31. Greg's chances for success in the debate were considered <u>dismal</u> by his supporters and coaches.

    A. gloomy
    B. bright
    C. possible
    D. expected

32. Despite their close friendship and long-term association, the two coworkers' day-to-day interactions were considered by many to be <u>tumultuous.</u>

    A. turbulent
    B. hilarious
    C. friendly
    D. calm

33. <u>Tedious</u> most nearly means.

    A. exciting
    B. interesting
    C. stimulating
    D. monotonous

34. The panda's antics were <u>endearing</u> to the visiting public.

    A. offensive
    B. frightening
    C. appealing
    D. surprising

35. <u>Garbled</u> most nearly means.

    A. annoying
    B. significant
    C. unsightly
    D. confused

STOP! DO NOT TURN THIS PAGE UNTIL TIME IS UP FOR THIS TEST. IF YOU FINISH BEFORE TIME IS UP, CHECK OVER YOUR WORK ON THIS TEST ONLY.

PART 4. PARAGRAPH COMPREHENSION

THE TEST ADMINISTRATOR WILL READ THE FOLLOWING ALOUD TO YOU:

Turn to Part 4 and read the directions for Paragraph Comprehension silently while I read them aloud.

This is a test of your ability to understand what you read. In this section you will find one or more paragraphs of reading material followed by incomplete statements or questions. You are to read the paragraph and select one of four lettered choices which BEST completes the statement or answers the question. When you have selected your answer, blacken the space on your answer sheet that has the same number and letter as your answer.

Your score on this test will be based on the number of questions you answer correctly. You should try to answer every question. DO NOT SPEND TOO MUCH TIME on any one question. If you finish before time is called, go back and check your work in this part ONLY.

Now find the section of your answer sheet that is marked PART 4. When you are told to begin, start with question number 1 in Part 4 of your test booklet and answer space number 1 in Part 4 on your separate answer sheet.

DO NOT TURN THE PAGE UNTIL TOLD TO DO SO. You will have 13 minutes to complete the 15 questions in this part. Are there any questions?

Begin.

Some young people make the serious mistake of getting involved with drugs. Some who think that "street drugs" are too dangerous may instead try experimenting with certain common household products—not realizing that these substances can be just as harmful. One such category of dangerous substances is inhalants. Inhalants are substances or fumes from products such as glue or paint thinner that are sniffed or "huffed" to cause an immediate high. Even though household products like glue and air freshener have legal, useful purposes, when they are used as inhalants they are harmful and dangerous.

Inhalants include a large group of chemicals that are found in such household products as aerosol sprays, cleaning fluids, glue, paint, paint thinner, gasoline, propane, nail polish remover, correction fluid, and marker pens. None of these are safe to inhale—they all can kill you.

Inhalants affect your brain and can cause you to suddenly engage in violent, or even deadly, behavior. You could hurt yourself or the people you love. Inhalants affect your brain with much greater speed and force than many other substances, and they can cause irreversible physical and mental damage before you know what's happened. Inhalants affect your heart because they starve the body of oxygen and force the heart to beat irregularly and more rapidly—and that can be dangerous for your body.

Inhalants damage other parts of your body. People who use inhalants can lose their sense of smell; experience nausea and nosebleeds; and develop liver, lung, and kidney problems. Chronic use can lead to muscle wasting and reduced muscle tone and strength. Inhalants can cause sudden death. Inhalant users can die by suffocation, choking on their vomit, or having a heart attack.

Before you risk it, get the facts. Inhalants can kill you the very first time you use them. They can permanently damage your body and brain. Chronic inhalant abusers may permanently lose the ability to perform everyday functions like walking, talking, and thinking. The vast majority of teens aren't using inhalants. According to a 1998 study, only 1.1 percent of teens are regular inhalant users and 94 percent of teens have never even tried inhalants.

1. According to the passage, inhalants affect a person's heart by

   A. making it beat more slowly
   B. making it beat irregularly
   C. causing it to pump more blood
   D. increasing the amount of bad cholesterol

2. Use of inhalants is a serious problem because of which of the following?

   A. Inhalants can kill you.
   B. Inhalants might make you high.
   C. Inhalants are illegal substances.
   D. Inhalants can make you feel intoxicated.

3. Which of the following is the best title for this passage?

   A. Inhalants Are Found in Common Substances
   B. Get the Facts
   C. Inhalants Can Damage and Kill You
   D. Help Your Friends Beat the Habit

4. Based on the passage, which of the following is NOT a way that inhalants can hurt your body?

   A. loss of the sense of smell
   B. liver problems
   C. nosebleeds
   D. hair loss

5. Based on the passage, why might young people think that inhalants are not harmful?

   A. Young people rarely come into contact with products containing inhalants.
   B. Inhalants are not very harmful.
   C. Inhalants are not used by many young people.
   D. Inhalants are found in common household products.

Alcohol is readily available from home or at stores. But the fact that it is easily available is no reason to think it is safe.

Alcohol can damage every organ in your body. It is absorbed directly into your bloodstream and can increase your risk for a variety of life-threatening diseases, including cancer. Alcohol also depresses your central nervous system and affects your brain. The results may include loss of coordination, slowed reflexes, distorted vision, and even "blackouts" (episodes of forgetting what you did while drinking). Other common results are loss of self-control, lowered inhibitions, and poor judgment. Drinking can lead to risky behaviors, including having unprotected sex. This may expose you to HIV/AIDS and other sexually transmitted diseases or cause unwanted pregnancy. Alcohol can even kill you. Drinking large amounts of alcohol can lead to coma or even death. Alcohol can also cause fatal accidents; in 1998, 35.8 percent of traffic deaths of 15- to 20-year-olds were alcohol-related. Mixing alcohol with medications or illicit drugs is extremely dangerous and can lead to accidental death. For example, alcohol-medication interactions may be a factor in at least 25 percent of emergency room admissions. Alcohol can also make you gain weight and give you bad breath.

You may have a friend who has a drinking problem. Sometimes it's tough to tell. There are signs you can look for. If your friend has one or more of the following warning signs, he or she may have a problem with alcohol: problems remembering things he or she recently said or did, getting drunk on a regular basis, lying about how much alcohol he or she is using, believing that alcohol is necessary to have fun, having frequent hangovers, feeling run-down or depressed or even suicidal, having "blackouts," having problems at school, or getting in trouble with the law. Encourage your friend to stop or seek professional help [http://www.freevibe. com/Drug_Facts/#top (government site)].

6. According to the passage, what percent of traffic deaths of youths in 1998 were attributed to alcohol use?

A. 10.9 percent
B. 23.2 percent
C. 35.8 percent
D. 47.4 percent

7. What is the main idea of this passage?

A. You should help a friend who has a drinking problem.
B. Alcohol is a dangerous substance.
C. Alcohol use is against the law for young people.
D. Alcohol is harmful to your body.

8. Which of the following is NOT mentioned as a danger of alcohol overuse?

   A. choking
   B. blackouts
   C. hangovers
   D. bad breath

9. According to the passage, which of the following can result from the effects of alcohol on your brain?

   A. cancer
   B. poor judgment
   C. weight gain
   D. hair loss

10. According to the passage, which of the following is a sign that a friend might be abusing alcohol?

   A. frequent drug use
   B. HIV/AIDS infection
   C. sleeping late
   D. problems at school

The illicit trade in art and cultural artifacts has increased dramatically in recent years, including pillaging archaeological sites and illegally exporting objects protected by international laws.

Back in 1987 in northern Peru, the ruins of the Moche (pronounced mo-chay) civilization, which flourished from about 100 B.C. to 700 A.D., were being studied by archaeologists. Unfortunately, thieves broke into the royal tomb of the Lord of Sipan and got away with unbelievable treasures.

One of the most valuable artifacts stolen from the royal tomb was an extremely rare Moche backflap, part of the royal costuming worn by elite members of the Moche civilization. A backflap weighs about 2.5 pounds and is made of gold, copper, and silver. Moche warrior-priests would wear the backflap as armor during battle to shield their backsides.

Ten years later, in August 1997, black market smugglers Denis Garcia and Orlando Mendez were looking for a buyer for a rare Peruvian artifact—a gold backflap. Garcia contacted an art brokerage firm in New York to see if he could arrange a sale. But, unbeknownst to him, the company was part of an FBI undercover operation targeting art theft, and he was referred to an undercover FBI agent who posed as an art broker. The undercover agent contacted Garcia, who described the item. Feeling sure he had a buyer, Garcia added his selling price—a cool $1.6 million.

Garcia gave the "art broker" a few days to contemplate the offer before calling him back and arranging a face-to-face meeting. This meeting took place on September 5, 1997. Garcia, who didn't have the backflap with him, said it was en route to New York from Peru and he had to make arrangements with his contact "Frank," an employee of the Panamanian Consulate in New York. A deal was made to contact the agent when the backflap was ready for delivery. So, while Garcia and Mendez made their arrangements, the FBI agents were making their own arrangements: how the takedown would be executed when the appropriate time came.

Nearly four weeks later, on October 2, Mendez called the agent to say that the backflap was in New York and they were ready to do business.

They arranged to meet on October 7. The FBI agents arrived first. Then, a black limo bearing diplomatic tags pulled up—it was Garcia, Mendez, and "Frank," aka Francisco Iglesias, who introduced himself as the consul general of Panama and presented his business card. Garcia got the backflap out of the trunk of the car. At that point, several FBI agents and detectives from a local police department surrounded the group and arrested them.

11. Based on the passage, what is the meaning of the word *pillage*?

    A. steal
    B. protect
    C. renovate
    D. replenish

12. According to the passage, why was the backflap so valuable?

    A. It was worn by a king.
    B. It was rare.
    C. It was embellished with rare jewels.
    D. It was very famous.

13. Based on the passage, it can be assumed that

    A. the backflap was returned to the Panamanian government
    B. the jewels in the backflap were authenticated
    C. the perpetrators were brought to trial
    D. Garcia got his $1.6 million

14. What was the purpose of the backflap?

    A. decoration
    B. competition
    C. preparation
    D. protection

15. Where did this story take place?

    A. Peru
    B. New York
    C. Panama
    D. Sipan

STOP! DO NOT TURN THIS PAGE UNTIL TIME IS UP FOR THIS TEST. IF YOU FINISH BEFORE TIME IS UP, CHECK OVER YOUR WORK ON THIS TEST ONLY.

PART 5. MATHEMATICS KNOWLEDGE

THE TEST ADMINISTRATOR WILL READ THE FOLLOWING ALOUD TO YOU:

Now turn to Part 5 and read the directions for Mathematics Knowledge silently while I read them aloud.

This is a test of your ability to solve general mathematics problems. You are to select the correct response from the choices given. Then mark the space on your answer sheet that has the same number and letter as your choice. Use your scratch paper to do any figuring you wish to do.

Your score on this test will be based on the number of questions you answer correctly. You should try to answer every question. DO NOT SPEND TOO MUCH TIME on any one question. If you finish before time is called, go back and check your work in this part ONLY.

Now find the section of your answer sheet that is marked PART 5. When you are told to begin, start with question number 1 in Part 5 of your test booklet and answer space number 1 in Part 5 on your separate answer sheet.

DO NOT TURN THE PAGE UNTIL TOLD TO DO SO. You will have 24 minutes to complete the 25 questions in this part. Are there any questions?

Begin

1. $x + 9 = 14, x = ?$

   A. 3
   B. 4
   C. 5
   D. 13

2. $3^2 + 4(6 - 3) =$

   A. 21
   B. 36
   C. 39
   D. 40

3. $2\frac{1}{4} \times 2\frac{1}{2}$

   A. 2

   B. $3\frac{1}{4}$

   C. $3\frac{3}{4}$

   D. $5\frac{5}{8}$

4.   The square root of 121 =

   A. 4
   B. –8
   C. 9
   D. –11

5.   What is the value of the following expression if $x = 3$ and $y = 4$?

   $2x^3y^2$

   A. 112
   B. 256
   C. 864
   D. 912

6.   Add:

   $3x^2 + 3xy + 4y + 2y^2$
   $+ 3x^2 + xy + 9y + y^2$

   A. $2x^2 + 4xy + y + 3y^2$
   B. $6x^2 + 4xy + 13y + 3y^2$
   C. $2x^2 + 5xy + 2y + 2y^2$
   D. $4x^2 + 5xy + y$

7.   Factor the following expression: $y^2 - 16y + 48$

   A. $(y - 1)(y + 48)$
   B. $(y - 4)(y - 12)$
   C. $(y - 4)(y + 4)$
   D. $(y + 1)(y - 16)$

8.   Solve for x.

   $12x - 6 = 8x + 10$

   A. $x = 1$
   B. $x = 2$
   C. $x = 4$
   D. $x = 6$

9.   Solve for the two unknowns.

   $3y + 3x = 24$
   $6y + 3x = 39$

   A. $y = 3; x = 5$
   B. $y = 4; x = 6$
   C. $y = 5; x = 3$
   D. $y = 6; x = 2$

10. $\dfrac{x^{13}}{x^5}$

   A. x^{-8}
   B. x^8
   C. x^{18}
   D. x^{-16}

11.   Solve for y.

   $y^2 + 7y = -10$

   A. $y = -5; y = -2$
   B. $y = 1; y = -10$
   C. $y = -2; y = 6$
   D. $y = 5; y = -1$

12.   Multiply:

   $\dfrac{6y}{10} \times \dfrac{3}{5x}$

   A. $6y + 5x = 30$
   B. $12y + 55x$

   C. $\dfrac{9y}{25x}$

   D. $\dfrac{3y}{5x}$

13. Divide:

$$\frac{6y}{10} \div \frac{3}{5x}$$

A. xy

B. $\frac{15xy}{11}$

C. $\frac{12}{55xy}$

D. $30\,xy$

14. $\sqrt[3]{27} =$

A. 2.25
B. 3
C. 4
D. 5

15. Solve for g. $\frac{g}{h} = a$

A. $g = \frac{h}{a}$

B. $g = \frac{a}{h}$

C. $g = ah$

D. $g = a - h$

16. Which of the following is an isosceles triangle?

A.

B.

C.

D.

17. What is the perimeter of the following rectangle?

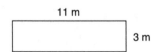

A. 12 m
B. 18 m
C. 24 m
D. 28 m

18. What is the circumference of the following circle?

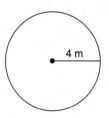

A. 6.56 m
B. 12.56 m
C. 25.12 m
D. 35.12 m

19. In an equilateral triangle, what is the measure of each angle?

A. 30°
B. 45°
C. 60°
D. 90°

20. In the figure below, if $\angle 1$ is 33°, what is the measure of $\angle 2$?

A. 56°
B. 110°
C. 147°
D. 180°

21. In the following right triangle, what is the length of side AB?

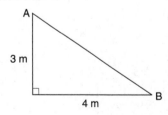

A. 3 m
B. 5 m
C. 7 m
D. 12 m

22. What is the area of the following triangle?

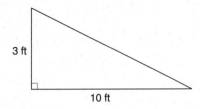

3 ft

10 ft

    A. 8 ft^2
    B. 12 ft^2
    C. 15 ft^2
    D. 16 ft^2

23. What is the diameter of the following circle?

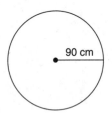

90 cm

    A. 40 cm
    B. 80 cm
    C. 160 cm
    D. 180 cm

24. If lines *A* and *B* are parallel and are intersected by line *C* and 2 is 31º, what is the measure of 7?

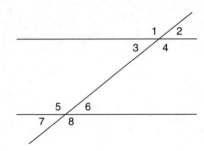

    A. 31º
    B. 50º
    C. 111º
    D. 149º

25. What is the volume of a cylinder with a height of 15 m and a radius of 5 m?

    A. 235.50 m^3
    B. 1,177.50 m^3
    C. 1,280.25 m^3
    D. 1,340.25 m^3

STOP! THIS IS THE END OF PRACTICE TEST FORM 1. IF YOU FINISH BEFORE TIME IS UP, CHECK OVER YOUR WORK ON THIS TEST ONLY.

AFQT Practice Test Form 1: Answers and Explanations

PART 2. ARITHMETIC REASONING

Scoring Your Test

Compare your answer to the correct answer. Mark an X in the column if you got the item correct. Total the number correct.

Item Number	Correct Answer	Mark X if You Picked the Correct Answer
1	D	
2	C	
3	A	
4	A	
5	D	
6	D	
7	C	
8	C	
9	B	
10	C	
11	B	
12	D	
13	B	
14	D	
15	D	
16	C	
17	C	
18	B	
19	A	
20	B	
21	A	
22	D	
23	A	
24	D	
25	C	
26	C	
27	D	
28	A	
29	B	
30	A	
Total Correct		

Gauging Your Level of Performance

In the following chart, find the number of items that you got correct. See the suggestions listed for your performance.

30	This is pretty good work. Review the explanations of the answers you got incorrect.
29	
28	
27	
26	
25	You are doing pretty well. Review the explanations for the items that you answered incorrectly. If you have time, review the other explanations and you will learn even more.
24	
23	
22	
21	
20	You need to keep studying and practicing. Pay close attention to the explanations for each item, even for the ones you got correct.
19	
18	
17	
16	
15	
14	
13	Spend time working on Chapter 9, "Sharpen Your Word Problem Skills," in Part 2 of this book. It will help you understand how to think through, set up, and solve the problems
12	
11	
10	
9	
8	
7	Keep working and reworking problems until you are comfortable with the processes.
6	
5	
4	
3	
2	
1	
0	

Explanations

1. **D** This is a simple addition problem. Add the amounts to get the total of $17.55.

2. **C** This problem has two steps. First, you need to add the amount spent. Then you need to subtract that amount from the $100 bill. The total amount spent is $81.94, so, subtracting that from $100, the change is $18.06.

3. **A** In order to calculate the percent, you must divide the number of items answered correctly by the total number of items. So divide 45 by 75 to get 0.60. To change that to a percent, move the decimal point two places to the right and add the percent sign to get 60%.

4. **A** To find the average, add up the numbers and divide by the number of numbers. In this problem, the numbers add to 415. Dividing that by 5 gives the correct result of 83 as the average.

5. **D** This problem needs to be completed in two steps. First, you need to determine what percent of the chocolates have nuts. Then you must subtract that percent from 100% to determine what percent do not have nuts. To find the percent that have nuts, divide: $9 \div 45 = 0.2 = 20\%$. $100\% - 20\% = 80\%$ of the chocolates do not have nuts.

6. **D** To find the ratio of one number to another, create a fraction to show the relationship. In this problem. there are 6 female club members to a total of 48 members. So the fraction that shows the relationship is $\frac{6}{48}$. This fraction needs to be simplified to $\frac{1}{8}$, the correct answer. You might see a ratio written as 1:8 on the ASVAB test. $\frac{1}{8}$ and 1:8 mean the same thing.

7. **C** If Jessica has 315 pages of reading and reads 65 pages each day, on Monday she has read 65 pages, on Tuesday she has read 2(65) or 130 pages, on Wednesday she has ready 3(65) or 195 pages, and on Thursday she has read 4(65) or 260 pages. On Friday, Jessica would need to read only 55 more pages to complete the assignment. Friday is the correct answer. Another way to do this is to divide 315 by 65 to get 4.85. If Monday is 1, Tuesday is 2, Wednesday is 3, Thursday is 4, and Friday would be 5. On Friday she would complete the assignment.

8. **C** Probability = number of favorable outcomes/ number of possible outcomes. In this problem, a favorable outcome would be selecting a penny. There are 150 pennies or favorable outcomes. The number of possible outcomes is the sum of all the coins, or $150 + 56 + 98 + 46 = 350$. So

$$\text{Probability} = \frac{150}{350}$$

Simplified, this is $\frac{3}{7}$.

9. **B** Simple interest problems use the formula $I = prt$, where I is the amount of interest, p is the principal or the amount saved or invested, r is the rate of interest, and is the amount of time that the interest is accruing. In this problem, you are asked to find the interest, given that the principal is $4,000, the rate of interest is 2%, and the amount of time is 1 year. Substitute this information into the formula:

$$I = 4,000(0.02)(1) = \$80 \text{ of interest}$$

10. **C** Set this up as a proportion.

$$\frac{5,200 \text{ miles}}{9 \text{ hours}} = \frac{x \text{ miles}}{1 \text{ hour}}$$

Cross multiply:

$$9x = 5,200$$
$$x = 577.77 \text{ miles per hour}$$

11. **B** The Science Club now has 250 members and wants to have a total of 376 members in 90 days. So the club needs to attract $376 - 250 = 126$ new members. To do this in 90 days, the club must attract $126 \div 90 =$ an average of 1.4 new members each day.

12. **D** Here you need to calculate the number of square meters in the garden and then determine how many ounces of fertilizer are needed. The area of a rectangular garden is calculated by multiplying the length $\times$ the width. In this problem the area is $4 \times 7 = 28 \text{ m}^2$. If you need 2 oz of fertilizer for every square meter, then you need to multiply the number of square meters by 2: $28 \times 2 = 56$ oz.

13. **B** Calculate the cost of the two CDs:

$$\$14.99 \times 2 = \$29.98$$

Reduce that amount by 25% by multiplying the total cost by 0.25:

$$0.25 \times 29.98 = \$7.495 \text{ Rounded to } \$7.50$$

Subtract $7.50 from the original cost:

$$\$29.98 - \$7.50 = \$22.48$$

A faster way to do this (and speed is important on the ASVAB) is to multiply the original cost by 75% or 0.75 because that is the cost of the items after the discount.

$$0.75 \times \$29.98 = \$22.48$$

14. **D** Use the following formula:

$$\text{Percent change} = \frac{\text{amount of change}}{\text{starting point}}$$

In this problem, the starting point is $67.50. The amount of change is the difference between the starting price and the ending price of $87.75.

$$\$87.75 - \$67.50 = \$20.25$$

Substitute the information into the formula:

$$\text{Percent change} = \frac{\$20.25}{\$67.50} = 0.3$$

Change that number to a percent by moving the decimal place two places to the right and adding the percent sign.

$$0.3 = 30\%$$

15. **D** Set this up as an equation.

A number plus 2 times that number is 300.

$$x + 2x = 375$$

Solve for x.

$$3x = 375$$
$$x = 125$$

So one number is 125 and the other is twice that or 250.

16. **C** To answer this question, you need to know the perimeter of the frame. For a rectangle, the perimeter is $2l + 2w$. If $w = 18$ and $l = 24$, then the perimeter $= 2(18) + 2(24) = 84$ inches. At $0.50 per inch, multiply $84 \times \$0.50$ to get the price of the wood.

$$84 \times \$0.50 = \$42.00$$

17. **C** To find the circumference of a circle, use the formula $C = \pi d$. In this problem, you are given the diameter. The diameter is 75 yards Substitute the information into the formula.

$$C = \pi 75$$
$$C = (3.14)(75) = 235.5 \text{ yds}$$

Note that you can skip a step if you remember the formula $C = \pi d$. Substitute the information you have.

$$C = \pi\,(75) = 235.5 \text{ yd}$$

18. **B** In this problem, you need to find 1/5 of 55. $55 \div 5 = 11$.

19. **A** Create an equation to solve this problem.

$$\text{Lindsey} = \text{Paula} - 2$$

You are told that Paula is 17. Substitute that information into the formula.

$$\text{Lindsey} = 17 - 2$$
$$\text{Lindsey} = 15$$

20. **B** Create equations to solve this problem.

$$\text{Al} = 3(\text{Bill})$$
$$\text{Bill} = 2(\text{Charlie})$$
$$\text{Charlie} = \$12.55$$

Solve for Al.
Substitute what you know into the formulas.

$$\text{Bill} = 2(\$12.55)$$
$$\text{Bill} = \$25.10$$

To find Al, substitute what you know about Bill.

$$\text{Al} = 3(\$25.10)$$
$$\text{Al} = \$75.30$$

21. **A** In this problem you need to calculate the number of 26-mpg units there are in 858. Do this by dividing 858 by 26.

$$858 \div 26 = 33 \text{ gallons}$$

22. **D** To solve this problem, use the formula $V = lwh$. You have been given the dimensions $l = 44$ ft, $w = 26$ ft, and $h = 6$ ft. Substitute that information into the formula.

$$V = (44)(26)(6)$$
$$V = 6,864 \text{ ft}^3$$

23. **A** You need to calculate the perimeter of the garden. The perimeter is the sum of all the sides, or you can use the formula $P = 2l + 2w$. You are given the dimensions of 12 feet and 30 feet. Substitute that information into the formula.

$$P = 2(12) + 2(30)$$
$$P = 84 \text{ ft}$$

24. **D** To calculate 14% of 7,000, multiply 7,000 by 0.14.

$$7,000 \times 0.14 = 980 \text{ votes}$$

25. **C** To calculate the volume of a cylinder, use the formula $V = \pi r^2 h$. In this problem the radius is 9 m. The height is given as 3.5 m. Substitute that information into the formula.

$$V = (3.14)(9^2)(3.5)$$
$$V = (3.14)(81)(3.5)$$
$$V = 890.19 \text{ or } 890.2 \text{ m}^3$$

26. **C** Use the formula $C = 2\pi r$ or $C = \pi d$.

You are given a diameter of 8,000 miles. Substitute that into the formula.

$$C = \pi(8,000)$$
$$C = 3.14(8,000)$$
$$C = 25,120 \text{ mi}$$

27. **D** To calculate the answer to this question, add up the amount of the checks and subtract that from the current amount in the checking account.

$$\$12,444.12 - (\$8,204.94 + \$890.99) = \$3,348.19$$

28. **A** Multiply $1,085.00 by 0.25 to get $271.25.

29. **B** Calculate the total cost of the items and then multiply by 15% to determine how much Danny will save.

$$\$750 + \$398.75 + \$149.98 + \$24.99 = \$1,323.72$$

$$\$1,323.72 \times 0.15 = \$198.56 \text{ savings due to the sale.}$$

30. **A** In this problem you know two of the three angles; one measures 65° and the other measures 90°, since the building forms a 90° angle with the ground. Together those two angles measure 155°. Since a triangle has a total of 180°, the third angle must measure $180° - 155° = 25°$.

PART 3. WORD KNOWLEDGE
Scoring Your Test

Compare your answer to the correct answer. Mark an X in the column if you got the item correct. Total the number correct.

Gauging Your Level of Performance

In the following chart, find the number of items that you got correct. See the suggestions listed for your performance.

Item Number	Correct Answer	Mark X if You Picked the Correct Answer
1	B	
2	C	
3	B	
4	A	
5	C	
6	B	
7	A	
8	D	
9	B	
10	D	
11	A	
12	B	
13	B	
14	A	
15	C	
16	C	
17	D	
18	B	
19	A	
20	C	
21	D	
22	A	
23	C	
24	B	
25	B	
26	A	
27	C	
28	B	
29	B	
30	C	
31	A	
32	A	
33	D	
34	C	
35	D	
Total Correct		

35	This is pretty good work. Review the explanations of the answers that you got incorrect.
34	
33	
32	
31	
30	You are doing pretty well. Review the explanations for the items that you answered incorrectly. If you have time, review the other explanations and you will learn even more.
29	
28	
27	
26	
25	You need to keep studying. Pay close attention to the explanations for each item, even for the ones you got correct.
24	
23	
22	
21	
20	
19	
18	
17	Spend time working on Chapter 6, "Sharpen Your Word Knowledge Skills," in Part 2 of this book.
16	
15	
14	
13	
12	Keep reading and identifying words that you don't know.
11	
10	
9	
8	
7	
6	
5	
4	
3	
2	
1	
0	

Explanations

1. **B** *Seethed* (choice D) means "was angry," "blew up," or "flamed up." *Danced* (choice C) is clearly incorrect. Choice A, *feared,* is opposite in meaning to what is intended, so it is incorrect as well. To *yearn* means "to seek, aspire, or wish for." Choice B, *longed,* is the correct answer.

2. **C** *Trivial* (choice D) means "small and insignificant" and is not the correct answer. *Dowdy* (choice A) means "drab" and is not correct. *Foolish* (choice B) means "simple" or "silly" and is incorrect. Choice C, *royal,* means "majestic" or "resplendent" and is the correct answer.

3. **B** *Height* (choice D) makes no sense and is not the correct answer. A *termination* is an ending, so choice A is not correct. His *physique,* presuming that he was strong, might have helped him, but this is not the best answer, so choice C is incorrect. *Resolve* means "tenacity" and "perseverance," so choice B is the correct answer.

4. **A** *Eased* (choice D) is not the correct answer. Danger might have *scrambled* or *erased* thoughts, but neither of these is the best answer, so choices B and C are incorrect. Choice A, *permeated,* is correct.

5. **C** *Indignant* means "irate" or "mad," so choice C, *angry,* is the correct answer.

6. **B** *Common* (choice A) means the opposite of *inimitable* and is incorrect. *Intimidated* (choice C) and *friendly* (choice D) are also incorrect. *Inimitable* means "matchless" or "unique," so *peerless* (choice B) is the correct answer.

7. **A** An *onslaught* is an attack or assault. In this instance, the family received so many warm wishes that it was overwhelmed. To the family, the flood of warm wishes seemed almost like an attack. Choice A is the correct answer.

8. **D** Although winning the lottery can dramatically change one's life, *upset* (choice A) is not the correct answer. *Frightened* (choice B) and *suspicious* (choice C) are also incorrect. The correct answer is *joyous,* choice D.

9. **B** *Ridiculous* (choice D) and *punctual* (choice C) are incorrect. *Graceful* has the opposite meaning to *maladroit,* so choice A is incorrect. Choice B, *clumsy,* is the correct answer.

10. **D** *Humorous* (choice A) and *successful* (choice B) are incorrect. Based on the sentence, you might be fooled into thinking that the correct answer is choice C, *unexpected.* That would have been a good guess if you didn't know that the best answer is choice D, *wicked.* To be *despicable* is to be contemptible or shameful.

11. **A** The context clues here are important. Lance wanted to take courses other than English composition, but it appears that he didn't have a choice. *Easy* (choice D) is not correct. The courses may be *important* (choice C), but that is also incorrect. If the courses were *optional* (choice B), Lance probably would not be upset. Choice A, *required,* is the correct answer.

12. **B** *Poignant* (choice A), *critical* (choice C), and *useful* (choice D) are incorrect. *Critical* in this sense means the opposite of *extraneous.* Choice B, *unrelated,* is correct.

13. **B** *Diminished* means "reduced or made smaller or weaker." *Acceptable* (choice A), *appropriate* (choice C), and *acknowledged* (choice D) are clearly incorrect. Choice B, *suppressed,* is the correct answer. To *suppress* means "to make smaller or stifle."

14. **A** Gina may have wanted to *chastise* (choice D) an angry person, but that is not the correct answer. *Recognize* (choice B) and *oust* (choice C) are not correct either. *Placate* means "to mollify or pacify someone," so choice A is the correct answer.

15. **C** Some legal documents might be so confusing that a *translation* seems necessary, but choice A is not correct. Jimmy may also have wanted to give the confusing document a *rejection* (choice B) or to hold a *conference* about it (choice D), but those answers are incorrect. To

clarify means "to explain or clear up." Choice C, *explanation*, is the correct answer.

16. **C** *Massive* means "weighty," "heavy," "huge," or "immense." Based on this, it is clear that choice C, *gigantic*, is the correct answer.

17. **D** Someone who is *deluded* has been tricked or deceived. Given that, *enhanced* (choice A) and *sharpened* (choice B) are clearly not correct. *Explained* (choice C) is not a relevant answer. The best answer is *misled*, choice D, which means nearly the same as "tricked or deceived."

18. **B** *Enhanced* means "heightened, increased, or boosted." *Subdued* (choice A) is clearly the opposite of that idea. *Ruined* (choice C) and *reflected* (choice D) are clearly incorrect. Choice B, *magnified*, is the correct answer.

19. **A** To be *engulfed* means "to be overcome or overwhelmed." *Withdrawn* (choice B), *affected* (choice C), and *destroyed* (choice D) are incorrect. Choice A, *immersed*, is closest in meaning to *engulfed* and is the correct answer.

20. **C** *Inflated* means "blown up, made bigger, pumped up, or expanded." Although Jordan must have felt *supported* (choice A), that is not the correct answer. He may have been *mystified* (choice D) by the applause and felt that he was *acknowledged* (choice B) by the audience, but those responses are also not correct. Choice C, *magnified*, is the correct answer.

21. **D** *Ratified* means "authorized, confirmed, or sanctioned." Although ratified items would certainly be *accepted* (choice B), the word is not strong enough to convey the real meaning of *ratified*. Clearly, *rejected* (choice A) and *revised* (choice C) are incorrect. *Endorsed* (choice D), a stronger meaning of *accepted*, is the correct answer.

22. **A** *Meager* means "insufficient, small, and inadequate." Choice C, *plentiful*, is the opposite of that concept. *Lonely* (choice B) and *outrageous* (choice D) are clearly incorrect. The only word that matches the meaning is *sparse*. Choice A is the correct answer.

23. **C** *Detriment* means "loss, harm, or injury." Choice A, *advantage*, is the opposite of that concept and is clearly wrong. *Closure* (choice B) and *protection* (choice D) are also wrong. Choice C, *damage*, conveys the message of harm or injury. Choice C is the correct answer.

24. **B** The decision may have been *logical*, but choice C is not the correct answer. *Pretentious* (choice D) means "showy or pompous" and is not correct. *Predictable*, choice A, is the opposite of the correct answer. Since *capricious* means "variable or impulsive," the best answer is *whimsical*. Choice B is the correct answer.

25. **B** The word *exorbitant* means "overpriced or absurdly inflated." *Fair* (choice C) and *difficult* (choice D) do not relate to this idea, so they are incorrect. Being overpriced might be *confusing* (choice A), but that answer is also incorrect. The correct answer is choice B, *excessive*.

26. **A** To *reinvigorate* means "to revitalize or restore to a previous level." *Exhaust* (choice D) has the opposite meaning and is incorrect. *Depress* (choice B) and *excite* (choice C) are also incorrect. Choice A, *refresh*, is the word that most nearly means *reinvigorate*.

27. **C** *Impromptu* means "unplanned or unrehearsed." Choice D, *planned*, is the opposite of this idea and is the wrong answer. *Boisterous* means "loud and chaotic," so choice B is not the correct answer. The celebration may have been *extravagant* (choice A), but that answer is also not correct. *Spontaneous* (choice C) is the correct answer.

28. **B** The word *implicit* refers to something that is not stated directly but is understood or implied by an action. *Specified* (choice A), *stated* (choice C), and *described* (choice D) are the opposite of that concept and are clearly incorrect. *Understood*, choice B, is the correct answer.

29. **B** To be *negligent* means "to be careless or remiss due to inattention." Based on that information, *punctual* (choice A) does not seem to fit. *Furious* (choice C) and *welcome* (choice D)

are clearly incorrect. Choice B, *inattentive*, is the best answer.

30. **C** To be *unscathed* means "to be unharmed and unhurt." Choice B, *injured*, is opposite in meaning and is clearly incorrect. The accident might have made Kevin *scared* (choice A) and his friends *relieved* (choice D), but these answers are also incorrect. Choice C, *intact*, is the correct answer.

31. **A** The word *dismal* conveys the notion of dreariness, dullness, and low expectations. *Bright* (choice B) is certainly not reflective of that concept. The words *possible* (choice C) and *expected* (choice D) are also incorrect. Of the choices, the word that most closely matches *dismal* is *gloomy*. Choice A is the correct answer.

32. **A** The word *tumultuous* means "confused, chaotic, and agitated." Choice D, *calm*, certainly does not convey that message, so it is incorrect. *Hilarious* (choice B) and *friendly* (choice C) do not relate to *tumultuous* at all. The only word that describes chaos and confusion is *turbulent*. Choice A is the correct answer.

33. **D** *Tedious* means "dull, dreary, overly detailed, and unexciting." *Exciting* (choice A), *interesting* (choice B), and *stimulating* (choice C) don't convey the same meaning at all. Choice D, *monotonous*, is the correct answer.

34. **C** *Endearing* means "attractive, charming, or engaging." *Offensive* (choice A) does not match this idea, nor does *frightening* (choice B). *Surprising* (choice D) is also incorrect. Choice C, *appealing*, is the correct answer.

35. **D** *Garbled* means "distorted, muddled, and confused." That is not the same as *annoying* (choice A), *significant* (choice B), or *unsightly* (choice C). Choice D, *confused*, is the correct answer.

PART 4. PARAGRAPH COMPREHENSION

Scoring Your Test

Compare your answer to the correct answer. Mark an X in the column if you got the item correct. Total the number correct.

Item Number	Correct Answer	Mark X if You Picked the Correct Answer
1	B	
2	A	
3	C	
4	D	
5	D	
6	C	
7	B	
8	A	
9	B	
10	D	
11	A	
12	B	
13	C	
14	D	
15	B	
Total Correct		

Gauging Your Level of Performance

In the following chart, find the number of items that you got correct. See the suggestions listed for your performance.

15	This is pretty good work. Review the explanations of the answers that you got incorrect.
14	
13	You are doing pretty well. Review the explanations for the items that you answered incorrectly. If you have time, review the other explanations and you will learn even more.
12	
11	
10	
9	
8	
7	You need to keep studying. Pay close attention to the explanations for each item, even for the ones that you got correct. This will help you understand why the answer is correct.
6	
5	
4	
3	Spend time reviewing Chapter 7, "Sharpen Your Paragraph Comprehension Skills," in Part 2 of this book. Keep reading books and newspapers.
2	
1	
0	

Explanations

1. **B** The passage indicates that use of inhalants can cause your heart to beat irregularly.

2. **A** The passage indicates that the most serious consequence of using inhalants is the potential of death, even on the first attempt.

3. **C** Although all the answers are possible, the major thrust of the passage it that inhalants are very dangerous to your health and that one consequence of using them can be death.

4. **D.** The passage mentions loss of the sense of smell (choice A), liver damage (choice B), and nosebleeds (choice C) as possible outcomes of using inhalants. Losing hair is not mentioned in the passage as a possible outcome of using inhalants, so choice D, hair loss, is the correct answer.

5. **D** The passage indicates that certain common household products contain dangerous substances that can cause problems when they are inhaled. According to the passage, people might believe that these products are safe, but the products were not created to be inhaled.

6. **C** The passage specifies that 35.8 percent of deaths of 15- to 20-year-olds in 1998 were alcohol-related.

7. **B** Although it is true that alcohol can harm your body (choice D), that it is against the law for people who are underage (choice C), and that you should help a friend who has a drinking problem (choice A), the basic premise of the passage is that alcohol involves more dangers than just the harm you do to yourself by drinking. For example, you can be killed by a drunk driver.

8. **A** The passage mentions the potential of blackouts (choice B), hangovers (choice C), and bad breath (choice D) as some of the results and dangers of alcohol use. Choking (choice A) is not mentioned in the passage.

9. **B** Cancer (choice A) and weight gain (choice C) are possible results of drinking, but they are not related to alcohol's effects on the brain. Hair loss (choice D) is not mentioned in the passage. Poor judgment (choice B) is listed in the passage as one result of alcohol's effect on the brain.

10. **D** The passage indicates that if your friend has memory lapses, gets drunk on a regular basis, lies about how much alcohol he or she is using, believes that alcohol is necessary to have fun, has frequent hangovers, feels run-down or depressed or even suicidal, has "blackouts" (episodes of forgetting what he or she did while drinking), has problems at school, or gets in trouble with the law, he or she may have a drinking problem.

11. **A** The passage tells a story about objects that were stolen from an ancient royal tomb. Therefore, it makes sense to conclude that *pillage* means "rob, plunder, or steal." Choice A is the correct answer.

12. **B** The passage indicates that the backflap was a rare archaeological find. Choice B is the correct answer.

13. **C** The backflap was from Peru, so there is no reason for it to have been returned to the Panamanian government. The passage does not say whether the jewels were or were not authenticated, or if the $1.6 million was paid. Since the perpetrators were caught by the FBI, it can be assumed that they were brought to trial.

14. **D** The passage indicates that the warrior-priests would wear the backflap as armor during battle to shield their backsides, so the backflap was worn for protection. Choice D is the correct answer.

15. **B** Although Peru and Panama are mentioned in the passage, the events described took place in New York. Choice B is the correct answer.

PART 5. MATHEMATICS KNOWLEDGE

Scoring Your Test

Compare your answer to the correct answer. Mark an X in the column if you got the item correct. Total the number correct.

Gauging Your Level of Performance

In the following chart, find the number of items that you got correct. See the suggestions listed for your performance.

Item Number	Correct Answer	Mark X if You Picked the Correct Answer
1	C	
2	A	
3	D	
4	D	
5	C	
6	B	
7	B	
8	C	
9	C	
10	B	
11	A	
12	C	
13	A	
14	B	
15	C	
16	A	
17	D	
18	C	
19	C	
20	C	
21	B	
22	C	
23	D	
24	A	
25	B	
Total Correct		

25	This is pretty good work. Review the explanations of the answers that you got incorrect.
24	
23	
22	You are doing pretty well. Review the explanations for the items that you answered incorrectly. If you have time, review the other explanations and you will learn even more.
21	
20	
19	
18	
17	You need to keep studying. Pay close attention to the explanations for each item, even for the ones that you got correct.
16	
15	
14	Spend time working on Chapter 8, "Sharpen Your Math Skills," in Part 2 of this book. Work and rework the problems until you fully understand the processes.
13	
12	
11	
10	You need to work the problems to the point that you are very comfortable with the processes used. If you can get to this point, the problems will be very easy for you.
9	
8	
7	
6	Learning the procedures on this test will also help you on the Arithmetic Reasoning test.
5	
4	
3	
2	
1	

Explanations

1. **C** Isolate the unknown on one side of the equation.

   Subtract 9 from each side.

   $$x = 14 - 9$$
   $$x = 5$$

2. **A** Perform the operations in the parentheses first, then the exponents, and then the remaining operations.

   $$9 + 4(3)$$
   $$= 9 + 12$$
   $$= 21$$

3. **D** Change the mixed numbers to improper fractions. Carry out the operation by multiplying the two numerators and the two denominators.

   $$\frac{9}{4} \times \frac{5}{2}$$
   $$= \frac{45}{8}$$
   $$= 5\frac{5}{8}$$

4. **D** $-11 \times -11 = 121$

5. **C** Substitute 2 for x and 4 for y into the expression.

   $$2(3)^3(4)^2$$

   Multiply out the exponents.

   $$2(27)(16)$$
   $$= 54 \times 16$$
   $$= 864$$

6. **B** When adding such expressions, place all similar terms under each other. Then perform the necessary operations. For this particular problem, place all the x^2 terms under each other and add the numbers, giving $6x^2$. Then go to the next terms (xy) and add those. Adding these terms gives you $4xy$. Next, add the y terms. Adding these terms results in $13y$. Next, add the y^2 terms, giving you $3y^2$. The answer is $6x^2 + 4xy + 13y + 3y^2$.

7. **B** Note the minus sign in the middle term and the plus sign in the third term. This should tell you that the factors will contain a minus sign in each term. In this problem, the fact that both of the terms will have a minus sign should lead you to the correct answer, as only one answer has a minus sign in each term. However, not all questions of this type will have that kind of clue. Note that the first term in each factor will be y. Now you need to find two numbers that multiply to 48 and add to 16. Those numbers are 4 and 12. This gives the factors $(y - 4)(y - 12)$.

8. **C** To solve such problems, move all the terms with an unknown to one side of the equal sign and the numbers to the other. In this problem, subtract 6 from both sides to move the numbers to the right side, giving you $12x = 8x + 10 + 6$. Next, work on the $8x$ term by subtracting $8x$ from both sides, giving $12x - 8x = 10 + 6$. Combine the terms, resulting in $4x = 16$. Solve for x: $x = 4$.

9. **C** Set each equation equal to zero. Next, arrange one of the equations so that when it is subtracted from or added to the other equation, one of the terms results in a zero and drops out of the equation. Next, solve for the remaining unknown.

   In this problem:

   $$3y + 3x = 24$$
   $$6y + 3x = 39$$

   Set each equation to zero:

   $$3y + 3x - 24 = 0$$
   $$6y + 3x - 39 = 0$$

   Note that each equation contains the term $3x$. If you subtract the second equation from the first, the x term will drop out.

   $$3y + 3x - 24 = 0$$
   $$-6y - 3x + 39 = 0$$

   Subtracting the terms results in $-3y + 15 = 0$. Solve for y:

   $$-3y = -15$$
   $$y = 5$$

To solve for x, take that result and substitute it into one of the original equations.

$$3(5) + 3x - 24 = 0$$
$$15 + 3x - 24 = 0$$
$$3x = 24 - 15$$
$$3x = 9$$
$$x = 3$$

The answer to the problem is $y = 5; x = 3$.

10. **B** To divide numbers with exponents, subtract the exponents. In this problem, subtract the 5 from the 13, leaving x^8 as the correct answer.

11. **A** Set the equation equal to zero:

$$y^2 + 7y + 10 = 0$$

Factor the equation.

$$(y + 5)(y + 2) = 0$$

Solve for y by setting each factor equal to 0:

$$y + 5 = 0; y = -5$$
$$y + 2 = 0; y = -2$$

The correct answer is $y = -5, y = -2$.

12. **C** To multiply fractions, multiply the numerators and denominators. Simplify where possible.

$$\frac{6y}{10} \times \frac{3}{5x}$$

$$\frac{18y}{50x} = \text{Simplify.}$$

$$\frac{9y}{25x} = \text{This cannot be simplified any further, so it is the final answer.}$$

13. **A** To divide fractions, invert the second term and multiply. Simplify where possible.

$$\frac{6y}{10} \div \frac{3}{5x} = \text{Invert and multiply.}$$

$$= \frac{6y}{10} \times \frac{5x}{3}$$

$$= \frac{30xy}{30} = \text{Simplify.}$$

$$= \frac{xy}{1} = xy$$

14. **B** The cube root is the number that, when multiplied by itself three times, results in the number given. In this instance, $3 \times 3 \times 3 = 27$, so the cube root of $27 = 3$.

To answer most questions of this type on the AFQT, you just need to memorize some basic cubes. It would be wise to memorize all the cubes from 2 to 15, just to prepare for the test item possibilities.

15. **C** Isolate the variable of interest on one side of the equation. In this problem, you must multiply each side by h, leaving g on the left side of the equation and h on the right side. Therefore, the answer is $g = ah$.

16. **A** An isosceles triangle has two equal sides and angles, so A is the correct answer.

17. **D** To find the perimeter of a quadrilateral, add the lengths of the four sides. In this instance, 11 m + 11 m + 3 m + 3 m = 28 m, the correct answer.

18. **C** The formula for the circumference of a circle is πd. The figure gives the radius, which is 1/2 the length of the diameter. To find the diameter, multiply the radius by 2. In this problem, the diameter is 8 meters. Multiplying 8 by π gives the correct answer of 25.12 meters. You can also use the formula $C = 2\pi r$ to get the same answer.

19. **C** An equilateral triangle has three equal angles. A triangle has a total of 180°, so each angle must be 60°.

20. **C** A straight line or straight angle is 180°. So if $\angle 1$ is 33°, the other angle is the difference between 180° and 33°, or 147°.

21. **B** $\angle C$ is a right angle, so you can employ the Pythagorean Theorem $a^2 + b^2 = c^2$ to get your answer. $3^2 + 4^2 = c^2$. So $9 + 16 = 25$. $c^2 = 25$ and $c = 5$.

22. **C** This is a right triangle, so 3 ft is the height of the triangle and 10 ft is the base. The formula for the area of a triangle is $\frac{1}{2}bh$. Substituting the information into the formula gives $\frac{1}{2}(3)(10)$, making the correct answer 15 ft^2.

23. **D** The diameter is $2r$. $r = 90$ cm, so the diameter is 180 cm.

24. **A** $\angle 2$ and $\angle 7$ are alternate exterior angles and therefore are equal in measure. So both $\angle 2$ and $\angle 7$ are 31°.

25. **B** The formula for finding the volume of a cylinder is $V = \pi r^2 h$. In this problem, the cylinder has a height of 15 m and a radius of 5 m. Substituting that information into the formula gives $\pi (5)^2 (15)$, making the correct answer 1,177.50 m^3.

AFQT Practice Test Form 2

The following practice test form is designed to be just like the real AFQT portion of the ASVAB test. It matches the actual test in content coverage and level of difficulty. The test is in four parts: Arithmetic Reasoning, Word Knowledge, Paragraph Comprehension, and Mathematics Knowledge.

On this test, the parts are numbered from 2 through 5. (When you take the real ASVAB, Part 1 will be a test of General Science. It is not included here.)

This practice test form will be an accurate reflection of how you'll do on test day if you treat it as if it were the real examination. Here are some hints on how to take the test under conditions similar to those of the actual exam:

- Find a quiet place to work and set aside a period of approximately an hour and a half when you will not be disturbed.
- Work on only one part at a time, and use your watch or a timer to keep track of the time limits for each test part.
- Tear out your answer sheet and mark your answers by filling in the ovals for each question. If you take the computer adaptive version of the ASVAB, you will mark your answers by using your mouse or the keyboard.
- Become familiar with the directions for each part of the test. You'll save time on the actual test day by already being familiar with this information.

At the end of the test, you'll find answer keys for each part and explanations for every question. After you check your answers against the keys, you can complete self-scoring charts that will show you how you did on each part of the test and what test topics you might need to study more. Then review the explanations, paying particular attention to the ones for the questions that you answered incorrectly.

GENERAL DIRECTIONS:

IF YOU ARE TAKING THE PAPER-AND-PENCIL VERSION OF THE ASVAB, THE TEST ADMINISTRATOR WILL READ THE FOLLOWING ALOUD TO YOU:

DO NOT WRITE YOUR NAME OR MAKE ANY MARKS in this booklet. Mark your answers on the separate answer sheet. Use the scratch paper which was given to you for any figuring you need to do. Return this scratch paper with your other papers when you finish the test.

If you need another pencil while taking this test, hold your pencil above your head. A proctor will bring you another one.

This booklet contains eight tests. *[Note: This practice test form for the AFQT contains only four of the eight tests.]* Each test has its own instructions and time limit. When you finish a test, you may check your work in that test ONLY. Do not go on to the next test until the examiner tells you to do so. Do not turn back to a previous test at any time.

For each question, be sure to pick the BEST ONE of the possible answers listed. Each test has its own instructions and time limit. When you have decided which one of the choices given is the best answer to the question, blacken the space on your answer sheet that has the same number and letter as your choice. Mark only in the answer space. BE CAREFUL NOT TO MAKE ANY STRAY MARKS ON YOUR ANSWER SHEET. Each test has a separate section on the answer sheet. Be sure you mark your answers for each test in the section that belongs to that test.

Here is an example of correct marking on an answer sheet.

S1   A triangle has

    A. 2 sides

    B. 3 sides

    C. 4 sides

    D. 5 sides

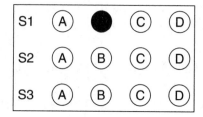

S1. [oval A] [oval B, blackened] [oval C] [oval D]

The correct answer to Sample Question S1 is B.

Next to the item, note how space B opposite number S1 has been blackened. Your marks should look just like this and be placed in the space with the same number and letter as the correct answer to the question. Remember, there is only ONE BEST ANSWER for each question. If you are not sure of the answer, make the BEST GUESS you can. If you want to change your answer, COMPLETELY ERASE your first answer mark.

Answer as many questions as possible. Do not spend too much time on any one question. Work QUICKLY, but work ACCURATELY. DO NOT TURN THE PAGE UNTIL TOLD TO DO SO. Are there any questions?

AFQT PRACTICE TEST FORM 2

Answer Sheet

Note: **When you take the real ASVAB, Part 1 will be a test of General Science. This test is *not* part of the AFQT and is *not* included here.**

PART 2-AR	PART 3-WK	PART 4-PC	PART 5-MK
1 (A)(B)(C)(D)	1 (A)(B)(C)(D)	1 (A)(B)(C)(D)	1 (A)(B)(C)(D)
2 (A)(B)(C)(D)	2 (A)(B)(C)(D)	2 (A)(B)(C)(D)	2 (A)(B)(C)(D)
3 (A)(B)(C)(D)	3 (A)(B)(C)(D)	3 (A)(B)(C)(D)	3 (A)(B)(C)(D)
4 (A)(B)(C)(D)	4 (A)(B)(C)(D)	4 (A)(B)(C)(D)	4 (A)(B)(C)(D)
5 (A)(B)(C)(D)	5 (A)(B)(C)(D)	5 (A)(B)(C)(D)	5 (A)(B)(C)(D)
6 (A)(B)(C)(D)	6 (A)(B)(C)(D)	6 (A)(B)(C)(D)	6 (A)(B)(C)(D)
7 (A)(B)(C)(D)	7 (A)(B)(C)(D)	7 (A)(B)(C)(D)	7 (A)(B)(C)(D)
8 (A)(B)(C)(D)	8 (A)(B)(C)(D)	8 (A)(B)(C)(D)	8 (A)(B)(C)(D)
9 (A)(B)(C)(D)	9 (A)(B)(C)(D)	9 (A)(B)(C)(D)	9 (A)(B)(C)(D)
10 (A)(B)(C)(D)	10 (A)(B)(C)(D)	10 (A)(B)(C)(D)	10 (A)(B)(C)(D)
11 (A)(B)(C)(D)	11 (A)(B)(C)(D)	11 (A)(B)(C)(D)	11 (A)(B)(C)(D)
12 (A)(B)(C)(D)	12 (A)(B)(C)(D)	12 (A)(B)(C)(D)	12 (A)(B)(C)(D)
13 (A)(B)(C)(D)	13 (A)(B)(C)(D)	13 (A)(B)(C)(D)	13 (A)(B)(C)(D)
14 (A)(B)(C)(D)	14 (A)(B)(C)(D)	14 (A)(B)(C)(D)	14 (A)(B)(C)(D)
15 (A)(B)(C)(D)	15 (A)(B)(C)(D)	15 (A)(B)(C)(D)	15 (A)(B)(C)(D)
16 (A)(B)(C)(D)	16 (A)(B)(C)(D)		16 (A)(B)(C)(D)
17 (A)(B)(C)(D)	17 (A)(B)(C)(D)		17 (A)(B)(C)(D)
18 (A)(B)(C)(D)	18 (A)(B)(C)(D)		18 (A)(B)(C)(D)
19 (A)(B)(C)(D)	19 (A)(B)(C)(D)		19 (A)(B)(C)(D)
20 (A)(B)(C)(D)	20 (A)(B)(C)(D)		20 (A)(B)(C)(D)
21 (A)(B)(C)(D)	21 (A)(B)(C)(D)		21 (A)(B)(C)(D)
22 (A)(B)(C)(D)	22 (A)(B)(C)(D)		22 (A)(B)(C)(D)
23 (A)(B)(C)(D)	23 (A)(B)(C)(D)		23 (A)(B)(C)(D)
24 (A)(B)(C)(D)	24 (A)(B)(C)(D)		24 (A)(B)(C)(D)
25 (A)(B)(C)(D)	25 (A)(B)(C)(D)		25 (A)(B)(C)(D)
26 (A)(B)(C)(D)	26 (A)(B)(C)(D)		
27 (A)(B)(C)(D)	27 (A)(B)(C)(D)		
28 (A)(B)(C)(D)	28 (A)(B)(C)(D)		
29 (A)(B)(C)(D)	29 (A)(B)(C)(D)		
30 (A)(B)(C)(D)	30 (A)(B)(C)(D)		
	31 (A)(B)(C)(D)		
	32 (A)(B)(C)(D)		
	33 (A)(B)(C)(D)		
	34 (A)(B)(C)(D)		
	35 (A)(B)(C)(D)		

PART 2. ARITHMETIC REASONING

THE TEST ADMINISTRATOR WILL READ THE FOLLOWING ALOUD TO YOU:

Turn to Part 2 and read the directions for Arithmetic Reasoning silently while I read them aloud.

This is a test of arithmetic word problems. Each question is followed by four possible answers. Decide which answer is CORRECT, and then blacken the space on your answer sheet that has the same number and letter as your choice. Use your scratch paper for any figuring you wish to do.

Here is a sample question. DO NOT MARK your answer sheet for this or any further sample questions.

S1   A student buys a sandwich for 80 cents, milk for 20 cents, and pie for 30 cents. How much did the meal cost?

   A. $1.00
   B. $1.20
   C. $1.30
   D. $1.40

The total cost is $1.30; therefore, C is the right answer. Your score on this test will be based on the number of questions you answer correctly. You should try to answer every question. DO NOT SPEND TOO MUCH TIME on any one question. If you finish before time is called, go back and check your work in this part ONLY.

Now find the section of your answer sheet that is marked PART 2. When you are told to begin, start with question number 1 in Part 2 of your test booklet and answer space number 1 in Part 2 on your separate answer sheet.

DO NOT TURN THIS PAGE UNTIL TOLD TO DO SO. You will have 36 minutes for the 30 questions. Are there any questions?

Begin.

1. Andre had a birthday party and spent $12.98 on balloons, $47.23 on party favors, $22.97 on a cake, $14.77 on ice cream, and $15.00 on invitations. How much did Andre spend on the party?

   A. $87.25
   B. $112.95
   C. $125.20
   D. $127.30

2. High school students were asked to pick their favorite kind of birthday party. The results are shown in the chart below. What percent of the students picked a laser tag party?

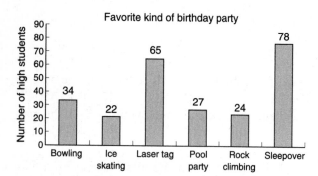

   A. 26
   B. 37
   C. 42
   D. 44

3. Bob's iPod contains 800 songs. If 256 songs are either jazz or rap songs, what percent of his collection is jazz or rap?

   A. 12%
   B. 24%
   C. 27%
   D. 32%

4. Matt took a biking trip. On the first day he rode 15 miles. On the second day he rode 35 miles, and on the third day he rested. On the fourth day he rode 57 miles, and on the fifth day he rode 43 miles. What was the average number of miles that he rode per day?

   A. 25
   B. 27
   C. 30
   D. 32

5. Blair's athletic specialty is the long jump. In his last competitions, he jumped 120 cm, 240 cm, 210 cm, 200 cm, 190 cm, and 190 cm. What is his average long jump?

   A. 133.86 cm
   B. 191.66 cm
   C. 199.26 cm
   D. 221.66 cm

6. A volleyball team won 25 games during a season of 85 games. What is the ratio of wins to losses?

   A. $\frac{5}{12}$
   B. $\frac{5}{6}$
   C. $\frac{1}{3}$
   D. $\frac{1}{2}$

7. A certain relay team has eight members. If each team member runs 5.2 kilometers, how many meters is the race?

   A. 116.6
   B. 416.6
   C. 41,600
   D. 43,600

8. The local shopping mall is conducting a survey of people's favorite fast foods. The results so far are as follows:

Type of Fast Food	Number of Persons
Pizza	602
Pasta	411
Hamburgers	589
Sushi	214
Chinese food	78
Barbecue	514

What is the probability that the next randomly selected person will say that his or her favorite fast food is pizza?

A. $\frac{1}{4}$

B. $\frac{1}{3}$

C. $\frac{4}{5}$

D. $\frac{6}{7}$

9. Sally and Peter are saving to buy a house. They deposit $15,000 in a savings bond that pays simple interest at a rate of 8% per year. If the down payment they need is $18,000, after how many years will they have enough money for a down payment?

A. 3
B. 5
C. 6
D. 7

10. First-class postage is $0.44 for the first ounce and $0.17 for each additional ounce. What is the cost for an 8-oz parcel?

A. $0.97
B. $1.12
C. $1.42
D. $1.63

11. Aaron has 256 cans of soup that he needs to pack into boxes that hold 30 cans each. How many cans of soup are left over after he fills as many boxes as possible?

A. 4
B. 16
C. 18
D. 22

12. Kelly wants to tile a wall in her bathroom. The wall is 10 feet by 12 feet. Each tile is 6 inches by 8 inches. How many tiles will she need to finish the job?

A. 124 tiles
B. 360 tiles
C. 412 tiles
D. 514 tiles

13. The Metro Fitness Center has a joining fee of $250.00 per person. The center runs a special promotion every January, offering a deal in which two persons can join for one joining fee, at a discount of 25% off the regular fee. If two friends want to join, what would each person pay?

A. $80.00
B. $93.75
C. $100.00
D. $112.25

14. Blythe sees a computer that she wants to buy. It costs $1,800. The store manager says that next week the computer will be on sale for $350 less. What percent will Blythe save if she waits a week before purchasing the computer?

A. 12.8%
B. 15.3%
C. 19.4%
D. 21.3%

15. Two numbers add to 1,500. One number is four times the size of the other. What are the two numbers?

A. 300; 1,200
B. 200; 1,300
C. 500; 1,000
D. 750; 750

16. Miles is starting a tree farm. His plot of land is triangular, with one side being 60 feet and the other two sides being 50 feet each. The height of this triangle-shaped plot is 40 feet. If each tree needs 20 square feet of space to grow, how many trees can Miles plant?

A. 60
B. 65
C. 70
D. 76

17. A meteor made a circular crater with a circumference of 56.52 meters. What is the diameter of the crater?

A. 9 m
B. 12 m
C. 15 m
D. 18 m

18. The wing of an airplane is shaped like a triangle. If one angle is 112° and another is 47°, what is the size of the third angle?

A. 12°
B. 21°
C. 24°
D. 37°

19. In 1968 the population of Belgium was 8,435,978. In 1998, the population was 10,544,972. By what percent did the population increase in 30 years?

A. 13%
B. 18%
C. 21%
D. 25%

20. Steve is measuring the growth of a tomato plant. The chart below indicates his measurements for the past five weeks. Based on the information in the chart, what should he predict will be the height of the plant at week 6?

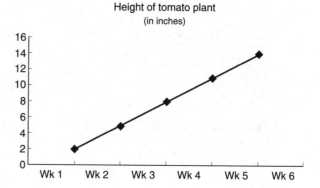

Height of tomato plant
(in inches)

A. 15 inches
B. 17 inches
C. 18 inches
D. 21 inches

21. Jose is training to run a 12-kilometer race. His training program has him running 3 kilometers per day for the first week and increasing that amount by 15% each week. How many kilometers will he be running per day in the fourth week?

A. 3.45 km
B. 3.97 km
C. 4.57 km
D. 4.97 km

22. A swimming pool is 3 meters deep, 50 meters long, and 25 meters wide. If it takes 5 grams of chlorine for every 15 cubic meters of water to keep the pool clean and healthy, how many grams of chlorine are needed?

A. 980 grams
B. 1,125 grams
C. 1,150 grams
D. 1,250 grams

23. A person needs 1,500 milligrams of calcium each day. For breakfast, Joel eats a bowl of cereal with milk that has 250 milligrams of calcium, a bagel with cream cheese that has 100 milligrams of calcium, and a small container of yogurt that has 225 milligrams of calcium. What percent of the daily calcium requirement does he get at breakfast?

   A. 24%
   B. 38%
   C. 44%
   D. 49%

24. A circular baking pan is 4 inches high with a diameter of 16 inches. How much cake batter can it hold?

   A. 404.2 in.^{3}
   B. 512.7 in.^{3}
   C. 788.8 in.^{3}
   D. 803.8 in.^{3}

25. A basketball has a diameter of 12 inches. What is its volume?

   A. 150.72 in.^{3}
   B. 516.06 in.^{3}
   C. 904.32 in.^{3}
   D. 1,316.12 in.^{3}

26. A box of laundry soap contains 200 oz. If the cost for one ounce is 3.5 cents, how much does the box of soap cost?

   A. $5.12
   B. $7.00
   C. $7.12
   D. $8.01

27. Melanie's credit card bill was $4,000 in February. If her monthly interest is 14%, what will her bill be in March if she makes no payments and has no new purchases?

   A. $4,440
   B. $4,560
   C. $4,720
   D. $4,890

28. In a jar, there are 45 green marbles, 32 red marbles, 13 purple marbles, 16 orange marbles, and 29 yellow marbles. If Duke selects one marble at random, what is the probability that the marble will be red or purple?

   A. 1:3
   B. 2:5
   C. 3:5
   D. 3:7

29. A corner table is in the shape of a right triangle. The sides that form the right angle measure 3 feet and 4 feet. What is the area of the table top?

   A. 6 ft^2
   B. 7.2 ft^2
   C. 8 ft^2
   D. 8.5 ft^2

30. Arnold signs an agreement with the A-1 car rental company for a car at $29 per day plus 22 cents per mile driven. If Arnold rents the car for two days and drives 200 miles, how much does he owe the company?

   A. $94.00
   B. $102.00
   C. $111.00
   D. $112.00

STOP! DO NOT TURN THIS PAGE UNTIL TIME IS UP FOR THIS TEST. IF YOU FINISH BEFORE TIME IS UP, CHECK OVER YOUR WORK ON THIS TEST ONLY.

PART 3. WORD KNOWLEDGE

THE TEST ADMINISTRATOR WILL READ THE FOLLOWING ALOUD TO YOU:

Now turn to Part 3 and read the directions for Word Knowledge silently while I read aloud.

This is a test of your knowledge of word meanings. These questions consist of a sentence or phrase with a word or phrase underlined. From the four choices given, you are to decide which one MEANS THE SAME OR MOST NEARLY THE SAME as the underlined word or phrase. Once you have made your choice, mark the space on your answer sheet that has the same number and letter as your choice.

Look at the sample question.

S1 The weather in this geographic area tends to be <u>moderate</u>.

    A. severe
    B. warm
    C. mild
    D. windy

The correct answer is "mild," which is choice C. Therefore, you would have blackened in space C on your answer sheet.

Your score on this test will be based on the number of questions you answer correctly. You should try to answer every question. DO NOT SPEND TOO MUCH TIME on any one question. If you finish before time is called, go back and check your work in this part <u>ONLY</u>.

Now find the section of your answer sheet that is marked PART 3. When you are told to begin, start with question number 1 in Part 3 of your test booklet and answer space number 1 in Part 3 on your separate answer sheet.

DO NOT TURN THE PAGE UNTIL TOLD TO DO SO. You will have 11 minutes to complete the 35 questions in this part. Are there any questions?

Begin.

1. <u>Deprecate</u> most nearly means

   A. compliment
   B. belittle
   C. encourage
   D. await

2. Despite the daily smog alerts, the capital's <u>complacent</u> inhabitants always said that they would never live anywhere else.

   A. thrilled
   B. surprised
   C. anxious
   D. satisfied

3. George was <u>incredulous</u> when he learned the surprising results of the survey.

   A. incredible
   B. unlawful
   C. impeccable
   D. skeptical

4. Peter had a <u>disinclination</u> for attending functions that involved lots of people and loud music.

   A. predisposition
   B. distaste
   C. desire
   D. indifference

5. Benny's statement about the end of the world was considered by his friends and acquaintances to be <u>hyperbole</u>.

   A. exaggeration
   B. revolutionary
   C. repulsive
   D. understatement

6. Barney, the puppy, was smaller than the other neighborhood dogs, but was definitely the most <u>pugnacious</u>.

   A. flawed
   B. aggressive
   C. transitional
   D. lucid

7. Jake enjoyed the <u>hiatus</u> between graduation and his first job.

   A. vacation
   B. excitement
   C. gap
   D. boredom

8. <u>De facto</u> most nearly means

   A. actual
   B. unreal
   C. inappropriate
   D. false

9. <u>Inculcate</u> most nearly means

   A. indoctrinate
   B. recommend
   C. misperceive
   D. infer

10. <u>Succor</u> most nearly means

    A. aid
    B. laugh
    C. hinder
    D. investigate

11. <u>Miscreant</u> most nearly means

    A. mistake
    B. villain
    C. misrepresentation
    D. objective

12. Although his neighbors were generous with their charity, their good will was not enough to <u>supplant</u> the despair he felt over the loss of his possessions.

    A. repair
    B. describe
    C. replace
    D. comply

13. Randy knew that his move to this town would be <u>transient.</u>

    A. happy
    B. impeccable
    C. impeachable
    D. temporary

14. Laura had a <u>proclivity</u> for desserts made of chocolate.

    A. aversion
    B. bias
    C. dislike
    D. distaste

15. Samantha was delighted with the new garden, which was a fascinating <u>labyrinth</u> of huge bushes, trees, and pathways.

    A. area
    B. forest
    C. maze
    D. playground

16. After hearing the motivational speaker, the audience thought that the congressman's speech sounded <u>pedestrian.</u>

    A. uninspired
    B. controversial
    C. exciting
    D. informative

17. They usually ignored Sally because her demeanor tended to be perpetually <u>peevish.</u>

    A. depressing
    B. grumpy
    C. elated
    D. haughty

18. Brian was <u>penitent</u> because he had mistakenly overcharged his customer.

    A. annoyed
    B. angry
    C. remorseful
    D. joking

19. It was highly unusual to have such a <u>balmy</u> day in the middle of January in Minnesota.

    A. frigid
    B. festive
    C. quiet
    D. pleasant

20. Jonathan's garden was a <u>medley</u> of colorful fruits and vegetables.

    A. mixture
    B. disaster
    C. basket
    D. partition

21. The attorney <u>facilitated</u> the discussion, bringing the group to consensus in record time.

    A. impeded
    B. receded
    C. enabled
    D. rejected

22. The story that Leon told the audience sounded remarkable, but it was actually <u>fabricated.</u>

    A. ordinary
    B. fictitious
    C. spectacular
    D. mundane

23. The trans-Atlantic trip was fraught with delays, making it more <u>arduous</u> than usual.

    A. fleeting
    B. difficult
    C. annoying
    D. informative

24. In this day and age, Jason's ideas about technology were considered <u>archaic</u> by his contemporaries.

    A. creative
    B. ridiculous
    C. fanciful
    D. outdated

25. The logic behind Larry's claims was so compelling that his conclusion was <u>indisputable</u>.

    A. questionable
    B. irrefutable
    C. silly
    D. shocking

26. By his <u>selfless</u> rescue efforts, Wayne helped many people to escape the burning building.

    A. unwanted
    B. destructive
    C. noble
    D. counterproductive

27. It was a <u>tactical</u> decision to stock up on food and water as the hurricane approached.

    A. planned
    B. fruitful
    C. useless
    D. lucky

28. Lily's devotion to her company was <u>steadfast</u> even though business had been poor for several months.

    A. questioning
    B. expected
    C. unfaltering
    D. wavering

29. Brandon's elderly grandmother was the <u>titular</u> head of the family.

    A. arrogant
    B. royal
    C. actual
    D. supposed

30. The visiting team <u>trounced</u> the home team in the last game of the season.

    A. welcomed
    B. disrespected
    C. crushed
    D. fought

31. His response was as <u>predictable</u> as the rising sun.

    A. elevating
    B. expected
    C. glorious
    D. shocking

32. The celebrations at midnight <u>ushered</u> in the new year.

    A. escorted
    B. identified
    C. overshadowed
    D. followed

33. The crowd protesting the injustice was especially <u>vociferous</u> today.

    A. friendly
    B. cooperative
    C. colorful
    D. loud

34. Mr. Clark's elegant clothing suited his <u>stature</u> in society.

    A. job
    B. status
    C. activity
    D. preference

35. Brian's remarks relating to the embarrassing incident were <u>disingenuous</u>.

    A. direct
    B. candid
    C. sincere
    D. dishonest

STOP! DO NOT TURN THIS PAGE UNTIL TIME IS UP FOR THIS TEST. IF YOU FINISH BEFORE TIME IS UP, CHECK OVER YOUR WORK ON THIS TEST ONLY.

PART 4. PARAGRAPH COMPREHENSION

THE TEST ADMINISTRATOR WILL READ THE FOLLOWING ALOUD TO YOU:

Turn to Part 4 and read the directions for Paragraph Comprehension silently while I read them aloud.

This is a test of your ability to understand what you read. In this section you will find one or more paragraphs of reading material followed by incomplete statements or questions. You are to read the paragraph and select one of four lettered choices which BEST completes the statement or answers the question. When you have selected your answer, blacken the space on your answer sheet that has the same number and letter as your answer.

Your score on this test will be based on the number of questions you answer correctly. You should try to answer every question. DO NOT SPEND TOO MUCH TIME on any one question. If you finish before time is called, go back and check your work in this part ONLY.

Now find the section of your answer sheet that is marked PART 4. When you are told to begin, start with question number 1 in Part 4 of your test booklet and answer space number 1 in Part 4 on your separate answer sheet.

DO NOT TURN THE PAGE UNTIL TOLD TO DO SO. You will have 13 minutes to complete the 15 questions in this part. Are there any questions?

Begin.

Some of the things you can do to prepare for the unexpected, such as making an emergency supply kit and developing a family communications plan, are the same for both a natural and a man-made emergency. However, there are important differences among natural disasters that will affect the decisions you make and the actions you take. Some natural disasters are easily predicted; others happen without warning. Planning what to do in advance is an important part of being prepared.

Find out what natural disasters are most common in your area. You may be aware of some of your community's risks; others may surprise you. Historically, flooding is the nation's single most common natural disaster. Flooding can happen in every U.S. state and territory. Earthquakes are often thought of as a West Coast phenomenon, yet 45 states all across the country, as well as many U.S. territories, are at moderate to high risk from earthquakes. Other disasters may be more common in certain areas. Tornadoes are nature's most violent storms and can happen anywhere. However, states located in "Tornado Alley," as well as areas in Pennsylvania, New York, Connecticut, and Florida, are at the highest risk for tornado damage. Hurricanes are severe tropical storms that form in the southern Atlantic Ocean, the Caribbean Sea, the Gulf of Mexico, and the eastern Pacific Ocean. Scientists can now predict hurricanes, but people who live in coastal communities should plan what they will do if they are told to evacuate.

Natural disasters include earthquakes, extreme heat, fires, floods, hurricanes, landslides and mudslides, thunderstorms, tsunamis, volcanoes, wildfires, winter storms, and extreme cold.

1. According to the passage, what is the most common natural disaster?

   A. tornadoes
   B. hurricanes
   C. tropical storms
   D. flooding

2. According to the passage, which of the following states is at the highest risk for tornadoes?

   A. Pennsylvania
   B. Wyoming
   C. California
   D. Utah

3. The passage indicates that the best way to be prepared for disasters is to

    A. have a battery-powered radio
    B. plan ahead
    C. read the newspapers to keep track of disasters
    D. live in a safe part of the country

4. According to the passage, which of the following is true?

    A. Hurricanes occur only along the Atlantic coast of the United States.
    B. Most states can be affected by earthquakes.
    C. Mountainous areas are most likely to be affected by flooding.
    D. Natural disasters cannot be predicted.

5. In order to plan ahead, the passage suggests that a person

    A. have an emergency supply kit and constantly replenish it
    B. listen to the radio for news of natural and man-made disasters
    C. stay in constant contact with family members and emergency relief personnel
    D. find out what natural disasters are most common in the area

The life blood of any business is money. You can't start, grow, or simply exist in business without sufficient money to pay the bills and provide you with some income. Here are some questions you'll need to answer as you consider starting or growing your business.

- How much money do I need to either get started or grow my business?
- Will I use my personal money?
- Should I ask someone else for a loan?
- Can I apply for a credit card?
- Will a vendor or a supplier be willing to give me trade credit? [This usually means that you have an extended period of time to pay your bill—typically 30 days from date of invoice.]
- To minimize costs, should I start my business in my home?
- If I use someone else's money, will my business generate enough money to be able to repay the loan (principal and interest)?

Many entrepreneurs start businesses at home using their own personal funds. Some ask friends and family for help to manage their business and, in some cases, ask friends to provide the initial or ongoing capital. When a business has been established for a while, the entrepreneur goes to his or her local bank for capital. Banks may consider giving you a line of credit, or possibly a small commercial loan, if you and/or your parents do your banking there.

Relationships are critical to succeeding in business. Know your suppliers. Make sure that you develop a relationship with them so that if you ever have difficulty in paying them, they may allow you some slack.

Developing a relationship with your bank and your personal banker also is important. Prior to seeking a loan from the bank, you need to establish a savings or checking account. Banks generally prefer to lend to their existing clients or clients who will bring the bank additional business (other new clients who will establish both personal and business accounts).

It is important to get to know your personal banker because she or he makes the final decisions about your loan. In most cases, your personal banker serves as your advocate, supporting your application before the bank's loan committee. Keep in mind when you apply for a loan that you and your parents must co-sign the loan.

Finally, establishing and maintaining a good credit history is critical to getting money for your business. Always pay your bills on time, and make sure that you periodically check your credit history. Your credit is like your name—do not abuse it.

6. According to the passage, which of the following is critical to succeeding in business?

   A. the type of products you are selling
   B. relationships with suppliers and banks
   C. the margin of profit for each item sold
   D. your credit line

7. Based on the information in the passage, what factor is important in maintaining a good credit history?

   A. knowing your banker
   B. obtaining a large loan
   C. having a supportive family
   D. paying bills on time

8. Which of the following is the best title for this passage?

    A. Money Means Business
    B. Bankers Make Loans
    C. Borrow from Your Family
    D. Profit Makes Perfect

9. Based on this passage, it can be inferred that

    A. you cannot be successful unless your suppliers believe in you
    B. you should not get your family and friends involved in your business
    C. you are more likely to get a loan from a bank if you already have accounts with that bank
    D. your business partners should be close friends

10. What is meant by the term *credit history*?

    A. the lending practices of your bank over the last several years
    B. whether your parents have accounts with the particular bank from which you are seeking a loan
    C. the length of time your bank has been in business
    D. your track record of paying bills.

If you'd lived in the California deserts a few thousand years ago, you could have owned lakefront property. Watch for "playas," or dry lake beds—those salt flats out on low valley floors—as you drive in the desert. At the end of the last ice age, when the weather here was a lot wetter, those were all freshwater lakes. Lake Manly, in Death Valley, was 600 feet deep and nearly 100 miles long. But as the climate changed, the lakes became saltier and eventually dried up. There are more than 50 playas (*playa* means "beach" in Spanish) in our deserts. Their cracked surfaces remain dry except after heavy storms.

When the water goes, only salt remains; we mine these former lakes for borax, chlorides, and other salts.

Five hundred million years ago, you could have sailed the *Titanic* over our deserts and never hit an iceberg, let alone a sand dune. Ancient tropical seas—much like the Caribbean—covered southern California at least twice. Back then, the ocean reached all the way to eastern California.

The limestone rocks and mountains we see today were formed back then. Sediments from land along with the shells and skeletons of millions of generations of corals, algae, and oysters and other shellfish built up in layers of muddy ooze. The weight of new layers compressed and hardened older ones, creating limestone. Eventually, the movement of the Earth's tectonic plates pushed the rock up into mountains.

You can see evidence of these ancient sea creatures in Death Valley National Park. Titus Canyon is an ideal area to explore some of the 20,000 feet of limestone deposits. In Providence Mountains State Recreation Area, Mitchell Caverns are being carved as water slowly dissolves away the limestone rock.

Wind caves, located in the Coyote Mountains (a designated wilderness area), are covered with exposed marine fossils raised hundreds of feet above sea level. The caves were created by wind and water erosion of the sandstone.

11. According to the passage, *playa* means

   A. dune
   B. recreational area
   C. geological formation
   D. beach

12. Which of the following is the best title for this passage?

   A. Wind Caves and Water
   B. Oceans to Deserts—Historical Changes
   C. Mystery Climates
   D. Marine Animals Lived Long Ago

13. Which of the following is NOT a piece of evidence that deserts were once under the ocean?

    A. salts and other minerals
    B. evidence of icebergs
    C. limestone
    D. fossil corals

14. Which of the following is mentioned in the passage as a positive attribute of California's deserts?

    A. There are no problems with flooding.
    B. They provide warmth that allows plants and animals to flourish.
    C. The climate is favored by humans.
    D. Important minerals can be mined there.

15. What explains the fact that marine animal fossils are found in the mountains of the Death Valley area?

    A. Land that was once under the sea was pushed upward during the formation of mountains.
    B. Marine animals lived in the mountains at one time because the climate was better.
    C. Marine animals migrated from the sea to the mountains over time.
    D. The mountains were once under oceans until the oceans dried up over time.

STOP! DO NOT TURN THIS PAGE UNTIL TIME IS UP FOR THIS TEST. IF YOU FINISH BEFORE TIME IS UP, CHECK OVER YOUR WORK ON THIS TEST ONLY.

PART 5. MATHEMATICS KNOWLEDGE

THE TEST ADMINISTRATOR WILL READ THE FOLLOWING ALOUD TO YOU:

Now turn to Part 5 and read the directions for Mathematics Knowledge silently while I read them aloud.

This is a test of your ability to solve general mathematics problems. You are to select the correct response from the choices given. Then mark the space on your answer sheet that has the same number and letter as your choice. Use your scratch paper to do any figuring you wish to do.

Your score on this test will be based on the number of questions you answer correctly. You should try to answer every question. DO NOT SPEND TOO MUCH TIME on any one question. If you finish before time is called, go back and check your work in this part <u>ONLY</u>.

Now find the section of your answer sheet that is marked PART 5. When you are told to begin, start with question number 1 in Part 5 of your test booklet and answer space number 1 in Part 5 on your separate answer sheet.

DO NOT TURN THE PAGE UNTIL TOLD TO DO SO. You will have 24 minutes to complete the 25 questions in this part. Are there any questions?

Begin

1. $z + 9 = 24.$ $z = ?$

   A. 6
   B. 15
   C. 24
   D. 36

2. $4^2 + 3(2 - 6) =$

   A. 4
   B. 12
   C. -4
   D. -12

3. 60 is what percent of 90?

   A. 30
   B. 33
   C. 45
   D. 67

4. What is the mean of the following numbers?

   24, 34, 12, 16, 34, 104, 890

   A. 14.12
   B. 56.24
   C. 159.14
   D. 450.34

5. Divide by $\frac{2}{3}$ by $\frac{5}{6}$.

   A. $\frac{4}{5}$

   B. $\frac{5}{18}$

   C. $\frac{15}{6}$

   D. $2\frac{1}{2}$

6. Factor the following expression:

   $x^2 - 100$

   A. $(x + 10)(x + 10)$
   B. $2x(100)$
   C. $(x - 10)(x - 10)$
   D. $(x + 10)(x - 10)$

7. Subtract:

   $12x^2 + 6y - 3$
   $3x^2 - 9y + 12$

   A. $9x^2 + 15y - 15$
   B. $15x^4 + 4y + 9$
   C. $15x^2 + 4y + 9$
   D. $9x^2 + 4y + 9$

8. Solve for x.

   $$\frac{r}{j} = \frac{x}{y}$$

   A. $\frac{yr}{j} = x$

   B. $x = \frac{rx}{jy}$

   C. $x = \frac{rx}{jy}$

   D. $jy = x$

9. Solve for the two unknowns.

   $3a + 4b = 12$
   $2a + 2b = 15$

   A. $a = 12; b = 10$
   B. $a = -10; b = 12$
   C. $a = -4; b = 9.5$
   D. $a = 18; b = -10.5$

10. $\dfrac{x^5 y^7}{x^7 y^2} -$

    A. $x^{-3} y^8$
    B. $x^3 y^8$
    C. $\dfrac{y^5}{x^2}$
    D. $\dfrac{y^4}{x^3}$

11. If $\dfrac{2}{25} = \dfrac{n}{500}$, what is n?

    A. 20
    B. 40
    C. 60
    D. 80

12. Multiply:

$$\frac{9}{x+1} \times \frac{3x+3}{5}$$

  A. $\frac{27x+27}{5x+1}$

  B. $5\frac{2}{5}$

  C. $30(3x^2 + 1)$

  D. $18\,x^2 + 30$

13. Divide:

$$\frac{5}{x+1} \div \frac{9}{3x+3}$$

  A. $\frac{45}{3x^2 + 6x + 3}$

  B. $\frac{45}{(x+1)(3x+1)}$

  C. $\frac{15x}{6x^2}$

  D. $1\frac{2}{3}$

14. $\sqrt[3]{216} =$

  A. 3
  B. 5
  C. 6
  D. 11

15. Solve for y.

$$\frac{v}{y} = \frac{s}{t}$$

  A. $y = \frac{vs}{yt}$

  B. $y = \frac{s}{vt}$

  C. $y = \frac{vt}{s}$

  D. $y = vst$

16. If the value of the expression $x + 2 < 12$, which of the following could be the value of x?

  A. 9
  B. 10
  C. 12
  D. 15

17. What is the perimeter of the following parallelogram?

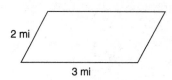

  A. 9 mi
  B. 10 mi
  C. 12 mi
  D. 14 mi

18. Round the following number to the nearest hundredth.

1,478.966

  A. 1,478.99
  B. 1,500.00
  C. 1,478.97
  D. 1,478.970

19. If the following is a right triangle and $\angle 2$ is 59°, what is the measure of $\angle 1$?

  A. 26°
  B. 31°
  C. 43°
  D. 52°

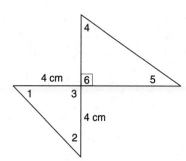

20. In the following figure, if $\angle 6$ measures 90°, what is the measure of $\angle 1$?

  A. 25°
  B. 35°
  C. 45°
  D. 55°

21. Subtract the following:

$$14y^2 + y + 6x^2 + 9x - 12$$
$$y^2 + 3y + 6x^2 + 2x + 12$$

A. $15y^2 + y + 6x^2 + 9x - 12$
B. $14y^2 + y + 9x$
C. $14y^2 + y + 6x^2 + 9x - 24$
D. $13y^2 - 2y + 7x - 24$

22. What is the volume of the following rectangular solid?

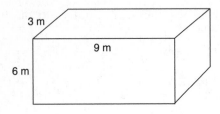

A. 36 m^3
B. 99 m^3
C. 121.5 m^3
D. 162 m^3

23. Factor $y^2 + 8y - 20$.

A. $(y + 10)(y + 2)$
B. $(y + 2)(y + 6)$
C. $(y - 10)(y + 2)$
D. $(y + 10)(y - 2)$

24. What is 2% of 5,000?

A. 10
B. 80
C. 100
D. 105

25. What is the volume of a sphere that has a radius of 3 meters?

A. 12.56 m^3
B. 37.68 m^3
C. 75.36 m^3
D. 113.04 m^3

STOP! THIS IS THE END OF PRACTICE TEST FORM 2. IF YOU FINISH BEFORE TIME IS UP, CHECK OVER YOUR WORK ON THIS TEST ONLY.

AFQT Practice Test Form 2: Answers and Explanations

PART 2. ARITHMETIC REASONING

Scoring Your Test

Compare your answer to the correct answer. Mark an X in the column if you got the item correct. Total the number correct.

Item Number	Correct Answer	Mark X if You Picked the Correct Answer
1	B	
2	A	
3	D	
4	C	
5	B	
6	A	
7	C	
8	A	
9	A	
10	D	
11	B	
12	B	
13	B	
14	C	
15	A	
16	A	
17	D	
18	B	
19	D	
20	B	
21	C	
22	D	
23	B	
24	D	
25	C	
26	B	
27	B	
28	A	
29	A	
30	B	
Total Correct		

Gauging Your Level of Performance

In the following chart, find the number of items that you got correct. See the suggestions listed for your performance.

30	This is pretty good work. Review the explanations of the answers that you got incorrect.
29	
28	
27	
26	
25	You are doing pretty well. Review the explanations for the items that you answered incorrectly. If you have time, review the other explanations and you will learn even more.
24	
23	
22	
21	
20	You need to keep studying and practicing. Pay close attention to the explanations for each item, even for the ones you got correct.
19	
18	
17	
16	
15	
14	
13	
12	Spend time working on Chapter 9, "Sharpen Your Word Problem Skills," in Part 2 of this book. If you are having trouble with these items, you will not perform well on the AFQT.
11	
10	
9	
8	
7	
6	
5	Keep working and reworking problems until you are comfortable with the processes.
4	
3	
2	
1	
0	

Explanations

1. **B** This is a simple addition problem. Add the amounts of $12.98, $47.23, $22.97, $14.77, $15.00 to get the total of $112.95.

2. **A** This problem has two steps. First you need to add the number of people, then you need to determine the percent who said that they preferred a laser tag party.

   $$34 + 22 + 65 + 27 + 24 + 78 = 250$$

   Now divide the number who preferred laser tag parties by the total number: $65/250 = 0.26$. To get the percent, move the decimal point two places to the right and add the percent sign: 26%.

3. **D** In order to calculate the percent, you need to divide the number of jazz and rap songs by the total number of songs: $256 \div 800 = 0.32$. To change that to a percent, move the decimal point two places to the right and add the percent sign to get the correct answer of 32%.

4. **C** To find the average, add up the numbers and divide by the number of numbers. In this instance, Matt rode $15 + 35 + 0 + 57 + 43 = 150$ miles. The number of numbers is 5, so the average number of miles he rode per day was 30. Don't make the mistake of dividing by 4 because on one day his number of miles was 0. That number needs to be used in calculating the average.

5. **B** To find the average, add up the numbers and divide by the number of numbers. In this problem, Blair's six jumps total to 1,150 cm. Since he has jumped 6 times, his average jump is $1,150 \div 6 = 191.66$ cm.

6. **A** To find the ratio of one number to another, create a fraction to show the relationship. In this problem, there are 25 wins in a total of 85 games. The question asks for the ratio of wins to losses, so you need to calculate the number of losses. $85 - 25 = 60$ losses. So the ratio of wins to losses is $\frac{25}{60}$, which simplifies to $\frac{5}{12}$.

7. **C** Set this up as a proportion. If each member runs 5.2 km, how many kilometers do eight members run? The proportion would look like this: $\frac{1}{5.2} = \frac{8}{x}$. Cross multiply and solve. $x = 8(5.2)$ or $x = 41.6$ km. However, the problem asks for an answer in meters. Since 1 km = 1,000 meters, 41.6 km = 41,600 meters.

8. **A** Probability = number of favorable outcomes/number of possible outcomes. In this problem, the number of favorable outcomes is the number of people selecting pizza as their favorite fast food. The number of possible outcomes is the number of all those surveyed, or $602 + 411 + 589 + 214 + 78 + 514 = 2,408$. So substituting into the formula, $\frac{602}{2,408}$. This simplifies to $\frac{1}{4}$, the correct ratio.

9. **A** To solve this problem, use the formula $I = prt$ for each year and then see in what year they have the total amount needed.

   Year 1: $(\$15,000 \times 0.08) = \$1,200$;
   $\$15,000 + \$1,200 = \$16,200$

   Year 2: $(\$16,200 \times 0.08) = \$1,296$;
   $\$16,200 + \$1,296 = \$17,496$

   Year 3: $(\$17,496 \times 0.08) = \$1,399.68$;
   $\$17,496 + \$1,399.68 = \$18,895.68$

   They reach the down payment of $18,000 after year 3.

10. **D** The first ounce is $0.44. There are seven additional ounces at $0.17 each. The total cost would be $\$0.44 + 7(\$0.17) = \$0.44 + \$1.19 = \$1.63$.

11. **B** If Aaron has 256 cans of soup to pack into boxes of 30, he can fill $256 \div 30$ boxes = 8 boxes with 16 cans left over.

12. **B** The formula for calculating area is $A = \ell w$. Since the tiles are measured in inches, calculate the area of the wall in square inches.

    $$10 \text{ ft} \times 12 \text{ in.} = 120 \text{ in.}$$
    $$12 \text{ ft} \times 12 \text{ in.} = 144 \text{ in.}$$
    $$120 \text{ in.} \times 144 \text{ in.} = 17,280 \text{ in.}^2$$

    Each tile has an area of 6×8 in. or 48 in.^{2}

    $$17,280 \text{ in.}^2 \div 48 \text{ in.}^2 = 360 \text{ tiles}$$

13. **B** The cost of the joining fee is $250.00.

Reduce that amount by 25% by multiplying the total cost by 0.25.

$$\$250.00 \times 0.25 = \$62.50$$

Subtract $62.50 from the original cost.

$$\$250 - 62.50 = \$187.50$$

Dividing that reduced membership fee by two people gives a fee of $93.75 for each person.

14. **C** Use the following formula:

$$\text{Percent change} = \frac{\text{amount of change}}{\text{starting point}}$$

In this problem, we know that the amount of change is $350 and the starting price of the computer is $1,800. Substitute that information into the formula:

$$\text{Percent change} = \frac{\$350.00}{\$1800.00} = 0.1944$$

Change that number to a percent by moving the decimal place two places to the right and adding the percent sign.

$$0.1944 = 19.44\%$$

15. **A** You are told that two numbers add to 1,500, with one number being four times the other. Create an equation.

$$x + 4x = 1,500$$

Solve for x.

$$5x = 1,500$$
$$x = 300$$
$$4x = 1,200$$

So the two numbers are 300 and 1,200.

16. **A** To calculate the area of a triangle, use the formula $A = \frac{1}{2}bh$.

In this instance, the base is 60 feet and the height is 40 feet.

$$A = \frac{1}{2}(60)(40)$$
$$A = \frac{1}{2}(2,400)$$
$$A = 1,200 \text{ ft}^2$$

If each tree needs 20 ft^2, divide that into the area.

$$\frac{1,200 \text{ ft}^2}{20 \text{ ft}^2} = 60 \text{ ft}^2$$

17. **D** Use the formula $C = 2\pi r$ or $C = \pi d$.

If the circumference is 56.52 meters, substitute that into the formula.

$$56.52 = \pi d$$

Solve for d by dividing both sides by π.

$$\frac{56.52}{3.14} = d$$
$$d = 18 \text{ m}$$

18. **B** A triangle has 180°. If one angle is 112° and another is 47°, that totals 159°. $180° - 159° = 21°$.

19. **D** Use the following formula:

$$\text{Percent change} = \frac{\text{amount of change}}{\text{starting point}}$$

The starting point is 8,435,978. The amount of change is the difference between 10,544,972 and 8,435,978. You find the difference by subtracting those two numbers.

$$10,544,972 - 8,435,978 = 2,108,994$$

Substitute that information into the equation.

$$\text{Percent of Change} = \frac{2108994}{8435978} = 0.2499 \text{ or } 25\%$$

20. **B** It appears that the plant grew by 3 inches each week. To find the height at week 6, add 3 inches to 14 to get 17 inches.

21. **C** Treat this like a compound interest problem where you calculate the increase in kilometers each week, using the increased amount as the amount to use in the calculations for the next week.

Week 1

$$3 \text{ km}$$

Week 2

$$3 \text{ km} + 0.15(3) = 3.45 \text{ km}$$

Week 3

$$3.45 \text{ km} + 0.15(3.45) = 3.97 \text{ km}$$

Week 4

$$3.97 + 0.15(3.97) = 4.57 \text{ km}$$

22. **D** To solve this problem, use the formula $v = \ell w h$. You have been given the dimensions of $l = 50$ m, $w = 25$ m, and $h = 3$ m.

Substitute that information into the formula.

$$V = (50)(25)(3)$$
$$V = 3{,}750 \text{ m}^3$$

If 5 grams of chlorine are required for every 15 m^3, calculate how many units of 15 m^3 there are in the total volume of 3,750 m^3.

$$3{,}750 \text{ m}^3 \div 15 \text{ m}^3 = 250 \text{ units}$$
$$250 \text{ units} \times 5 \text{ grams} = 1{,}250 \text{ grams of chlorine}$$

23. **B** In this problem, you need to find the amount of calcium that Joel eats at breakfast. Add 250, 100, and 225 to get his calcium intake of 575 mg. To calculate the percentage, divide 575 by the required amount.

$$\frac{575}{1500} = 38\%$$

24. **D** To calculate the volume of a cylinder, use the formula $V = \pi r^2 h$.

In this problem, the diameter is 16 in., so the radius is 8 in. The height is given as 4 in. Substitute that information into the formula.

$$V = (3.14)(8^2)(4)$$
$$V = (3.14)(64)(4)$$
$$V = 803.84 \text{ or } 803.8 \text{ in.}^3$$

Be sure to pay attention to the information you are given. You could have made an error by using the diameter rather than the radius because the diameter was given in the problem.

25. **C** To calculate the volume of a sphere, use the formula $V = \frac{4}{3}\pi r^3$.

You are given a diameter of 12 in., so the radius is 6 in. Substitute that information into the formula.

$$V = \frac{4}{3}\pi(6)^3$$
$$V = \frac{4(3.14)(216)}{3}$$
$$V = \frac{2712.96}{3} = 904.32 \text{ in.}^3$$

26. **B** To calculate the answer, multiply 200 by 0.035.

$$200 \times 0.035 = \$7.00$$

27. **B** Her bill will be $4,000 plus additional interest of 14%. Multiply $4,000 by 1.14 to get $4,560. Her bill will be $4,560 if she makes no payments and no new purchases.

28. **A** Probability = number of favorable outcomes/number of possible outcomes. Favorable outcomes would be red or purple marbles.

$$\text{Probability} = \frac{32 + 13}{45 + 32 + 13 + 16 + 29}$$
$$= \frac{45}{135} = \frac{1}{3}$$

29. **A** Use the formula for finding the area of a triangle: $A = \frac{1}{2}bh$. The height of this right triangle is 3 feet, and the base is 4 feet. Substitute that information into the formula.

$$A = \frac{1}{2}(4)(3)$$
$$A = 6 \text{ ft}^2$$

30. **B** For the basic rental, the cost is $29 \times 2 = \$58$. For the mileage, multiply 200 miles times 22 cents. $200 \times 0.22 = \$44$. Together the costs are $58 + $44 = $102.

PART 3. WORD KNOWLEDGE

Scoring Your Test

Compare your answer to the correct answer. Mark an X in the column if you got the item correct. Total the number correct.

Item Number	Correct Answer	Mark X if You Picked the Correct Answer
1	B	
2	D	
3	D	
4	B	
5	A	
6	B	
7	C	
8	A	
9	A	
10	A	
11	B	
12	C	
13	D	
14	B	
15	C	
16	A	
17	B	
18	C	
19	D	
20	A	
21	C	
22	B	
23	B	
24	D	
25	B	
26	C	
27	A	
28	C	
29	D	
30	C	
31	B	
32	A	
33	D	
34	B	
35	D	
Total Correct		

Gauging Your Level of Performance

In the following chart, find the number of items that you got correct. See the suggestions listed for your performance.

35	This is pretty good work. Review the explanations of the answers that you got incorrect.
34	
33	
32	
31	
30	You are doing pretty well. Review the explanations for the items that you answered incorrectly. If you have time, review the other explanations and you will learn even more.
29	
28	
27	
26	
25	You need to keep studying. Pay close attention to the explanations for each item, even for the ones that you got correct.
24	
23	
22	
21	
20	
19	
18	
17	Spend time working on Chapter 6, "Sharpen Your Word Knowledge Skills," in Part 2 of this book.
16	
15	
14	
13	
12	Keep reading and identifying words that you don't know.
11	
10	
9	
8	
7	
6	
5	
4	
3	
2	
1	
0	

Explanations

1. **B** To *deprecate* means "to express disapproval, to criticize, to denigrate, or to deplore." The words *compliment* (choice A) and *encourage* (choice C) have the opposite meaning. The word *await* (choice D) is not related at all to the meaning of *deprecate*. *Belittle*, choice B, is the best answer.

2. **D** *Complacent* most nearly means "self-satisfied, contented, smug, and happy to ignore real problems." *Thrilled* (choice A), *surprised* (choice B), and *anxious* (choice C) do not fit that concept. Only *satisfied*, choice D, fits the notion of being happy with things as they are and blissfully unaware of trouble.

3. **D** *Incredulous* means "unwilling to believe or showing doubt." *Unbelieving*, *doubtful*, and *unconvinced* are synonyms. Of the possible answers, *incredible* (choice A), *unlawful* (choice B), and *impeccable* (choice C) are not related to the definition of *incredulous*. Choice D, *skeptical*, is the correct answer.

4. **B** The prefix *dis-* means "the opposite of." So a *disinclination* is the opposite of an *inclination*. An *inclination* is a bias or tendency in favor of a particular situation. A *disinclination* is therefore a bias or tendency against a particular situation. *Predisposition* (choice A) and *desire* (choice C) are closer in meaning to *inclination* than to *disinclination*. *Indifference* (choice D) is a neutral concept and is incorrect. Choice B, *distaste*, is the best answer.

5. **A** *Hyperbole* is an overstatement for the purpose of effect. It should not be taken seriously. *Understatement*, choice D, is the opposite of that meaning, so it cannot be the correct answer. The words *revolutionary* (choice B) and *repulsive* (choice C) are not related to the definition, leaving choice A, *exaggeration*, as the correct answer.

6. **B** *Pugnacious* means "eager and ready to fight, aggressive, and contentious." *Flawed* (choice A), *transitional* (choice C), and *lucid* (choice D) do not relate to the definition. *Aggressive*, choice B, is the correct answer.

7. **C** A *hiatus* is a pause or a break. *Vacation* (choice A), *excitement* (choice B), and *boredom* (choice D) are not related to the definition. *Gap*, choice C, is the correct answer.

8. **A** *De facto* is a Latin phrase describing something that exists "in fact" but is not officially approved or recognized. "Actually" and "in effect" are other definitions. The words *unreal* (choice B) and *false* (choice D) have the opposite meaning. *Inappropriate* (choice C) does not relate to the definition. *Actual*, choice A, is the best answer.

9. **A** To *inculcate* means "to impress upon the mind by persistent urging." "Instill" and "teach by repeating over and over" are other definitions. *Misperceive* (choice C) and *infer* (choice D) are not related to the definition. *Recommend* (choice B), although somewhat related to the definition, does not seem strong enough. *Indoctrinate*, choice A, is the correct answer.

10. **A** *Succor* means "to help in time of need." *Support* and *comfort* are some related words. *Hinder* (choice C) seems to be the opposite in meaning, while *laugh* (choice B) and *investigate* (choice D) seem to be unrelated to the definition. *Aid*, choice A, is the correct answer.

11. **B** The prefix *mis-* means "to do wrongly or poorly." A *miscreant* is a criminal, troublemaker, or scoundrel. The words *mistake* (choice A), *misrepresentation* (choice C), and *objective* (choice D) do not seem to relate to the definition. *Villain*, choice B, is the correct answer.

12. **C** *Supplant* means "to take the place of" or "to remove something in order to replace it." *Repair* (choice A), *describe* (choice B), and *comply* (choice D) do not relate to the definition. *Replace*, choice C, is the correct answer.

13. **D** *Transient* means "lasting only a short time, passing quickly, fleeting, brief, and momentary." The words *happy* (choice A), *impeccable* (choice B), and *impeachable* (choice C) do not fit the definition. *Temporary*, choice D, is the correct answer.

14. **B** A *proclivity* is a preference or leaning toward something. The words *aversion* (choice A), *dislike* (choice C), and *distaste* (choice D) are all opposites of this idea. Choice B, *bias*, is the correct answer.

15. **C** A *labyrinth* is a web, tangle, or jumble of something. A labyrinth certainly exists in an *area* (choice A), but that is not the correct answer. *Forest* (choice B) and *playground* (choice D) are incorrect. *Maze*, choice C, is the correct answer.

16. **A** The word *pedestrian* can mean "a person who walks," but it can also mean "dull and drab." The word *exciting*, choice C, is the opposite of that meaning. The speech may have been *controversial* (choice B) or *informative* (choice D), but the correct answer is choice A, *uninspired*.

17. **B** To be *peevish* is to be crabby or ill tempered. Choice A, *depressing*, is incorrect. *Elated* (choice C) is the opposite of the correct meaning. *Haughty* means "proud," making choice D incorrect. Choice B, *grumpy*, is the correct answer.

18. **C** Brian was probably *annoyed* (choice A) and perhaps even *angry* (choice B) with himself for overcharging the customer, but these answers do not relate to the meaning of *penitent*. *Joking* (choice D) also does not reflect the correct answer. To be *penitent* means "to be repentant, sorrowful, or contrite." Choice C, *remorseful*, is the correct answer.

19. **D** January in Minnesota is typically *frigid*, so choice A is incorrect. It is possible that winter in Minnesota is *festive*, so choice B is also incorrect. It is also possible that a January day could be *quiet*, so choice C is incorrect. *Balmy* means "warm, temperate, and gentle." *Pleasant*, choice D, most nearly fits that meaning and is the correct answer.

20. **A** *Medley* means "a combination or assortment." *Disaster* (choice B) is not correct. *Basket* (choice C) and *partition* (choice D) are not related to the meaning of *medley* and are also incorrect. The correct answer is *mixture*, choice A.

21. **C** *Facilitated* means "smoothed the way or made possible." *Impeded* (choice A) means "prevented," so that is clearly incorrect. *Receded* (choice B) means "moved away," so that also is incorrect. *Rejected* (choice D) is also an incorrect answer. *Enabled*, choice C, is the correct answer.

22. **B** *Fabricated* means "made up or invented and not really true." The word *ordinary* (choice A) does not have this meaning. Leon's story might be *spectacular* (choice C) or *mundane* (choice D), but in either case it could also be true, so these are also incorrect. Choice B, *fictitious*, reflects the correct meaning of the word *fabricated* and is the correct answer.

23. **B** The word *arduous* means "laborious, challenging, hard, and demanding." That does not necessarily mean that the trip was *informative* (choice D). If the trip was fraught with delays, it certainly wasn't *fleeting* (choice A). The trip was probably more *annoying* (choice C) than usual, but the correct answer is choice B, *difficult*.

24. **D** The word *archaic* means "ancient, dated, and out of date." Clearly, *creative* (choice A), *ridiculous* (choice B), and *fanciful* (choice C) are all incorrect. Choice D, *outdated*, is the correct answer.

25. **B** *Indisputable* means "undeniable and unquestionable." Given that, *questionable* (choice A) is incorrect. *Silly* (choice C) and *shocking* (choice D) do not seem related to the definition given. Choice B, *irrefutable*, is the word that most closely means *indisputable* and is the correct answer.

26. **C** The word *selfless* means "unselfish, altruistic, or generous." *Unwanted* (choice A), *destructive* (choice B), and *counterproductive* (choice D) do not relate to the definition of *selfless*. The word that most nearly means *selfless* is choice C, *noble*.

27. **A** The word *tactical* means "made or carried out with a particular goal in mind." A tactical decision might be *fruitful* (choice B), *useless* (choice C), or *lucky* (choice D), but the word that most nearly means *tactical* is choice A, *planned*.

28. **C** To be *steadfast* means "to be unquestioning, resolute, and committed." Given this definition, *questioning* (choice A) is the opposite in meaning. *Expected* (choice B) and *wavering* (choice D) are clearly wrong answers. Choice C, *unfaltering*, is the correct answer.

29. **D** The word *titular* means "in name only, not actual or real." *Arrogant* (choice A) and *royal* (choice B) are not related to that meaning. *Actual* (choice C) has the opposite meaning and is incorrect as well. Choice D, *supposed*, is the correct answer.

30. **C** *Trounced* means "defeated by a wide margin." *Welcomed* (choice A), *disrespected* (choice B), and *fought* (choice D) do not match that meaning and are incorrect. *Crushed* (choice C) is the correct answer.

31. **B** *Predictable* means "certain to happen; easy to foretell or foresee." *Elevating* (choice A) is not correct. *Glorious* (choice C) and *shocking* (choice D) may describe the rising sun, but these words do not match the meaning of *predictable*. Choice B, *expected*, is the correct answer.

32. **A** *Ushered* means "brought in, announced, or introduced." *Identified* (choice B) and *overshadowed* (choice C) do not adhere to that meaning. *Followed* (choice D) means somewhat the opposite. Choice A, *escorted*, is the word that most closely means *ushered*.

33. **D** To be *vociferous* means "to be highly vocal or raucous." That is not the same as being *friendly* (choice A) or *cooperative* (choice B). The protest might have been *colorful* (choice C) to some extent, but that also is incorrect. Choice D, *loud*, is the correct answer.

34. **B** *Stature* means "standing or importance." *Job* (choice A), *activity* (choice C), and *preference* (choice D) are not good answers. Choice B, *status*, conveys the right meaning and is the correct answer.

35. **D** *Disingenuous* means "false, feigned, or insincere." The words *direct* (choice A), *candid* (choice B), and *sincere* (choice C) hold the opposite meaning. Choice D, *dishonest*, is the word that most nearly resembles *disingenuous*.

PART 4. PARAGRAPH COMPREHENSION
Scoring Your Test

Compare your answer to the correct answer. Mark an X in the column if you got the item correct. Total the number correct.

Item Number	Correct Answer	Mark X if You Picked the Correct Answer
1	D	
2	A	
3	B	
4	B	
5	D	
6	B	
7	D	
8	A	
9	C	
10	D	
11	D	
12	B	
13	B	
14	D	
15	A	
Total Correct		

Gauging Your Level of Performance

In the following chart, find the number of items that you got correct. See the suggestions listed for your performance.

15	This is pretty good work. Review the explanations of the answers that you got incorrect.
14	
13	You are doing pretty well. Review the explanations for the items that you answered incorrectly. If you have time, review the other explanations and you will learn even more.
12	
11	
10	
9	
8	You need to keep studying. Pay close attention to the explanations for each item, even for the ones that you got correct. This will help you understand why the answer is correct.
7	
6	
5	
4	Spend time reviewing Chapter 7, "Sharpen Your Paragraph Comprehension Skills," in Part 2 of this book. Keep reading books and newspapers.
3	
2	
1	
0	

Explanations

1. **D** The passage mentions several kinds of natural disasters, but it specifically says that flooding is the nation's single most common natural disaster.

2. **A** The passage mentions that the parts of the country that make up "Tornado Alley," as well as areas in Pennsylvania, New York, Connecticut, and Florida, are at the highest risk for tornado damage. Even if you don't know which states are in Tornado Alley, Pennsylvania (choice A) is on the list of highest-risk states, so it must be the correct answer.

3. **B** All these answers are reasonable ways to prepare for disasters, but the best answer out of the four is to "plan ahead." Choice B is the correct answer.

4. **B** The passage indicates that some natural disasters can be predicted, so choice D must be incorrect. There is no indication that flooding is more likely in mountainous areas, so choice C must be incorrect. Hurricanes are said to occur in the Gulf of Mexico and in the Pacific Ocean as well as in the Atlantic Ocean, so choice A must be incorrect. However, the passage does indicate that 45 of the 50 U.S. states are vulnerable to earthquakes, so choice B must be the correct answer.

5. **D** All of these answers are good suggestions, but the one mentioned by the passage is to determine what natural disasters are most common in the area in which you live. Choice D is the correct answer.

6. **B** Certainly your margin of profit (choice C) is important to success, and the type of product you are selling (choice A) also matters. Your credit line (choice D) may be important if your need to borrow money to make your business work. The passage, however, indicates that the most important factor in your success is your relationships with suppliers and banks. Choice B is the correct answer.

7. **D** Knowing your banker (choice A) would help in obtaining a line of credit, but it has nothing to do with your credit history. Having a supportive family (choice C) is helpful in business, but again, it has nothing to do with your credit history. The passage makes it clear that maintaining a good credit history requires always paying your bills on time and making sure that you periodically check your credit history. Choice D, paying your bills on time, is the correct answer.

8. **A** The basic premise of the entire passage is that it takes money to start and operate a business. Thus choice A, "Money Means Business," is the best title.

9. **C** The passage stresses the importance of maintaining a good relationship with your banker. It says nothing about the need to have your suppliers believe in you (choice A), to keep your family and friends out of your business (choice B), or to be close friends with your business partners (choice D). Being in good stead with your banker by keeping accounts at the bank will make it easier for you to get a loan for your business.

10. **D** Credit history has nothing to do with your bank and its practices (choices A and C) or with your parents' banking history (choice B). Credit history has to do with you and your track record of paying bills on time. Choice D is the correct answer.

11. **D** The passage clearly indicates that *playa* means "beach." Choice D is the correct answer.

12. **B** The main idea of this passage is that parts of California that are now deserts were at one time covered with water. The best answer of the alternatives given is choice B, "Oceans to Deserts—Historical Changes."

13. **B** The passage mentions fossil corals (choice D), which are animals that live in the water. Limestone (choice C) is formed in deep seas, and salt and other minerals (choice A) are also found in the water. Icebergs are mentioned in the passage, but only as part of a reference to a famous ship, the *Titanic*. They are not one of the pieces of evidence the writer offers to support the claim that California was once beneath the ocean. Choice B is the correct answer.

14. **D** The passage says that because California's deserts were once under the sea, these areas now contain deposits of minerals such as borax, chlorides, and other salts that we mine. Choice D is the correct answer.

15. **A** Marine animals live in the ocean, not in mountains where there is no water, so choices B and C are incorrect. Choice D is incorrect because the passage does not say that the oceans dried up to reveal underwater mountains; instead, it says that tectonic forces pushed the mountains up out of the ancient seabeds. Choice A is the correct answer.

PART 5. MATHEMATICS KNOWLEDGE

Scoring Your Test

Compare your answer to the correct answer. Mark an X in the column if you got the item correct. Total the number correct.

Gauging Your Level of Performance

In the following chart, find the number of items that you got correct. See the suggestions listed for your performance.

Item Number	Correct Answer	Mark X if You Picked the Correct Answer
1	B	
2	A	
3	D	
4	C	
5	A	
6	D	
7	A	
8	A	
9	D	
10	C	
11	B	
12	B	
13	D	
14	C	
15	C	
16	A	
17	B	
18	C	
19	B	
20	C	
21	D	
22	D	
23	D	
24	C	
25	D	
Total Correct		

25	This is pretty good work. Review the explanations of the answers that you got incorrect.
24	
23	
22	You are doing pretty well. Review the explanations for the items that you answered incorrectly. If you have time, review the other explanations and you will learn even more.
21	
20	
19	
18	
17	You need to keep studying. Pay close attention to the explanations for each item, even for the ones that you got correct.
16	
15	
14	
13	Spend time working on Chapter 8, "Sharpen Your Math Skills," in Part 2 of this book. Work and rework the problems until you fully understand the processes.
12	
11	
10	
9	You need to work the problems to the point that you are very comfortable with the processes used. If you can get to this point, the problems will be very easy for you.
8	
7	
6	Learning the procedures on this test will also help you on the Arithmetic Reasoning test.
5	
4	
3	
2	
1	
0	

Explanations

1. **B** Isolate the unknown on one side.

   Subtract 9 from both sides.

   $$z = 24 - 9$$
   $$z = 15$$

2. **A** Perform the operations in the parentheses first, then the exponents, and then the remaining operations.

   $$16 + 3(-4)$$
   $$16 + (-12) = 4$$

3. **D** $60 = x$ % of 90

   $60 = 90x$ Solve for x.

   $$x = \frac{60}{90}$$

   $$x = \frac{6}{9}$$

   $x = \frac{2}{3}$ Divide 2 by 3 to get 0.6666 or 67%

4. **C** When calculating the average or mean, add the numbers and then divide by the number of numbers. The sum of 24, 34, 12, 16, 34, 104, and 890 is 1,114, and 1,114 divided by 7 is 159.14.

5. **A** When dividing fractions, invert and multiply. See if you can simplify the fractions.

   $$\frac{2}{3} \div \frac{5}{6} = \frac{2}{3} \times \frac{6}{5} \text{ Multiply}$$

   $$\frac{12}{15} = \text{Simplify}$$

   $$= \frac{4}{5}$$

6. **D** In this problem, you should note three things. First, x times x gives x^2. Second, 10 times 10 gives 100. Last, note that there are only two terms in the expression and there is a minus sign. The minus sign tells you that the term in one factor needs to be a minus sign. This results in two factors: $(x + 10)(x - 10)$.

7. **A** When subtracting, change the sign and add. In this problem, $3x^2 - 9y + 12$ is changed to $-3x^2 + 9y - 12$ and then added to the first term.

   $$12x^2 + 6y - 3$$
   $$\underline{-3x^2 + 9y - 12}$$

   Add the terms. This results in the correct answer of $9x^2 + 15y - 15$.

8. **A** For this problem you want to isolate the x on one side of the equal sign. To do this, multiply each side by y, giving the correct answer: $\frac{yr}{j} = x$.

9. **D** Set each equation equal to zero. Next, arrange the equations so that when one is subtracted from or added to the other, one of the terms becomes zero and drops out of the result. Next, solve for the remaining unknown.

   In this problem,

   $$3a + 4b = 12$$
   $$2a + 2b = 15$$

   Set the equations equal to zero:

   $$3a + 4b - 12 = 0$$
   $$2a + 2b - 15 = 0$$

   Note that neither adding nor subtracting will eliminate a term, but if you multiply one equation by an appropriate term to make two terms equal, you can add or subtract as necessary to eliminate a term. For this problem, if you multiply the second equation by –2 and then add the equations, the b term can be eliminated.

   $$3a + 4b - 12 = 0$$
   $$-2(2a + 2b - 15) = 0$$

   $$3a + 4b - 12 = 0$$
   $$-4a - 4b + 30 = 0$$

   Add the two equations:

   $$-a + 18 = 0$$
   $$-a = -18$$
   $$a = 18$$

Substitute the value of a into one of the original equations.

$$2(18) + 2b - 15 = 0$$
$$36 + 2b - 15 = 0$$
$$21 + 2b = 0$$
$$2b = -21$$
$$b = -10.5$$

The correct answer is $a = 18$, $b = -10.5$

10. **C** To divide numbers with exponents, subtract the exponents. In this problem, subtract 7 from 5, giving –2 as the exponent for x, and 2 from 7, giving 5 as the exponent for y. The term thus becomes $x^{-2}y^5$. This also can be written as $\frac{y^5}{x^2}$, which is the correct answer listed in the selections.

11. **B** This item asks you to calculate a proportion. To do so, cross multiply so that the problem becomes $25n = 1,000$. Solve for n by dividing 25 into 1,000, giving you an n of 40.

12. **B** To multiply fractions, multiply the numerators and denominators. Simplify where possible.

$$\frac{9}{x+1} \times \frac{3x+3}{5}$$

$$\frac{27x+27}{5x+5}$$

Factor this fraction to get

$$\frac{27(x+1)}{5(x+1)}$$

To simplify, cancel the $x + 1$ terms, leaving $\frac{27}{5}$ or $5\frac{2}{5}$.

13. **D** To divide fractions, invert the second term and multiply. Simplify where possible.

$$\frac{5}{x+1} \div \frac{9}{3x+1} \text{ becomes } \frac{5}{x+1} \times \frac{3x+3}{9}$$

Multiply the numerators and denominators.

$$\frac{15x+15}{9x+9} \text{ Simplify by factoring.}$$

$$\frac{15(x+1)}{9(x+1)} \text{ Simplify by canceling.}$$

$$\frac{15}{9} = \frac{5}{3} = 1\frac{2}{3}$$

14. **C** The cube root is the number that, when multiplied by itself three times, results in the original number. In this case, $6 \times 6 \times 6 = 216$, so 6 is the correct answer.

15. **C** In this type of problem, where two fractions are separated by an equal sign, you can cross multiply and then solve for the variable of interest. Cross multiply to get $sy = vt$. Solving for y gives $\frac{vt}{s}$, the correct answer.

16. **A** Solve this as if it were an equation.

$$x + 2 < 12 \text{ Subtract 2 from both sides.}$$
$$x < 12 - 2$$
$$x < 10$$

In order to be correct, x must be less than 10. The only answer that satisfies this is 9. 10 is not correct because it equals 10 and therefore is not less than 10.

17. **B** A parallelogram has two equal lengths and two equal widths. The perimeter is the sum of the widths and lengths, or $2l + 2w$. Substituting in the measurements, we get $2(3) + 2(2)$. This gives a perimeter of 10 miles.

18. **C** The hundredths place is two places to the right of the decimal point. Underline the hundredths place. If the number to the right of it is less than 5, keep the number in that place the same. If it is 5 or greater, increase the number in the hundredths place by one. In this problem, the number to the right of the hundredths place is more than 5, so the number is rounded to 1,478.97, which is the correct answer.

19. **B** A right triangle has one angle that measures 90°. If a second angle measures 59°, that accounts for 149°. Subtracting that total from 180° gives the result of 31°.

20. **C** In this problem, $\angle 6$ is 90°. That makes $\angle 3$ 90°. Because the two sides of the triangle are equal, it is an isosceles triangle. That makes $\angle 1$ and $\angle 2$ equal. Since $\angle 3$ is 90°, that leaves 90° to be split equally between the two remaining angles. That would make each angle 45°.

21. **D** To subtract the two expressions, line up the similar terms so that the y^2s are lined up, the ys are lined up, the x^2s are lined up, and so on.

$$14y^2 + y + 6x^2 + 9x - 12$$
$$y^2 + 3y + 6x^2 + 2x + 12$$

To subtract, change the sign of the number you are subtracting and then add the terms.

$$\begin{array}{r} 14y^2 + y + 6x^2 + 9x - 12 \\ - y^2 - 3y - 6x^2 - 2x - 12 \\ \hline 13y^2 - 2y \qquad + 7x - 24 \end{array}$$

22. **D** The volume of a rectangular solid is its length × width × height. In the figure, the length is 3 m, the width is 9 m, and the height is 6 m. Multiplying 3 × 9 × 6 gives the correct answer of 162 m^3.

23. **D** Looking at the last term of –20, there are several possible factors: –2 and +10, –10 and +2, +4 and –5, –5 and +4, +1 and –20, and –20 and +1. Looking at the middle term indicates that the combination of numbers should produce a +8. The two numbers that could produce an 8 as a middle term would be –2 and +10 or –10 and +2. The first term is y because y times y is y^2.

So try $(y - 10)(y + 2)$; when multiplied, it gives you $y^2 - 8y - 20$. That is not the correct answer.

Try $(y + 10)(y - 2)$; when multiplied, it gives you $y^2 + 8y - 20$. That is the correct answer.

24. **C** 2% is the equivalent of 0.02. $0.02 \times 5{,}000 = 100$

25. **D** The volume of a sphere is found by using the formula $\frac{4}{3}\pi r^3$. Substituting the information into the formula gives $\frac{4}{3}(3.14)(3)^3$ or $4 \times 3.14 \times 27 \div 3$, making the correct answer 113.04 m^3.

Part 4

MATCHING YOUR SKILLS AND INTERESTS TO OCCUPATIONS

When you select an occupation or career, whether it's in the military or not, there are two important things to consider in finding the right occupation for you. One is your interests (what you like to do), and the other is your abilities (what you do well). The best jobs and occupations for you are those that match your interests and let you use your best abilities.

This section of the book will help you identify some of the best occupations for you. First, take the following interest inventory and find your strongest interest areas.

INTEREST CHECKLIST

The following pages ask you if you would like or not like to engage in a number of activities. Read each statement and mark the Ⓛ if you like or would like to do this activity or the Ⓓ if you dislike or would not like to do this activity. **When you are done with each section, count the number of LIKES and write it in the space provided.**

Part 1

	Like	Dislike
Take care of animals	Ⓛ	Ⓓ
Build kitchen cabinets	Ⓛ	Ⓓ
Drive a fire engine or delivery truck	Ⓛ	Ⓓ
Work on a farm	Ⓛ	Ⓓ
Repair household appliances	Ⓛ	Ⓓ
Operate a lawn mower	Ⓛ	Ⓓ
Paint houses	Ⓛ	Ⓓ
Fix a broken faucet	Ⓛ	Ⓓ
Perform lawn care services	Ⓛ	Ⓓ
Put out forest fires	Ⓛ	Ⓓ
Test the quality of parts before a shipment	Ⓛ	Ⓓ
Operate a machine on a production line	Ⓛ	Ⓓ
Frame a house	Ⓛ	Ⓓ
Repair computers	Ⓛ	Ⓓ
Repair telephone lines	Ⓛ	Ⓓ

Total Number of Likes _____

Part 2

	Like	Dislike
Investigate crimes	Ⓛ	Ⓓ
Study space travel	Ⓛ	Ⓓ
Research the cause of diseases	Ⓛ	Ⓓ
Study rocks and minerals	Ⓛ	Ⓓ
Study animal anatomy	Ⓛ	Ⓓ
Learn about new sources of energy	Ⓛ	Ⓓ
Study marine life	Ⓛ	Ⓓ
Study the movement of planets	Ⓛ	Ⓓ
Use a computer to solve problems	Ⓛ	Ⓓ
Develop a better way to predict weather	Ⓛ	Ⓓ
Identify the cause of atmospheric pollution	Ⓛ	Ⓓ
Study the effects of radiation on plants	Ⓛ	Ⓓ
Work in a biology or chemistry lab	Ⓛ	Ⓓ
Do research to improve solar power	Ⓛ	Ⓓ
Study weather conditions	Ⓛ	Ⓓ

Total Number of Likes _____

Part 3

	Like	Dislike
Sing in a choir	Ⓛ	Ⓓ
Act in a play	Ⓛ	Ⓓ
Dance on stage	Ⓛ	Ⓓ
Design sets for plays	Ⓛ	Ⓓ
Write a novel	Ⓛ	Ⓓ
Make pottery	Ⓛ	Ⓓ
Write words for a song	Ⓛ	Ⓓ
Design toys for a manufacturer	Ⓛ	Ⓓ
Play a musical instrument	Ⓛ	Ⓓ
Design artwork for a magazine	Ⓛ	Ⓓ
Write the script for a play	Ⓛ	Ⓓ
Perform jazz or dance	Ⓛ	Ⓓ
Write stories or articles for a magazine	Ⓛ	Ⓓ
Create dance routines for a show	Ⓛ	Ⓓ
Join a theater group	Ⓛ	Ⓓ

Total Number of Likes _____

Part 4

	Like	Dislike
Perform nursing duties	Ⓛ	Ⓓ
Teach people how to read	Ⓛ	Ⓓ
Work with disabled people	Ⓛ	Ⓓ
Work as a camp counselor	Ⓛ	Ⓓ
Host social events	Ⓛ	Ⓓ
Tutor students in school subjects	Ⓛ	Ⓓ
Teach in school	Ⓛ	Ⓓ
Act as a tour guide	Ⓛ	Ⓓ
Work as a lifeguard	Ⓛ	Ⓓ
Care for the elderly	Ⓛ	Ⓓ
Give first aid to people who need it	Ⓛ	Ⓓ
Help people with family-related problems	Ⓛ	Ⓓ
Organize field trips for disabled people	Ⓛ	Ⓓ
Work to help people who have had tragedies	Ⓛ	Ⓓ
Work in a health club	Ⓛ	Ⓓ

Total Number of Likes _____

Part 5

	Like	Dislike
Sell automobiles	Ⓛ	Ⓓ
Manage a clothing store	Ⓛ	Ⓓ
Start your own business	Ⓛ	Ⓓ
Negotiate contracts for professional athletes	Ⓛ	Ⓓ
Manage a department in a company or store	Ⓛ	Ⓓ
Sell real estate	Ⓛ	Ⓓ
Convince other people that your ideas are best	Ⓛ	Ⓓ
Present a case in front of a judge or jury	Ⓛ	Ⓓ
Manage a restaurant	Ⓛ	Ⓓ
Be a lawyer for sports figures	Ⓛ	Ⓓ
Run for political office	Ⓛ	Ⓓ
Manage a hotel	Ⓛ	Ⓓ
Act as the spokesperson for a major company	Ⓛ	Ⓓ
Design and present an advertising campaign	Ⓛ	Ⓓ
Develop a plan to boost business for a company	Ⓛ	Ⓓ

Total Number of Likes _____

Part 6

	Like	Dislike
Keep accurate financial records	Ⓛ	Ⓓ
Proofread documents for accuracy	Ⓛ	Ⓓ
Schedule conferences for an organization	Ⓛ	Ⓓ
Use a word processor to edit documents	Ⓛ	Ⓓ
Count the inventory of a small business	Ⓛ	Ⓓ
Enter data into a computer program	Ⓛ	Ⓓ
Operate a calculator	Ⓛ	Ⓓ
File letters and documents accurately	Ⓛ	Ⓓ
Photocopy letters and reports	Ⓛ	Ⓓ
Maintain employee records	Ⓛ	Ⓓ
Stamp, sort, and distribute mail for a company	Ⓛ	Ⓓ
Develop an office filing system	Ⓛ	Ⓓ
Takes notes during a meeting	Ⓛ	Ⓓ
Handle hotel or airline reservations	Ⓛ	Ⓓ
Review financial records of an organization	Ⓛ	Ⓓ

Total Number of Likes _____

Summarizing Your Results

List the number of likes for each of the six areas in the space below.

Interest Area

Part 1 _____ = Realistic (R)

Part 2 _____ = Investigative (I)

Part 3 _____ = Artistic (A)

Part 4 _____ = Social (S)

Part 5 _____ = Enterprising (E)

Part 6 _____ = Conventional (C)

Each part is now labeled with a term: Realistic, Investigative, Artistic, Social, Enterprising, and Conventional.

Which was your highest area? Was it Realistic, Investigative, Artistic, Social, Enterprising, or Conventional?

List it here. [   ]

Was there another interest area that was high? Was it Realistic, Investigative, Artistic, Social, Enterprising, or Conventional?

List it here. [   ]

What Do Your Interest Areas Mean?

Realistic (R). Realistic people and occupations deal with working with equipment, using tools and machines, working with animals, working with things, and working with your hands. Realistic activities often involve practical, hands-on problems and solutions.

Investigative (I). Investigative people and occupations relate to problem solving, using math, researching situations, learning about a new subject area, using your knowledge to solve problems, or creating things and ideas based on facts and investigations. Investigative activities involve learning about new subject areas or ideas and allow you to use your knowledge to solve problems.

Artistic (A). Artistic people and occupations deal with writing, creating artistic things, performing in plays, writing plays or novels, or creating original work through your imagination. Artistic activities allow you to be creative and use your imagination to do original work.

Social (S). Social people and occupations engage in helping others, interacting with people in a positive and helpful way, and making the world a better place. Social activities allow you to use your skills and talents to interact effectively with others.

Enterprising (E). Enterprising people and occupations deal with leading people and organizations, selling oneself or one's ideas to others, and leading and selling people, things, and ideas. Enterprising activities allow you to take a leadership role.

Conventional (C). Conventional people and occupations involve paying attention to details like organization, clerical situations, and accuracy. Conventional activities require attention to accuracy and detail.

FINDING OCCUPATIONS THAT MATCH YOUR INTERESTS

The following pages list occupations, both military and civilian, that relate to the various interest areas. They are organized by interest area: Realistic, Investigative, Artistic, Social, Enterprising, and Conventional. Go to the set of occupations that match your strongest and second strongest interest areas. These occupations will match your interests best.

Review the list of occupations in your top two interest areas to explore careers that match your dominant interests.

Explaining the Chart

Column 1. The first column gives the name of the occupation. These occupations include both civilian and military occupations that are representative of the world of work.

Column 2. For each occupation, a second interest area is listed. Occupations are generally some combination of the six interest areas. To understand the occupation better, take a look at the second interest area and see how it matches your own interest areas. The symbols used are:

R   Realistic
I   Investigative
A   Artistic
S   Social
E   Enterprising
C   Conventional

Column 3. This column includes an indication of the degree of importance of verbal skills for the occupation. This relates to your capability in reading and vocabulary—the Reading Comprehension and Word Knowledge ASVAB tests. These are two of the four tests that make up the AFQT. The occupations are identified as having Low, Medium, or High verbal skill importance.

Column 4. This column lists the degree of importance of math skills for the occupation. The occupations are identified as having Low, Medium, or High math skill importance. This relates to your Math Knowledge and Arithmetic Reasoning skills, two of the important ASVAB tests. The verbal and math tests make up the AFQT, the basic entry-level test for the military.

Column 5. The column Science and Technical skills is added to help you make a better decision. These skills relate to the importance of knowledge of general science, electronics information, and mechanical comprehension to the occupation. The importance can be High, Medium, or Low. The AFQT does not include these skills, but the full ASVAB battery does.

Column 6. Next, for each occupation, this column has an ME, which indicates that it is a military enlisted occupation, or MO, indicating that it is an officer occupation. If the column is blank, the occupation does not typically exist in the military but does exist in the nonmilitary world of work. The verbal and math requirements still matter in the nonmilitary world.

REALISTIC (R) OCCUPATIONS

Column 1 = Occupation Title

Column 2 = Second Interest Area (R, I, A, S, E, C)

Column 3 = Importance Level for Verbal Skills (L = Low; M = Medium; H = High)

Column 4 = Importance Level for Math Skills (L = Low; M = Medium; H = High)

Column 5 = Importance Level for Science and Technical Skills (L = Low; M = Medium; H = High)

Column 6 = Occupation is Enlisted (ME) or Officer (MO), if blank, neither

Occupational Title	Second Interest	Verbal	Math	Science and Technical	Military Enlisted or Officer
Agricultural and Food Science Technicians	I	M	H	H	
Agricultural Engineers	I	H	H	H	
Agricultural Inspectors	I	M	M	M	
Air Crew Members	C	L	H	H	ME
Air Crew Officers	C	M	H	H	MO
Aircraft Launch and Recovery Specialists	C	L	L	H	ME
Aircraft Mechanics and Service Technicians	I	M	H	H	ME
Aircraft Structure, Surfaces, Rigging, and Systems Assemblers	C	L	M	H	ME
Airline Pilots, Copilots, and Flight Engineers	E	H	H	H	ME MO
Amusement and Recreation Attendants	C	L	M	L	
Architectural and Civil Drafters	C	M	H	M	ME
Armored Assault Vehicle Crew Members	C	H	M	M	ME
Artillery and Missile Crew Members	C	L	H	H	ME
Automotive Body and Related Repairers	C	L	L	H	ME
Automotive Glass Installers and Repairers	C	L	L	H	

REALISTIC (R) OCCUPATIONS

Column 1 = Occupation Title
Column 2 = Second Interest Area (R, I, A, S, E, C)
Column 3 = Importance Level for Verbal Skills (L = Low; M = Medium; H = High)
Column 4 = Importance Level for Math Skills (L = Low; M = Medium; H = High)
Column 5 = Importance Level for Science and Technical Skills (L = Low; M = Medium; H = High)
Column 6 = Occupation is Enlisted (ME) or Officer (MO), if blank, neither

Occupational Title	Second Interest	Verbal	Math	Science and Technical	Military Enlisted or Officer
Automotive Service Technicians and Mechanics	C	L	M	H	ME
Aviation Inspectors	I	H	H	H	
Avionics Technicians	C/I	M	H	H	ME
Bakers	C	L	M	L	ME
Biological Technicians	I	L	M	M	
Brickmasons and Blockmasons	I	L	M	L	ME
Broadcast Technicians	E	M	M	H	ME
Bus Drivers, School	S	L	M	L	
Bus Drivers, Transit and Intercity	S	L	M	L	
Cabinetmakers and Bench Carpenters	A	L	M	H	
Carpenters	C	L	H	H	ME
Carpet Installers	C/E	L	M	M	
Chemical Technicians	I	M	H	H	
Civil Engineering Technicians	I	H	H	M	ME
Civil Engineers	I	H	H	H	MO
Cleaners of Vehicles and Equipment	C	L	L	L	
Commercial Divers	C	L	L	H	ME
Computer Hardware Engineers	I/C	H	H	H	MO

REALISTIC (R) OCCUPATIONS

Column 1 = Occupation Title

Column 2 = Second Interest Area (R, I, A, S, E, C)

Column 3 = Importance Level for Verbal Skills (L = Low; M = Medium; H = High)

Column 4 = Importance Level for Math Skills (L = Low; M = Medium; H = High)

Column 5 = Importance Level for Science and Technical Skills (L = Low; M = Medium; H = High)

Column 6 = Occupation is Enlisted (ME) or Officer (MO), if blank, neither

Occupational Title	Second Interest	Verbal	Math	Science and Technical	Military Enlisted or Officer
Computer Software Engineers	I/C	H	H	H	MO
Computer, Automated Teller and Office Machine Repairers	C	H	H	H	ME
Cooks, Institution and Cafeteria	C	L	M	L	ME
Cooks, Restaurant	E	L	M	L	
Cooks, Short Order	E	L	M	L	
Correctional Officers & Jailers	S	L	L	L	ME
Couriers & Messengers	C	L	M	L	
Crane & Tower Operators	C	L	M	M	ME
Dental Laboratory Technicians	I	L	L	M	ME
Desktop Publishers	A	M	L	M	
Dining Room & Cafeteria Attendants & Bartender Helpers	E/S	L	L	L	
Drywall Installers	C	L	M	M	
Electric Motor, Power Tool, & Related Repairers	C	L	M	H	ME
Electrical & Electronic Engineering Technicians	I	H	H	H	
Electrical & Electronics Repairers, Commercial & Industrial Equipment	I	H	H	H	ME

REALISTIC (R) OCCUPATIONS

Column 1 = Occupation Title
Column 2 = Second Interest Area (R, I, A, S, E, C)
Column 3 = Importance Level for Verbal Skills (L = Low; M = Medium; H = High)
Column 4 = Importance Level for Math Skills (L = Low; M = Medium; H = High)
Column 5 = Importance Level for Science and Technical Skills (L = Low; M = Medium; H = High)
Column 6 = Occupation is Enlisted (ME) or Officer (MO), if blank, neither

Occupational Title	Second Interest	Verbal	Math	Science and Technical	Military Enlisted or Officer
Electrical & Electronics Repairers, Powerhouse, Substation & Relay	C/I	H	H	H	ME
Electrical Engineering Technician	I	H	H	H	ME
Electrical Engineers	I	H	H	H	MO
Electricians	I	L	M	H	ME
Electro-Mechanical Technicians	I	M	M	H	ME
Elevator Installers & Repairers	C	L	M	H	
Farmers & Ranchers	E	M	H	H	
Farmworkers & Laborers Crop, Nursery, & Greenhouse	E	L	L	M	
Fire Fighters	S	M	M	M	ME
Fire Investigators	I	H	H	H	
Fish & Game Wardens	I	L	L	L	
Food Preparation Workers	C	L	L	M	ME
Forest & Conservation Workers	I	L	L	M	
Foresters	I	M	H	H	
Geological & Petroleum Technicians	I	M	H	H	
Hazardous Materials Removal Workers	C	L	M	M	ME

REALISTIC (R) OCCUPATIONS					

Column 1 = Occupation Title
Column 2 = Second Interest Area (R, I, A, S, E, C)
Column 3 = Importance Level for Verbal Skills (L = Low; M = Medium; H = High)
Column 4 = Importance Level for Math Skills (L = Low; M = Medium; H = High)
Column 5 = Importance Level for Science and Technical Skills (L = Low; M = Medium; H = High)
Column 6 = Occupation is Enlisted (ME) or Officer (MO), if blank, neither

Occupational Title	Second Interest	Verbal	Math	Science and Technical	Military Enlisted or Officer
Heating, Air Conditioning, & Refrigeration Mechanics & Installers	C	L	M	H	
Highway Maintenance Workers	C/E	L	L	M	
Industrial Machinery Mechanics	C	L	M	H	ME
Industrial Truck & Tractor Operators	C	L	M	M	ME
Infantry	C	L	L	L	ME
Inspectors, Testers, Sorters, Samplers, & Weighers	C	M	H	M	ME
Jewelers & Precious Stone & Metal Workers	C	L	M	M	
Landscape Architects	A	H	M	H	
Landscaping & Grounds-keeping Workers	I	L	L	M	
Laundry & Dry Cleaning Machine Operators & Tenders	C	L	L	M	
Lifeguards, Ski Patrol, & Other Recreational Protective Service Workers	S	M	L	M	
Locksmiths & Safe Repairers	C	L	L	H	
Logging Equipment Operators	C/E	L	L	H	
Machinists	I	M	H	H	ME

REALISTIC (R) OCCUPATIONS					

Column 1 = Occupation Title

Column 2 = Second Interest Area (R, I, A, S, E, C)

Column 3 = Importance Level for Verbal Skills (L = Low; M = Medium; H = High)

Column 4 = Importance Level for Math Skills (L = Low; M = Medium; H = High)

Column 5 = Importance Level for Science and Technical Skills (L = Low; M = Medium; H = High)

Column 6 = Occupation is Enlisted (ME) or Officer (MO), if blank, neither

Occupational Title	Second Interest	Verbal	Math	Science and Technical	Military Enlisted or Officer
Maintenance & Repair Workers, General	C	L	M	H	
Marine Engineers & Naval Architects	I	H	H	H	MO
Meat, Poultry, & Fish Cutters	C	L	L	L	
Mechanical Engineering Technicians	I	H	H	H	ME
Mechanical and Aerospace Engineers	I	H	H	H	MO
Medical & Clinical Laboratory Technicians	I	L	H	H	ME
Medical Appliance Technicians	I	M	M	H	ME
Medical Equipment Preparers	C	L	M	M	ME
Medical Equipment Repairers	I	M	M	H	ME
Mining and Geological Engineers, Including Mining Safety Engineers	I	M	H	H	
Mobile Heavy Equipment Mechanics	C	L	L	H	ME
Motorboat Operators	E	L	L	M	ME
Motorcycle Mechanics	C	L	L	H	
Musical Instrument Repairers & Tuners	A	L	M	M	
Nuclear Power Reactor Operators	C	M	M	H	ME
Nuclear Technicians	I	M	H	H	

REALISTIC (R) OCCUPATIONS

Column 1 = Occupation Title

Column 2 = Second Interest Area (R, I, A, S, E, C)

Column 3 = Importance Level for Verbal Skills (L = Low; M = Medium; H = High)

Column 4 = Importance Level for Math Skills (L = Low; M = Medium; H = High)

Column 5 = Importance Level for Science and Technical Skills (L = Low; M = Medium; H = High)

Column 6 = Occupation is Enlisted (ME) or Officer (MO), if blank, neither

Occupational Title	Second Interest	Verbal	Math	Science and Technical	Military Enlisted or Officer
Nursery Workers	C/E	L	L	L	
Operating Engineers & Other Construction Equipment Operators	C	L	L	M	ME
Ophthalmic Laboratory Technicians	C	L	M	M	ME
Outdoor Power Equipment & Other Small Engine Mechanics	C	L	L	H	
Packers & Packagers, and Material Movers	C	L	L	L	ME
Painters, Construction & Maintenance	C/E	L	L	M	
Painting, Coating, & Decorating Workers	C	L	L	M	
Paperhangers	C	L	L	M	
Parking Lot Attendants	E	L	L	L	
Pest Control Workers	C	L	M	M	
Petroleum Engineers	I	H	H	H	
Pilots, Ship	E	M	M	M	MO
Pipe Fitters and Steam Fitters	C/E	L	M	H	ME
Plasterers & Stucco Masons	C	L	L	M	ME
Plumbers	E	L	M	H	ME
Police Patrol Officers	S	H	L	L	ME
Power Plant Operators	C	L	M	H	ME
Printing Machine Operators	C	L	M	M	ME

REALISTIC (R) OCCUPATIONS

Column 1 = Occupation Title

Column 2 = Second Interest Area (R, I, A, S, E, C)

Column 3 = Importance Level for Verbal Skills (L = Low; M = Medium; H = High)

Column 4 = Importance Level for Math Skills (L = Low; M = Medium; H = High)

Column 5 = Importance Level for Science and Technical Skills (L = Low; M = Medium; H = High)

Column 6 = Occupation is Enlisted (ME) or Officer (MO), if blank, neither

Occupational Title	Second Interest	Verbal	Math	Science and Technical	Military Enlisted or Officer
Pump Operators, Except Wellhead Pumpers	C	L	M	H	ME
Radar and Sonar Technicians	C	L	M	H	ME
Radiologic Technologists & Technicians	I	M	M	M	ME
Refuse & Recyclable Materials Collectors	C	L	L	M	
Roofers	C	L	L	M	ME
Sailors & Marine Oilers	C	L	M	M	ME
Ship and Boat Captains	E	M	H	M	MO
Ship Engineers	E	M	M	H	MO
Sound Engineering Technicians	A	L	L	H	ME
Special Forces	E	M	M	H	ME MO
Surgical Technologists	S	L	M	H	ME
Surveying Technicians	C	L	M	M	ME
Taxi Drivers & Chauffeurs	E	L	L	L	
Telecommunications Line Installers & Repairers	C	L	M	H	ME
Tree Trimmers & Pruners	A	L	L	M	
Truck Drivers, Heavy & Tractor-Trailer	C	L	M	M	ME
Truck Drivers, Light or Delivery Services	C	L	M	M	ME
Upholsterers	C	L	M	M	

REALISTIC (R) OCCUPATIONS

Column 1 = Occupation Title

Column 2 = Second Interest Area (R, I, A, S, E, C)

Column 3 = Importance Level for Verbal Skills (L = Low; M = Medium; H = High)

Column 4 = Importance Level for Math Skills (L = Low; M = Medium; H = High)

Column 5 = Importance Level for Science and Technical Skills (L = Low; M = Medium; H = High)

Column 6 = Occupation is Enlisted (ME) or Officer (MO), if blank, neither

Occupational Title	Second Interest	Verbal	Math	Science and Technical	Military Enlisted or Officer
Veterinary Assistants & Laboratory Animal Caretakers	I	L	L	M	
Water & Liquid Waste Treatment Plant & System Operators	C	L	M	H	ME
Welders, Cutters, Solderers, & Brazers	C	L	M	H	ME
Welders, Production	C	L	L	H	ME
Woodworking Machine Setters & Set-up Operators, Except Sawing	C	L	M	H	

INVESTIGATIVE (I) OCCUPATIONS

Column 1 = Occupation Title

Column 2 = Second Interest Area (R, I, A, S, E, C)

Column 3 = Importance Level for Verbal Skills (L = Low; M = Medium; H = High)

Column 4 = Importance Level for Math Skills (L = Low; M = Medium; H = High)

Column 5 = Importance Level for Science and Technical Skills (L = Low; M = Medium; H = High)

Column 6 = Occupation is Enlisted (ME) or Officer (MO), if blank, neither

Occupational Title	Second Interest	Verbal	Math	Science and Technical	Military Enlisted or Officer
Aerospace Engineering & Operations Technicians	R	L	H	H	ME
Aerospace Engineers	R	M	H	H	MO
Anesthesiologists	R	H	H	H	MO
Anthropologists & Archeologists	A	H	H	M	
Archivists	C	H	M	M	
Astronomers	R	H	H	H	
Atmospheric & Space Scientists	R	H	M	H	MO
Biochemists & Biophysicists	R	M	H	H	MO
Biologists	R	H	M	H	MO
Biomedical Engineers	R	H	H	H	
Cardiovascular Technologists & Technicians	R	M	H	H	ME
Chemical Engineers	R	L	H	H	
Chemists	R	M	H	H	MO
Chiropractors	R	H	M	M	
Clinical, Counseling, & School Psychologists	S	H	M	M	MO
Compensation Benefits, & Job Analysis Specialists	C	H	H	L	
Computer Programmers	R	M	H	H	ME
Computer Security Specialists	R	H	M	H	ME

INVESTIGATIVE (I) OCCUPATIONS

Column 1 = Occupation Title

Column 2 = Second Interest Area (R, I, A, S, E, C)

Column 3 = Importance Level for Verbal Skills (L = Low; M = Medium; H = High)

Column 4 = Importance Level for Math Skills (L = Low; M = Medium; H = High)

Column 5 = Importance Level for Science and Technical Skills (L = Low; M = Medium; H = High)

Column 6 = Occupation is Enlisted (ME) or Officer (MO), if blank, neither

Occupational Title	Second Interest	Verbal	Math	Science and Technical	Military Enlisted or Officer
Computer Support Specialists	C	H	M	H	ME
Computer Systems Analysts	C	M	H	H	ME
Database Administrators	C	M	H	H	ME
Dentists, General	R	M	H	H	MO
Dietitians & Nutritionists	E	H	H	L	MO
Economists	E	H	H	L	
Electronics Engineers, Except Computer	R	M	M	H	MO
Environmental Science & Protection Technicians, Including Health	R	M	H	H	ME
Environmental Scientists & Specialists, Including Health	R	M	H	H	MO
Family & General Practitioners	E/S	H	H	H	MO
Financial Analysts	C	H	H	L	MO
Fire-Prevention & Protection Engineers	E	M	M	H	
Food Scientists & Technologists	R	M	H	H	MO
Forensic Science Technicians	C	H	H	H	
Geographers	R	H	H	H	
Geoscientist	R	M	H	H	MO
Historians	A	H	M	M	
Hydrologists	R	M	H	H	MO

INVESTIGATIVE (I) OCCUPATIONS

Column 1 = Occupation Title

Column 2 = Second Interest Area (R, I, A, S, E, C)

Column 3 = Importance Level for Verbal Skills (L = Low; M = Medium; H = High)

Column 4 = Importance Level for Math Skills (L = Low; M = Medium; H = High)

Column 5 = Importance Level for Science and Technical Skills (L = Low; M = Medium; H = High)

Column 6 = Occupation is Enlisted (ME) or Officer (MO), if blank, neither

Occupational Title	Second Interest	Verbal	Math	Science and Technical	Military Enlisted or Officer
Industrial Engineering Technicians	C	M	H	H	
Industrial-Organizational Psychologists	E	H	H	M	MO
Logisticians	E	H	H	M	MO
Management Analysts	E	H	H	M	MO
Market Research Analysts	E	H	H	L	
Mathematical Technicians	C/R	L	H	M	
Mathematicians	C	L	H	H	MO
Medical & Clinical Laboratory Technologists	R	M	H	H	ME
Network System & Data Communications Analysts	R	M	H	H	ME
Nuclear Engineers	R	M	H	H	MO
Nuclear Medicine Technologists	R	H	H	H	ME
Operations Research Analysts	C	H	H	M	MO
Optometrists	R	H	H	H	MO
Oral & Maxillofacial Surgeons	R	M	H	H	MO
Orthodontists	R	M	M	H	MO
Pediatricians, General	E/S	H	H	H	MO
Pharmacists	C	H	H	H	MO
Physician Assistants	S	H	H	H	MO
Physicists	R	H	H	H	MO

INVESTIGATIVE (I) OCCUPATIONS

Column 1 = Occupation Title

Column 2 = Second Interest Area (R, I, A, S, E, C)

Column 3 = Importance Level for Verbal Skills (L = Low; M = Medium; H = High)

Column 4 = Importance Level for Math Skills (L = Low; M = Medium; H = High)

Column 5 = Importance Level for Science and Technical Skills (L = Low; M = Medium; H = High)

Column 6 = Occupation is Enlisted (ME) or Officer (MO), if blank, neither

Occupational Title	Second Interest	Verbal	Math	Science and Technical	Military Enlisted or Officer
Political Scientists	A	H	H	L	MO
Product Safety Engineers	R	H	H	H	
Psychiatrists	S/A	H	H	H	MO
Range Managers	R	H	H	H	
Respiratory Therapists	R	H	H	M	ME
Social Science Research Assistants	C	H	H	M	
Sociologists	S/A	H	H	M	
Soil & Plant Scientists	R	H	H	H	
Soil & Water Conservationists	R	M	H	H	
Statisticians	C	M	H	M	
Surgeons	R	H	H	H	MO
Surveyors	E	H	H	H	ME
Urban & Regional Planners	E	H	M	M	
Veterinarians	R	H	H	H	MO
Zoologists & Wildlife Biologists	R	H	H	H	

ARTISTIC (A) OCCUPATIONS

Column 1 = Occupation Title

Column 2 = Second Interest Area (R, I, A, S, E, C)

Column 3 = Importance Level for Verbal Skills (L = Low; M = Medium; H = High)

Column 4 = Importance Level for Math Skills (L = Low; M = Medium; H = High)

Column 5 = Importance Level for Science and Technical Skills (L = Low; M = Medium; H = High)

Column 6 = Occupation is Enlisted (ME) or Officer (MO), if blank, neither

Occupational Title	Second Interest	Verbal	Math	Science and Technical	Military Enlisted or Officer
Actors	E	H	L	L	
Advertising and Promotions Managers	E	H	H	L	
Architects, Except Landscape & Naval	R	L	M	H	
Art Directors	E	M	L	M	
Art, Drama, & Music Teachers, Postsecondary	S	H	L	L	MO
Broadcast News Analysts	S	H	L	L	ME
Camera Operators, Television, Video, & Motion Picture	R	L	L	M	ME
Cartoonists	E	L	L	L	
Choreographers	S	M	L	L	
Commercial & Industrial Designers	R	M	M	H	
Copy Writers	E	H	L	L	ME
Costume Attendants	R	L	L	L	
Creative Writers	I	H	L	L	
Curators	I	H	M	L	
Dancers	S/R	L	L	L	
Directors—Stage, Motion Pictures, Television & Radio	E	H	L	M	MO
Editors	E/S	H	L	L	ME

ARTISTIC (A) OCCUPATIONS

Column 1 = Occupation Title
Column 2 = Second Interest Area (R, I, A, S, E, C)
Column 3 = Importance Level for Verbal Skills (L = Low; M = Medium; H = High)
Column 4 = Importance Level for Math Skills (L = Low; M = Medium; H = High)
Column 5 = Importance Level for Science and Technical Skills (L = Low; M = Medium; H = High)
Column 6 = Occupation is Enlisted (ME) or Officer (MO), if blank, neither

Occupational Title	Second Interest	Verbal	Math	Science and Technical	Military Enlisted or Officer
English Language & Literature Teachers, Postsecondary	S	H	L	L	MO
Fashion Designers	E	L	L	L	
Film & Video Editors	E	M	L	M	MO
Floral Designers	R	L	L	L	
Foreign Language & Literature Teachers, Postsecondary	S	H	L	L	MO
Graphic Designers	E	M	M	M	ME
Interior Designers	E	M	L	M	
Interpreters & Translators	S	H	L	L	ME
Librarians	C	H	L	L	
Makeup Artists, Theatrical & Performance	R	L	L	L	
Merchandise Displayers & Window Trimmers	R	L	L	L	
Models	E	L	L	L	
Museum Technicians & Conservators	R	L	L	L	
Music Arrangers & Composers	C/I	L	L	L	MO
Music Directors	E/S	L	L	L	MO
Musicians, Instrumental	E/S	L	M	L	ME
Painters, Sculptors & Illustrators	R	L	L	L	ME

ARTISTIC (A) OCCUPATIONS

Column 1 = Occupation Title

Column 2 = Second Interest Area (R, I, A, S, E, C)

Column 3 = Importance Level for Verbal Skills (L = Low; M = Medium; H = High)

Column 4 = Importance Level for Math Skills (L = Low; M = Medium; H = High)

Column 5 = Importance Level for Science and Technical Skills (L = Low; M = Medium; H = High)

Column 6 = Occupation is Enlisted (ME) or Officer (MO), if blank, neither

Occupational Title	Second Interest	Verbal	Math	Science and Technical	Military Enlisted or Officer
Photographers	R	L	L	M	ME
Photographic Process Workers	R	L	L	M	
Producers	E	H	M	L	MO
Radio & Television Announcers	S	H	L	L	ME
Reporters & Correspondents	I	H	L	L	ME
Set and Exhibit Designers	R	M	L	M	
Singers	E	L	L	L	ME
Talent Directors	E	H	M	L	
Technical Writers	I	H	L	L	

SOCIAL (S) OCCUPATIONS

Column 1 = Occupation Title
Column 2 = Second Interest Area (R, I, A, S, E, C)
Column 3 = Importance Level for Verbal Skills (L = Low; M = Medium; H = High)
Column 4 = Importance Level for Math Skills (L = Low; M = Medium; H = High)
Column 5 = Importance Level for Science and Technical Skills (L = Low; M = Medium; H = High)
Column 6 = Occupation is Enlisted (ME) or Officer (MO), if blank, neither

Occupational Title	Second Interest	Verbal	Math	Science and Technical	Military Enlisted or Officer
Adult Literacy, Remedial Education, & GED Teachers & Instructors	A	H	M	L	
Ambulance Drivers & Attendants, Except Emergency Medical Technicians	R	M	M	M	
Animal Control Workers	R	H	M	L	
Animal Trainers	R	M	M	M	
Athletic Trainers	R	H	M	H	
Audiologists & Speech Therapists	I	H	M	H	MO
Bailiffs	E	M	L	L	ME
Child Care Workers	A	M	L	L	
Child Support, Missing Persons, and Unemployment Insurance Fraud Investigators	E/C	H	M	L	
Child, Family, & School Social Workers	E/A	H	M	L	MO
Clergy	E/A	H	M	L	MO
Counseling Psychologists	I	H	M	L	MO
Dental Assistants	R	M	M	M	ME
Dental Hygienists	C	L	M	H	ME
Dietetic Technicians	R	M	H	L	

SOCIAL (S) OCCUPATIONS

Column 1 = Occupation Title

Column 2 = Second Interest Area (R, I, A, S, E, C)

Column 3 = Importance Level for Verbal Skills (L = Low; M = Medium; H = High)

Column 4 = Importance Level for Math Skills (L = Low; M = Medium; H = High)

Column 5 = Importance Level for Science and Technical Skills (L = Low; M = Medium; H = High)

Column 6 = Occupation is Enlisted (ME) or Officer (MO), if blank, neither

Occupational Title	Second Interest	Verbal	Math	Science and Technical	Military Enlisted or Officer
Directors, Religious Activities & Education	E	H	M	L	MO
Education Administrators, Elementary & Secondary School	E	H	M	L	
Education Administrators, Preschool & Child Care Center/Program	E	H	M	L	
Educational, Vocational, & School Counselors	A	H	M	L	ME
Elementary School Teachers	A/I	H	M	L	
Emergency Medical Technicians & Paramedics	R	H	M	H	ME
Employment Interviewers	E	H	M	L	
Equal Opportunity Representatives and Officers	E	H	M	L	
Fitness Trainers & Aerobic Instructors	R	H	L	M	
Funeral Attendants	E	L	L	L	
Health Educators	E/I	H	M	L	
Home Health Aids	R	M	L	L	
Kindergarten Teachers, Except Special Education	A	H	M	L	
Licensed Practical & Licensed Vocational Nurses	R	H	H	M	ME

SOCIAL (S) OCCUPATIONS

Column 1 = Occupation Title

Column 2 = Second Interest Area (R, I, A, S, E, C)

Column 3 = Importance Level for Verbal Skills (L = Low; M = Medium; H = High)

Column 4 = Importance Level for Math Skills (L = Low; M = Medium; H = High)

Column 5 = Importance Level for Science and Technical Skills (L = Low; M = Medium; H = High)

Column 6 = Occupation is Enlisted (ME) or Officer (MO), if blank, neither

Occupational Title	Second Interest	Verbal	Math	Science and Technical	Military Enlisted or Officer
Massage Therapists	R	L	L	L	
Medical & Public Health Social Workers	I	H	M	L	MO
Medical Assistants	C	M	M	M	ME
Mental Health & Substance Abuse Social Workers	I	H	M	L	MO
Mental Health Counselors	I	H	M	L	ME
Middle School Teachers	A/I	H	M	L	
Nursing Aides, Orderlies, & Attendants	R	M	M	L	ME
Nursing Instructors & Teachers, Postsecondary	I	H	H	M	
Occupational Health & Safety Specialists	E	H	M	H	ME
Occupational Therapist Aides	R	M	M	M	ME
Occupational Therapists	R	H	M	M	MO
Orthotists & Prosthetists	I	M	H	H	
Park Naturalists	R	H	M	L	
Personal & Home Care Aides	R	M	M	L	
Personal Financial Advisors	E	M	H	L	
Physical Therapist Aides	R	M	M	H	ME
Physical Therapists	R	H	M	M	MO
Police, Fire, & Ambulance Dispatchers	C	H	M	L	

SOCIAL (S) OCCUPATIONS

Column 1 = Occupation Title

Column 2 = Second Interest Area (R, I, A, S, E, C)

Column 3 = Importance Level for Verbal Skills (L = Low; M = Medium; H = High)

Column 4 = Importance Level for Math Skills (L = Low; M = Medium; H = High)

Column 5 = Importance Level for Science and Technical Skills (L = Low; M = Medium; H = High)

Column 6 = Occupation is Enlisted (ME) or Officer (MO), if blank, neither

Occupational Title	Second Interest	Verbal	Math	Science and Technical	Military Enlisted or Officer
Preschool Teachers	A	H	L	L	
Probation Officers & Correctional Treatment Specialists	C	H	M	L	
Psychiatric Aides	R	H	M	L	ME
Psychiatric Technicians	R	H	L	L	
Radiation Therapists	R	H	H	H	ME
Recreation Workers	A/R	H	M	L	
Recreational Therapists	A	H	L	L	
Registered Nurses	I	H	M	M	MO
Residential Advisors	C	H	L	L	
Secondary School Teachers	A/I	H	M	L	
Security Guards	E	L	L	L	ME
Sheriffs and Deputy Sheriffs	E	M	L	L	MO
Social & Community Service Managers	E	H	M	L	
Social & Human Service Assistants	C	H	L	L	
Special Education Teachers, Secondary School	A	H	M	L	
Speech-Language Pathologists	I	H	M	L	MO
Substance Abuse & Behavioral Disorder Counselors	I	H	L	L	ME

SOCIAL (S) OCCUPATIONS

Column 1 = Occupation Title

Column 2 = Second Interest Area (R, I, A, S, E, C)

Column 3 = Importance Level for Verbal Skills (L = Low; M = Medium; H = High)

Column 4 = Importance Level for Math Skills (L = Low; M = Medium; H = High)

Column 5 = Importance Level for Science and Technical Skills (L = Low; M = Medium; H = High)

Column 6 = Occupation is Enlisted (ME) or Officer (MO), if blank, neither

Occupational Title	Second Interest	Verbal	Math	Science and Technical	Military Enlisted or Officer
Teacher Assistants	C	H	L	L	
Tour Guides & Escorts	E	H	L	L	
Training & Development Specialists	E	H	L	L	MO
Vocational Education Teachers	A/I	H	M	M	
Waiters and Waitresses	E	M	M	L	

ENTERPRISING (E) OCCUPATIONS

Column 1 = Occupation Title

Column 2 = Second Interest Area (R, I, A, S, E, C)

Column 3 = Importance Level for Verbal Skills (L = Low; M = Medium; H = High)

Column 4 = Importance Level for Math Skills (L = Low; M = Medium; H = High)

Column 5 = Importance Level for Science and Technical Skills (L = Low; M = Medium; H = High)

Column 6 = Occupation is Enlisted (ME) or Officer (MO), if blank, neither

Occupational Title	Second Interest	Verbal	Math	Science and Technical	Military Enlisted or Officer
Administrative Services Managers	C	M	L	L	MO
Advertising Sales Agents	C/S	H	M	L	
Aircraft Launch and Recovery Officers	C	M	L	M	MO
Appraisers & Assessors of Real Estate	C	H	H	M	
Arbitrators, Mediators, & Conciliators	S	H	M	L	
Armored Assault Vehicle Officers	R	H	M	M	MO
Artillery and Missile Officers	R	H	H	H	MO
Athletes & Sports Competitors	R	L	L	L	
Chefs & Head Cooks	R	L	M	L	ME
Chief Executives	C	H	H	L	
Coaches and Scouts	R	H	L	L	
Command and Control Center Officers	I	H	M	H	MO
Compensation & Benefits Managers	S	H	M	L	
Computer & Information Systems Managers	C	H	H	H	MO
Construction Mangers	R	H	H	H	
Criminal Investigators and Special Agents	I	H	M	M	

ENTERPRISING (E) OCCUPATIONS

Column 1 = Occupation Title
Column 2 = Second Interest Area (R, I, A, S, E, C)
Column 3 = Importance Level for Verbal Skills (L = Low; M = Medium; H = High)
Column 4 = Importance Level for Math Skills (L = Low; M = Medium; H = High)
Column 5 = Importance Level for Science and Technical Skills (L = Low; M = Medium; H = High)
Column 6 = Occupation is Enlisted (ME) or Officer (MO), if blank, neither

Occupational Title	Second Interest	Verbal	Math	Science and Technical	Military Enlisted or Officer
Crop and Livestock Managers	R	M	M	L	
Demonstrators & Product Promoters	S/R	H	M	L	
Detectives & Criminal Investigators	C	H	M	M	ME
Driver/Sales Workers	R	L	L	L	
Education Administrators, Postsecondary	C/S	H	M	L	MO
Financial Examiners	S	H	H	L	
Financial Managers	C	H	H	L	MO
Flight Attendants	S	M	L	L	ME
Food Service Managers	C/S	M	H	L	MO
Funeral Directors	S	H	L	L	
Hairdressers, Hairstylists, & Cosmetologists	S/A	L	L	L	
Human Resources Managers	S	H	M	L	MO
Industrial Engineers	I	M	H	H	MO
Industrial Production Managers	C	M	M	M	
Infantry Officers	R	H	M	M	MO
Insurance Adjusters, Examiners, & Investigators	I	H	M	M	
Insurance Sales Agents	S	M	M	L	

ENTERPRISING (E) OCCUPATIONS

Column 1 = Occupation Title
Column 2 = Second Interest Area (R, I, A, S, E, C)
Column 3 = Importance Level for Verbal Skills (L = Low; M = Medium; H = High)
Column 4 = Importance Level for Math Skills (L = Low; M = Medium; H = High)
Column 5 = Importance Level for Science and Technical Skills (L = Low; M = Medium; H = High)
Column 6 = Occupation is Enlisted (ME) or Officer (MO), if blank, neither

Occupational Title	Second Interest	Verbal	Math	Science and Technical	Military Enlisted or Officer
Judges, Magistrate Judges, & Magistrates	S	H	M	L	MO
Lawyers	C	H	M	L	MO
Loan Officers	S	H	H	L	
Lodging Managers	C	H	M	L	
Manicurists & Pedicurists	S	L	L	L	
Marketing Managers	C	H	H	M	
Medical and Health Services Managers	S	H	M	M	MO
Meeting and Convention Planners	C	H	L	L	
Nursery & Greenhouse Managers	R	M	L	H	
Opticians, Dispensing	C	M	M	M	
Paralegals & Legal Assistants	C	H	L	L	ME
Parts Salespersons	R	M	L	M	
Personnel Recruiters	S	H	L	L	MO
Private Detectives & Investigators	S	H	M	L	
Property, Real Estate, & Community Association Managers	C	M	M	L	
Public Relations Specialists	A	H	L	L	MO
Purchasing Agents, Except Wholesale, Retail, and Farm Products	C	H	H	L	MO

ENTERPRISING (E) OCCUPATIONS
Column 1 = Occupation Title
Column 2 = Second Interest Area (R, I, A, S, E, C)
Column 3 = Importance Level for Verbal Skills (L = Low; M = Medium; H = High)
Column 4 = Importance Level for Math Skills (L = Low; M = Medium; H = High)
Column 5 = Importance Level for Science and Technical Skills (L = Low; M = Medium; H = High)
Column 6 = Occupation is Enlisted (ME) or Officer (MO), if blank, neither

Occupational Title	Second Interest	Verbal	Math	Science and Technical	Military Enlisted or Officer
Purchasing Managers	C	H	H	L	MO
Real Estate Sales Agents	C/S	H	M	L	
Retail Salespersons	S	M	M	L	ME
Sales Agents, Securities & Commodities	C	H	H	L	
Sales Managers	C	H	M	L	
Sales Representatives, Chemical and Pharmaceutical	S/R	H	M	L	
Special Forces Officers	R	H	M	M	MO
Telemarketers	C	H	L	L	
Training & Development Managers	S	H	L	L	MO
Transit & Railroad Police	S	M	L	L	
Transportation Storage & Distribution Managers	C	M	H	M	MO
Travel Guides	S	M	L	L	
Treasurers, Controllers, & Chief Financial Officers	C	H	H	L	MO
Wholesale & Retail Buyers, Except Farm Products	C	H	H	L	MO

CONVENTIONAL (C) OCCUPATIONS

Column 1 = Occupation Title

Column 2 = Second Interest Area (R, I, A, S, E, C)

Column 3 = Importance Level for Verbal Skills (L = Low; M = Medium; H = High)

Column 4 = Importance Level for Math Skills (L = Low; M = Medium; H = High)

Column 5 = Importance Level for Science and Technical Skills (L = Low; M = Medium; H = High)

Column 6 = Occupation is Enlisted (ME) or Officer (MO), if blank, neither

Occupational Title	Second Interest	Verbal	Math	Science and Technical	Military Enlisted or Officer
Accountants & Auditors	E	H	H	L	MO
Actuaries	I	M	H	L	
Air Traffic Controllers	R	H	M	M	ME
Assessors	E	M	H	L	
Bill & Accountant Collectors	E	H	M	L	
Bookkeeping, Accounting, & Auditing Clerks	E	L	H	L	ME
Brokerage Clerks	E	L	H	L	
Budget Analysts	E	H	H	L	MO
Cargo & Freight Agents	R	H	M	L	ME
Cartographers & Photogrammetrists	I/R	L	H	M	ME
Cashiers	E	L	H	L	ME
City Planning Aides	I	H	H	L	
Claims Examiners, Property & Casualty Insurance	E	M	H	L	
Construction & Building Inspectors	R	M	H	H	
Correspondence Clerks	E	H	M	L	ME
Cost Estimators	E	H	H	L	
Counter & Rental Clerks	E	M	M	L	
Court Clerks	E	H	M	L	
Credit Analysts	E	H	H	L	

CONVENTIONAL (C) OCCUPATIONS

Column 1 = Occupation Title

Column 2 = Second Interest Area (R, I, A, S, E, C)

Column 3 = Importance Level for Verbal Skills (L = Low; M = Medium; H = High)

Column 4 = Importance Level for Math Skills (L = Low; M = Medium; H = High)

Column 5 = Importance Level for Science and Technical Skills (L = Low; M = Medium; H = High)

Column 6 = Occupation is Enlisted (ME) or Officer (MO), if blank, neither

Occupational Title	Second Interest	Verbal	Math	Science and Technical	Military Enlisted or Officer
Credit Authorizers, Checkers, & Clerks	E	L	M	L	
Customer Service Representatives	E	H	M	L	
Dispatchers, Except Police, Fire, & Ambulance	R	M	M	M	
Electrical Drafters	R	M	H	H	ME
Executive Secretaries & Administrative Assistants	E	H	M	L	ME
File Clerks	E	H	M	L	
Fire Inspectors	R	H	M	H	ME
Freight & Cargo Inspectors	R	M	H	M	ME
Human Resources Assistants, Except Payroll & Timekeeping	E	H	M	L	ME
Immigration & Customs Inspectors	E	H	M	L	ME
Insurance Appraisers, Auto Damage	R	M	H	L	
Insurance Claims & Policy Processing Clerks	E	M	H	L	
Legal Secretaries	E	H	L	L	ME
Library Assistants, Clerical	R	M	M	L	
Library Technicians	S	H	M	L	
License Clerks	E	M	M	L	

CONVENTIONAL (C) OCCUPATIONS

Column 1 = Occupation Title
Column 2 = Second Interest Area (R, I, A, S, E, C)
Column 3 = Importance Level for Verbal Skills (L = Low; M = Medium; H = High)
Column 4 = Importance Level for Math Skills (L = Low; M = Medium; H = High)
Column 5 = Importance Level for Science and Technical Skills (L = Low; M = Medium; H = High)
Column 6 = Occupation is Enlisted (ME) or Officer (MO), if blank, neither

Occupational Title	Second Interest	Verbal	Math	Science and Technical	Military Enlisted or Officer
Licensing Examiners & Inspectors	E	M	M	L	
Loan Interviewers & Clerks	E	H	H	L	
Mail Clerks & Mail Machine Operators, Except Postal Service	R	L	L	M	ME
Mapping Technicians	R	L	H	M	ME
Medical Records & Health Information Technicians	R	M	M	L	ME
Medical Transcriptionists & Secretaries	E	H	M	L	ME
Meter Readers, Utilities	R	L	M	L	
Municipal Clerks	E	H	M	L	
Office Clerks, General	E/R	M	M	L	ME
Order Fillers, Wholesale & Retail Sales	E	L	M	L	
Parking Enforcement Workers	R	M	L	L	
Pharmacy Technicians	R	M	M	M	ME
Police Identification & Records Officers	R	M	M	M	ME
Postal Service Clerks	R	L	M	L	
Postal Service Mail Carriers	R	L	M	L	
Production, Planning, & Expediting Clerks	E	H	H	L	ME

CONVENTIONAL (C) OCCUPATIONS

Column 1 = Occupation Title

Column 2 = Second Interest Area (R, I, A, S, E, C)

Column 3 = Importance Level for Verbal Skills (L = Low; M = Medium; H = High)

Column 4 = Importance Level for Math Skills (L = Low; M = Medium; H = High)

Column 5 = Importance Level for Science and Technical Skills (L = Low; M = Medium; H = High)

Column 6 = Occupation is Enlisted (ME) or Officer (MO), if blank, neither

Occupational Title	Second Interest	Verbal	Math	Science and Technical	Military Enlisted or Officer
Proofreaders & Copy Markers	I	H	M	L	
Receptionists & Information Clerks	E	H	M	L	ME
Reservation & Transportation Ticket Agents & Travel Clerks	E	H	M	L	ME
Secretaries	E	H	M	L	ME
Shipping, Receiving, & Traffic Clerks	R	M	M	L	ME
Statistical Assistants	E	M	H	M	
Stock Clerks	R	L	M	L	ME
Tax Examiners, Collectors, & Revenue Agents	E	H	H	L	
Tax Preparers	E	H	H	L	
Telephone Operators	R	M	L	L	ME
Tellers	E	L	H	L	
Title Examiners, Abstractors, & Searchers	E	H	M	L	

WHAT DO YOU DO NEXT?

Use your interests and abilities to determine which occupations are best for you. When you work with a military recruiter, let the recruiter know which occupations you would be interested in. Most recruiters will try to fit you into areas that fit your interests and skills, but remember that the military has various needs that must be filled. The available jobs may or may not be directly related to your specific interests at the time.

The most important score, however, is your AFQT. If you perform well on the two verbal tests and two math tests on the ASVAB, your AFQT score will be high. This is the prime score that the military pays attention to. The better you do on the AFQT, the more options you will have in the military. This book gives you the necessary tools to score high on the AFQT.

Work hard, score well, serve well. Whatever the outcome, remember that there is no more honorable calling than serving your country.